D0207109

THE SPLENDID CENTURY

MORROW QUILL PAPERBACKS

The Splendid Century

W. H. LEWIS

MCMLIV

FIRST MORROW QUILL PAPERBACK EDITION 1978

Printed in the United States of America.

1   2   3   4   5   6   7   8   9   10

Library of Congress Catalog Card Number 53-9235

ISBN 0-688-06009-9

To My Brother

Acknowledgements

The author desires to thank the Oxford University Press for permission to reprint the chapter entitled, "The Galleys," which originally appeared under the title "The Galleys of France" in *Essays presented to Charles Williams*, Oxford University Press, 1947

Contents

Foreword

This book does not pretend to offer a comprehensive survey of the *Grand Siècle*, and, if long-winded titles were still the fashion, it might with more accuracy have been called "Some aspects of French life in the days of Louis XIV."

I have been forced to make it selective rather than comprehensive for two reasons: firstly, had I written on every aspect of the period which interests me, I should have swollen the book to unmanageable proportions: and secondly, because there are many achievements of the age with which I am not competent to deal. In the first category of omissions are chapters on the French Navy, on the *Parlements* and their struggles with the Crown, and on the Diplomatic and Civil Services; there should, I know, have been something on Hugues de Lyonne and his successors, those unscrupulously brilliant diplomatists who had so much to do with making Louis XIV the *Grand Monarque*, and on Colbert, Louis' greatest civil servant, who worked with such unavailing energy to give France the planned economy of a modern totalitarian state.

Within the second category fall Descartes and his world, Poussin,

Claude and the artists in general, Le Nôtre, the "Capability Brown" of his day, father of formal landscape gardening, Mansart, the creator of Versailles (and little though he dreamt of it, of the Euston Hotel).

For the omissions in the first category, I apologize; whilst as regards those in the second, I feel that it would be the height of impudence on my part to suppose that what I would have found tedious to write, anyone else would have found interesting to read.

Lastly, a word on the baffling problem of money. The value of French money fluctuated considerably during the century, and there is the further complication that Europe is now in a period of unstable exchange. The first difficulty I have dealt with by striking an average for the value of French currency throughout the reign, and the second by translating—very approximately—into the rates of exchange ruling. The result does not satisfy me, but only a monetary expert could find the right solution. Here, however, is a table which may give the reader a rough idea of the basis of my calculations:

1 livre (silver)=1 franc (17th. Cent.)=1 franc (1914)=$ .20 (1914)
6 livres (silver)=1 crown (silver)=6 francs (1914)=$1.22 (1914)
4 crowns (silver)=1 louis (gold)=24 francs (1914)=$4.87 (1914)

W. H. LEWIS

Headington Quarry,
Oxford.
2nd May 1953.

THE SPLENDID CENTURY

I

The King

We know both too much and too little about Louis XIV ever to succeed in capturing the whole man. In externals, in the mere business of eating, drinking, and dressing, in the outward routine of what he loved to call the *métier du roi*, no historical character, not even Johnson or Pepys, is better known to us; we can even, with the aid of his own writings, penetrate a little of the majestic façade which is *Le Grand Roi*. But when we have done so, we see as in a glass darkly. Hence the extraordinary number and variety of judgments which have been passed upon him; to one school, he is incomparably the ablest ruler in modern European history; to another, a mediocre blunderer, pompous, led by the nose by a succession of generals and civil servants; whilst to a third, he is no great king, but still the finest actor of royalty the world has ever seen. Courtesy, reticence, and an almost inhuman tranquillity of demeanour, are the qualities in Louis which strike us at the first glance: the latter so constant that when on a certain day he speaks roughly to his coachman, "usually a prime favourite," his entourage correctly deduces from this fact that a serious crisis has arisen. We never catch him off his guard or surprise his secrets: whether we meet the taciturn, faintly bored Louis of the private apartments, or the Sun-King whose "terrifying majesty" made so deep an impression on so many observers.

But let us begin at the beginning.

Louis XIV, son of Louis XIII (1601–43) and of his Spanish Queen, Anne of Austria (1601–67), was born in the *château* of St. Germain at two o'clock on the morning of 5th September 1638, the first child of parents who hated each other, and who had been married for twenty-three years. The birth was hailed as a miracle, the little Dauphin was given the name of *Dieudonné*, the wine ran free, and even the hungry were fed.

From his cold-blooded, shifty, suspicious father the child seems to have inherited nothing but a love of music and an interest in the minutiae of army administration, whilst to his mother he owed a magnificent constitution and his indomitable pride.

From the first, Louis was a solemn child, very well aware of who he was, and what he was to be. His earliest recorded utterance is characteristic; on the 21st April 1643, being then not five years old, he was taken to the bedside of his dying father. "Who is it?" said the King. "Louis XIV," replied his son. He had anticipated his inheritance by some three weeks only; on 14th May Louis XIII died. His will, under which the Queen-Mother would have been a puppet, was set aside by the Parlement, and Anne found herself Regent of France with Jules Mazarin (1602–61) as her Prime Minister. And perhaps as something very much more, for the relationship between Anne of Austria and Mazarin remains obscure to this day. Did the Cardinal make his position safe for life by marrying the Queen-Mother? There was nothing to prevent it, for he was never a priest, and there is much circumstantial evidence in favour of the supposition. What is certain is that this softly smiling, humble, deferential man, this piece of iron painted to look like a lath, acquired a complete ascendancy over the Regent, and treated the young King in a manner which is only to be explained on the assumption that he was his step-father. In the royal family the Cardinal's word was absolute and final: and whilst Mazarin was piling up a huge private fortune, the King, and even the Regent, had to petition him, often unsuccessfully, for a little pocket money for their daily needs. Here, at the very apex of the pyramid, one found a *petit bourgeois* ménage tyrannically controlled by an Italian Harpagon.

Few kings have had a worse upbringing than Louis XIV. His formative years were passed at an impoverished court, preoccupied with a seemingly endless continental war, and harassed by civil disturbances culminating in the open rebellion whereby the great nobles tried to restore the anarchy which Richelieu had extinguished. And Anne, though a fond mother, whose love her son returned, was not the woman to bother herself about her children's education. One great service she did render Louis, and that was to lay the foundations of his religious belief to such good effect that in after years, if his creed was in many respects faulty, he at least acquired a lasting fear of the Devil strong enough to throw a perpetual shadow over his enjoyment of the illicit pleasures of his more exuberant period. The evidence that Anne concerned herself personally in this matter is from a source that is beyond suspicion, a letter from Louis' first confessor, Fr. Paulin, S.J. (1593?–1653), giving a preliminary report on the young King to his Provincial after taking over his duties in 1646: ". . . in short, there is no lamb more gentle and more easily guided than our little king . . . and he has a piety which the Most Christian Queen, by her loving warnings and advice, has instilled into him from his first infancy." But religion and petting apart, Louis and his younger brother Philippe (1640–1701) seem to have been left pretty much to their own devices. Louis himself in one of his rare expansive moments, told Mme. de Maintenon how his childhood was spent; his governesses, he said, passed their days in gossip and cards, rarely knowing where he was. His mother's chamberwomen thought him beneath their notice, and it was to these chamberwomen's chamberwomen that he escaped for company when he could get away from his mother. At the Queen's mealtimes he and Philippe would take up a strategic position in the corridor and raid the dishes on their way from the kitchens, retiring into some hiding place to bolt a stolen omelette. The King's favourite companion was a peasant girl, daughter of one of the lower servants, to whom he acted as page, carrying her train, lighting her about the endless ante-rooms and passages, or pushing her round the gardens in a wheeled chair. So little care was taken of him, he

said, that once in his early days he was only saved by chance from
drowning in one of the fountains. These early contacts were to
have a profound influence on his mature life, for in the height of
his glory it was noticed with strong disapproval that he was never
so much at his ease as when in his own room with a favourite
valet, and that it was to his humbler servants that he invariably
showed the best and most human side of his character. These early
years cannot have been without their value; for in them the King
was brought into close touch with the people for the only time in
his life, and what is more, was treated by them *sans façon*. It must
have been from the intimates of his youth rather than by inheritance that he acquired that *solidité*, that common sense on which
he so rightly prided himself, and which was one of his most valuable qualities. And the influence of these peasants must have done
something to counteract the inherited and overweening pride
which his education, such as it was, fostered instead of attempting
to eradicate. In 1644, when he was only six, the *Educatio Regia*,
written for his especial benefit, instructs him to remind himself every morning that he is about to act God during the day, and to ask
himself every evening how far he has succeeded in doing so. At the
same time his writing master is setting him copies such as "Homage is due to Kings, they act as they please." And the geography
master has drawn for him a map of the western world labelled
l'Europe Françoise, so that the growth of his temporal pride may
keep pace with that of his spiritual. And, to crown all, he was
given as governor the Maréchal-Duc de Villeroi (1598–1685), a
man whose fitness for the post may best be gauged by his favourite
rule of conduct: "Always hold the pot for anyone who stands
firmly, and upset it over his head the minute his feet begin to slip."

Louis, already an observant judge of character, was the first to
ridicule his governor's sycophancy. "Oui, Sire" was a phrase so
often on the governor's lips that "Maréchal Ouisire" became his
nickname in the royal nursery. With such a governor Louis, as
may be imagined, learnt just as much as he pleased, and that was
remarkably little; for he early showed a distaste for books which
was to continue all his life, and which was so marked that when at
the urging of Olympe Mancini (1634–1708) he read a fashionable
romance, the fact was a subject for court gossip.

For Louis' deficient education Mazarin has been much blamed,
and with justice, but the charge that he deliberately stunted the

King's mental growth in order to rule alone seems to be quite unfounded. And indeed Louis himself admits his debt to Mazarin for initiating him into the art of statecraft. What was unpardonable in Mazarin's conduct was the sordid poverty in which he kept his sovereign; the young Louis looks every inch a King when he inspects his unpaid troops in his gold-laced coat and his diamond-buckled hat with the ostrich feather. But these were only his stage clothes, and at home things were very different. He had not a pair of sheets without large holes in them, his worn-out dressing gown came only half-way down his legs, and the upholstery of his shabby old coach hung in rags. Tradesmen with long outstanding accounts threatened to stop supplying the royal table, unpaid servants deserted their posts, and the very Pages of the Chamber had to be dismissed to save the cost of their food. It was the humiliation, not the hardship, which galled Louis so insufferably, and the lean years under Mazarin left an indelible mark on his character; the startling contrast between the lives of Louis the King and Louis the private individual may well have been the origin of that conscious playing a part, that distinct flavour of the *roi du théâtre* which is never quite absent from Louis the King, whilst the sumptuous extravagance of the personal reign almost certainly began as a reaction against the years of empty pockets.

Deeper still, and even more obviously influencing Louis for the rest of his life, sank the lessons of the Fronde, that tragi-comic civil war which lasted with brief intervals from 1649 to 1653.

The Fronde has often been compared with the contemporary civil war in England, but in fact the two revolts have nothing in common; for no matter of principle was at stake in the Fronde. It was merely an uneasy alliance between a large group of the nobility and the Parlement to wrest power from the Crown for purely selfish and sectional motives; democratic sentiment was as yet unborn, and had the Crown been defeated in the struggle, oligarchy, not democracy, would have succeeded autocracy. The Frondeur's objective was neither a limited monarchy nor a republic, but an impotent monarchy.

The year 1651 marks the lowest ebb of Louis XIV's fortunes; King, Cardinal, and Court found themselves blockaded in the Louvre by citizen guards, who also held the gates of Paris, examining outgoing coaches and wagons to make sure that the King was not attempting to escape from his capital. And on one black night that winter came an outrage foreshadowing the still distant revolution; on some rumour of the King's escape, the mob broke into the Louvre and insisted on seeing its Sovereign. There was nothing for it but to yield to *force majeure*. Anne, with such hidden transports of fury as may be imagined, ushered a deputation of the people into the King's bedroom where Louis lay pretending to be asleep, and then adroitly improved the situation by a friendly chat with one of the citizen officers who claimed her acquaintance on the ground that he had once been the lackey of one of her servants.

If Anne was furious it was nothing to the slow steady rage which possessed the young King. One may hazard the guess that for the rest of his long life not a week passed without his recalling his greatest humiliation; and its infliction set the course which the monarchy was to follow for the rest of its existence. The Versailles idea, which was to insulate Louis and his successors from all contact with their subjects, was born that night, and when the monarchy emerged triumphant from the civil war there were firmly implanted in Louis some maxims of government from which he never afterwards departed: principally, the reduction of the nobility to impotence and the transfer of all non-military employment to the hands of the *bourgeoisie:* and secondly, the reduction of the Parlement to the state of a legal instrument for the registration of the King's decisions. For good or ill, Louis was successful in both objects.

If Mazarin had not died in 1661, would Louis have continued to be his docile pupil for the next ten or perhaps twenty years? An idle but intriguing question. It is difficult to believe that the yoke was not beginning to fret a man of his temperament, yet he makes no such complaint; and right up to the day of his Prime Minister's death he remained his attentive, not to say obsequious, pupil.

It was at half-past two on the morning of the 8th March 1661 that Mazarin died; the event had been expected for some days, and when Louis woke later in the morning, the news was broken to him by his nurse, who, we note with astonishment, slept in the royal bedroom. Slipping quietly out of bed, Louis dressed himself and, passing into his study, locked the door. There he remained for two hours. We would give much to know his thoughts during the only two hours of his life which he ever spent in solitude, but unfortunately his memoirs do not even refer to the incident. All we can guess is that it was during this period of self-communing that he added another to his fundamental laws of statecraft, namely, that he would never again have a Prime Minister or admit a Churchman to his Council. "I would as soon take a Prime Minister," was henceforth to be his strongest expression in condemning some proposed innovation in matters of state.

On the same morning the King met his Heads of Departments and spoke to them for the first time *en roi*. No departmental decision was in future to be signed except by the King in person, and no requests were to be granted without his sanction. In future he himself would carry out all the duties which had hitherto been performed by the Cardinal: and the Minister's function from now onwards was to advise, not to initiate. The Ministers departed, grumbling at this unforeseen whim of the newly enfranchised apprentice, and looked forward to a tiresome week or so of uncertainty before the King tired of playing at the Premiership: little realizing that the personal reign had begun, and was to continue to the end of the chapter.

It is, of course, very easy to over-dramatize the scene: the timid, rather backward young man who locks himself up in his study and emerges as the *Grand Monarque* before whom even his Ministers tremble. Naturally nothing of the sort happened, and naturally during the earlier years Louis leant heavily on the very able staff which he had inherited from the Mazarin régime. But nevertheless it was early obvious that here was a king who really meant what he said, and who intended not only to reign, but also to govern.

What assets had he for the performance of his self-imposed task? Firstly, and by no means to be despised in a world even more prone than ours to judge by externals, he looked and acted the part to perfection; his enemies grudgingly admitted him to be the handsomest man in France, the beau ideal of a great French gentleman; he must have shone, we are told, even had he been born in a private station. He was an excellent dancer, a tolerable musician, a charming raconteur, and master of a perfect and discriminating politeness. The Prince de Condé (1621–86), who has been winning battles for over thirty years, returns from his last victory, Sneff, in 1674; he is now crippled with gout, and as he painfully climbs the great staircase of Versailles, at the head of which the King awaits him, he apologizes for his slowness. "Cousin," says Louis, "one who moves under such a load of laurels must of necessity move slowly." In 1689 he fits out the exiled James II for the invasion of Ireland. The moment of departure comes; Louis takes off his own sword, hands it to James, and kissing him, remarks, "I hope I never see your face again." An old noble tells the King that he is a ruined man, and must leave Court. "Marquis," says the King, "you and I have known each other too long to separate at a time of life when neither of us can afford to hunt for new friends; don't desert me": and the Marquis is given a pension. Another courtier receives a valuable appointment, and the patent is accompanied by a note in the King's hand—"May I be the first to rejoice with you as a friend on the post that I give you as master."

It is all charming no doubt, but unfortunately there is another side to Louis XIV. There is that selfishness which may be called sublime, and under which all his intimate circle had to suffer. His son's wife, and after her his grandson's, had to risk their lives in pregnancy because it was the King's pleasure that they should accompany him from one royal residence to another. Louis never loved anyone more dearly than his fascinating granddaughter, the Duchess of Burgundy (1685–1712). And how does he treat her? In 1708 she was with child when the King wanted to go to Fontainebleau; the doctors, backed by Mme. de Maintenon, pointed out that if the Duchess made the journey she would be in grave danger. Louis insisted upon her accompanying the Court, and the result was that she had a miscarriage. The news was broken to the King in the gardens in front of most of the Court, and this is how he received it: "What does it matter to me who succeeds me? Isn't the Duc de Berri of an age to marry and have children? Since she was to have a miscarriage, thank God it is over and I shall no longer be nagged by a pack of doctors and old women." Like all great egoists Louis hated scenes, he hated melancholy thoughts, and he hated unhappy faces; the Duchess had been tactless enough to produce all three, and the King felt that he had a legitimate grievance.

We find him adopting the same attitude towards his courtiers; you might have lost a dearly loved wife or an only son at the beginning of the week: but Louis would think that a disrespectful excuse for your failure to attend at Court before the week was out, and when you did attend, would have found it *fort mauvais* if you did not behave with that deferential gaiety which was expected of all courtiers in all circumstances. A very promininent Court lady, Mme. d'Espinois, dies, and Mme. de Maintenon in giving the news to a friend writes: "The death of Mme. d'Espinois was a surprise and nothing more. The King rids himself of unhappy ideas as soon as possible."

Louis' sister-in-law, Madame Palatine (1652–1722), was once in deep disgrace with him for several weeks. Louis had ravaged the Palatinate, her home country, and she had had the pleasure of hearing that her father's house was in ruins and the countryside a desert. Madame grieved instead of rejoicing, and the King found her conduct *fort mauvais*.

Neither the Queen nor the mistresses fared any better at his hands than did the rest of the household; indeed, being more necessary to his comfort, they fared worse. But Louis XIV's treatment of his Queen, if inexcusable, is at least explicable. The one great pure passion of his selfish life was for Marie Mancini (1640–1715), and when it was at its height he had been forced into a diplomatic marriage with the stupid little Infanta of Spain. It is easy to see that he could hardly have been expected to love her, but one finds it difficult to forgive him for forcing her to live on terms of intimacy with his mistresses. It was, however, an arrangement convenient to the King, and that was the only aspect of the matter that presented itself to him.

"The King was all his life a lover," says St. Simon with a touch of unexpected poetry. Well, that is, of course, one way of putting it, but I feel that another contemporary verdict, *il ne peut pas se passer des femmes* gives a truer picture. There is about Louis' sexual activities a coarseness, something of the farmyard, which upsets our conception of his character and seems curiously at variance with the standards by which he regulated all other departments of his dignified life. Madame, who knew him thoroughly, says that all women, peasants, chambermaids, servant's daughters, women of quality, were the same to him, provided only that they would make a pretence of loving him. Medical reasons partly account for his indiscriminate and insatiable appetite for women, but the explanation of its indulgence lies mainly in the base flattery which was so constantly at work to persuade him that kings were exempt from the restraints of the moral law. What self-control was to be expected from a handsome and vigorous man, the absolute ruler of a Court in which married women openly asserted that to give oneself to one's prince offended neither God, husband, nor parents?

Only one good thing can be said about this side of Louis' life: that he never allowed his mistresses the slightest political influence. He lived up to the advice which he bequeaths to his son on the management of these left-hand queens:

The second consideration, which is the more delicate, and the more difficult in practice, is that in surrendering one's heart one must remain the absolute master of one's head; let the beauty you enjoy have no share in your affairs and keep the two things absolutely separate. You know what I have already said on various occasions concerning the credit of a favourite, and that of a mistress is very much more dangerous still.

There was no place under Louis XIV for the political mistress of the next reign, and even Mme. de Maintenon, wife though she was, was excluded from all business as rigorously as were her predecessors. Hear her explain her own position in a letter to the Archbishop of Paris in 1698:

The King does not wish to hear matters of business spoken of except by the Ministers; he is displeased that the Nuncio should have addressed himself to me. Make the Nuncio listen to reason on this point once and for all, I beg of you. I can only, as occasion arises, offer general maxims, and I cannot do anything in particular instances, which indeed I rarely hear mentioned. I would be only too well recompensed for the slavery in which I live if I could do some good; but Monseigneur, there is nothing for it but to sigh at seeing the way matters are handled. I don't wish to say more . . . for I must keep my opinions to myself.

It may be objected that we are here seeing Louis in his sixties: what of the young Louis? Here he is, speaking on the same subject to a group of friends when he was in his early twenties: "You are all my friends, those of my kingdom of whom I am fondest, and in whom I have most confidence. I am young, and women usually have great power over men of my age. I order all of you, if you notice that any woman . . . shows the least sign of managing me, to warn me. I shall then need only twenty-four hours to get rid of her."

By the standards of his time and country, the King was not sex-

ually precocious. When, to use Court language, he entered the
lists of love, he was already in his eighteenth year, and in his rather sordid initiation he was the seduced, not the seducer. One of
his mother's Waiting Women, Mme. de Beauvais—*Cataut* to the
family circle—waylaid him as he was coming from his bath. It was
a purely physical adventure, which had no sequel other than awakening Anne to the fact that the sooner her son was married the
better. For Mme. de Beauvais it was, of course, a triumph which
conferred a certain prestige upon her for the rest of her long life;
forty years later she was still at Court, blind and bleary, but still
treated by Louis with marked consideration. What Anne said to
Cataut about the performance we don't know, but she had sense
enough to say nothing at all to her son, though it might perhaps
have been better if she had scolded. Louis would then probably
have taken Mme. de Beauvais as his mistress, whereas what actually
happened came near to being a disaster.

The story begins with Mazarin's importation of his widowed
sister and her four daughters after his triumphant return to power
in 1653. Olympe, the eldest girl and the beauty of the family, was
then fourteen, Marie thirteen, and the others still children. Two
years passed, years of growing anxiety on the Queen-Mother's part
as she saw Olympe's power over the King increasing daily; and
Anne had lost no time in arriving at an accurate estimate of
Olympe, "the serpent of the Mazarins," and as bad a lot as ever
came out of Italy. But in fact Anne's fears were without foundation; Olympe, frigid, greedy, and ambitious, was flattered by
Louis' obvious passion, but saw clearly that she had no chance of
marrying him and had no intention of entering on a liaison which
might have compromised her prospects of a brilliant settlement in
life. The danger lay elsewhere.

Of Marie, the second girl, an astrologer had predicted that she
would be a source of misfortune to her family: and the unfortunate child was in consequence detested by her mother and feared by
her uncle, who together agreed to make her the Cinderella of the
sisters. Whilst the others were being fêted at Court, Marie was
either at home with the servants or making a compulsory retreat in
some convent. Her mother died in 1656, and during Mme. Mancini's last illness Louis, at the orders of Mazarin, took to calling at
the Hôtel Mancini to ask how the sick woman did. In her ante-
room he would meet Marie, the neglected daughter, Marie with her

jet black hair and her shy admiration. She was sixteen, he eighteen. She was relegated to the background, so was he. As time passed Louis found himself looking forward to calling on Mme. Mancini; the tiresome duty dictated by Mazarin had become the chief pleasure of the day, for at the Hôtel Mancini he was sure to find Marie of the flashing black eyes who smiled a welcome which was at once flattering and challenging. The King would drive home reflecting on her pretty figure and hands, her swift changes of mood, her impulsive candour, all so strange and new to him. He was in fact in love, and, had he known it, so was she.

Oddly enough neither the Queen-Mother nor Mazarin seem to have felt any alarm at Louis' attentions to Marie; from the height of middle-age they apparently dismissed the matter as a boy and girl romance of no consequence, and even welcomed Marie into the family circle, whose boredom she mitigated by recitations from Corneille; and where Louis of an evening would play to her on the guitar, on which he was a more than passable performer.

It was not until 1658 that it became apparent to all France that this was no boy and girl flirtation; in that year Louis was taken dangerously ill on active service, and on his return to Court he found that the chief topic of conversation was the violent, indeed almost indecent, grief which Marie had shown in public during the crisis of his sickness. Fontainebleau was selected by the doctors for the King's convalescence, and there Louis had eyes for no one but Marie; it was a lovely autumn, and the two lovers developed a taste for rock climbing in the forest. Perched out of reach of their exasperated seniors, they held hands and dreamed golden dreams of a future in fairyland, while the now thoroughly alarmed Anne made arrangements to hurry on her son's marriage with all possible speed.

French policy, and Anne's personal inclination, pointed to the Infanta of Spain, Anne's niece, as the desirable bride for Louis; and in order to hasten the traditional dilatoriness of the Court of Madrid, Mazarin played a comedy after his own heart. The Duchess-Dowager of Savoy and her daughter Marguerite were invited to meet their French relatives *en famille* at Lyons, and a rumour was set on foot that the King would return from the party betrothed to Marguerite. On the 26th October the French Court set out for Lyons, and Marie Mancini was one of the entourage. The

King's behaviour on the journey did nothing to dispel the uneasiness of his mother; for Louis the carriage was always too hot, too cold, too stuffy, or too draughty, and he found that in order to avoid an attack of the vapours, he must take constant horse exercise. So day after day he and Marie rode side by side through the autumn country, "like a pair of lovers in a romance," as Mlle. de Montpensier sourly remarked, and when they reached the night's halting place, there were moonlit strolls through quiet streets, or a drive with Louis acting as coachman, followed by a picnic supper at Marie's lodgings.

Mazarin pretended not to see these junketings, for they served the useful purpose of preventing Louis from taking any inconvenient fancy for Marguerite of Savoy; but when Spain had come to heel with an offer of the Infanta's hand and the Court had returned to Paris, he felt that the time had come to end the romance. He was quite unaware of the fact that during the trip, Louis had engaged himself to Marie; for this was no *amourette*, and to neither of the lovers did the cynical worldly solution even occur; other kings had made love matches, thought Louis, and why not he? And he may have reflected that his mother, married to Mazarin, was in no position to raise strong objections to her son's marrying Mazarin's niece.

It was early in 1659 that the King formally offered himself to the Cardinal as a suitor for Marie's hand, and Mazarin was, or at any rate affected to be, horrified at the proposition. But it is by no means certain that Mazarin did not toy with the idea of making Marie Queen of France; what does appear to be sure is that he reported Louis' proposal to the Queen in colourless language which contained no expression of disapproval, and that Anne threw up her head and said that if her son so disgraced himself, she would lead a rebellion that would set fire to the four corners of France. There was a furious quarrel between mother and son, Marie and her sisters were exiled, and Louis, still writing daily to Marie, but yielding to irresistible pressure, was at last made to understand that he must set out for the Spanish frontier to honour his engagement to the Infanta. But the struggle was perhaps the hardest and certainly the most critical in which Mazarin ever engaged. His letters to the King during the height of the affair are interesting as showing very clearly that his relations with Louis must have rested on a more intimate basis than that of his Premiership. Had he not had an unshakable hold on the King, can we imagine so cautious an opportunist writing in this key?

With regard to (Marie's) feelings towards me which you are pleased to report, I am not surprised at your saying so; your passion prevents you from seeing her as she is . . . she has insatiable ambition, is very wrong-headed and passionate, despises everybody, has no restraint, and has a penchant for every kind of extravagance . . . in fact a thousand faults and not one single quality worthy of your affection.

And again, a few days later: "Can I, without neglecting my duty, abstain from letting you know that your own conduct is entirely lacking in *bienséance* when, on the eve of your marriage, you abandon yourself to a passion . . . which will end in your being unable to conceal your aversion for this (i.e. the Spanish) marriage?"

It was a sullen and despairing Louis who on the 9th June 1660 allowed himself to be married to the Infanta at St. Jean-de-Luz, and our sympathy goes out to the unfortunate little bride. As indeed did that of the French Court, which in the next few days noticed with compassionate amusement that the child had fallen madly in love with her husband. The naïve little Queen poured out her satisfaction to all who would listen to her; explaining how she had never before spoken to any man except her father and her confessor; how she had always hoped to be Queen of France; and how she had always loved Louis XIV since first she saw his portrait. "Pretty, and entirely lacking in charm," was France's verdict on the new Queen.

Louis was certainly not in love with his wife; but he was touched and flattered by her passion, and the first week of his married life passed off better than might have been expected. But on the homeward journey he left the slow Court to move northwards without him while he made a sentimental journey to the places of Marie's exile; and at Brouage, that sad little town in the salt marshes, he paced the melancholy shore in tears till late at night, coming back "with long sighs" to sleep in the room which had been Marie's.

Here ends the first and only romance of Louis' life. Marie was now at Paris where Mazarin, with his usual cunning, had manoeuvred her into the position of seeming to look favourably on the courtship of Prince Charles of Lorraine, who, as it happened, was really in love with her, though Mazarin had no idea of sanctioning his suit. Sarcastic letters went from the Cardinal to the King at Brouage, pointing out what a ridiculous figure he cut whilst sentimentalizing at the seaside over a girl who was queening it in Paris with a new lover; other letters, instigated by Mazarin, poured in upon Louis to confirm the Cardinal's news. Ridicule was perhaps the only thing in the world which Louis feared. On his return to Paris he greeted Marie with an icy politeness: Marie blazed out at him: Mazarin, with exquisite dexterity, prevented any explanations between the two: and the next year Marie disappeared from the French stage as the bride of Prince Colonna, Constable of Naples. The epilogue to the story was the bridegroom's openly expressed pleasure and surprise at the discovery that his wife was a virgin.

On the 1st April 1661 Louis' brother Philippe, *Monsieur* to the Court, was married at the Palais-Royal to Henriette Anne (1644–70), sister of Charles II of England. Louis had accepted the match without enthusiasm; he confessed publicly to sharing the national antipathy towards the English, and on the whole he rather disliked what he remembered of his cousin Henriette. Not so many years had passed since he had received a sharp scolding from his mother for not asking her to dance with him at the Louvre. And his explanation that he didn't like skinny little girls had not improved matters. Consequently he was completely taken by surprise by the beautiful girl of sixteen who was presented to him as his future sister-in-law. According to one account, "Minette," as Charles called her, had really no claim to good looks at all; but, adds our informant, once you had looked into her eyes, you forgot everything but your passion to please her. Even women, however, allowed her a lovely complexion, brilliant eyes, gleaming white teeth, and full red lips; but what was more to the point with the men, she had that indescribable something in comparison with which mere beauty is unimportant.

Henriette was a girl who understood the pitilessness of life in a way which was impossible to her French cousins. Her earliest memories were of a nightmare England full of evil, triumphant faces, and coarse voices without mercy; then the years of lonely poverty with a mother ever mourning for a murdered husband. She had indeed learnt in the expressive phrase of the time, how steep are the stairs of the charitable. And now had come her hour of triumph; for she knew that Louis XIV could have married her if he had chosen to do so, and she saw that he was now regretting that he hadn't.

There is perhaps no more striking tribute to Henriette's charm than the fact that her husband, by his own confession, was in love with her for a whole fortnight after his marriage; for in Mme. de Lafayette's tactful words, it was given to no woman to capture the heart of that prince. From his earliest years it had been his chief pleasure to dress himself as a girl and admire the result in his mirror, and he was the leading authority at Court on female underclothing. He had such favourites as such a man would naturally have, notably the Chevalier de Lorraine, "beautiful as an angel": and when they had been on active service together a few years earlier, and the Chevalier had had a touch of fever, Monsieur's wifely distress had been a source of scandalized amusement to his brother officers, and even to the troops. Philippe indeed flaunted a mistress, as was only seemly for a man of his age and rank, but that fortunate lady was in the enviable position of enjoying the wages of sin without the slightest danger to the welfare of her immortal soul. To finish with the character of this very unpleasant young man, we may say that his rapidly growing dislike of his bride was due to the discovery that the courtiers admired her charms more than they did his own.

We would sympathize more with Henriette if she had been forced into her marriage, but in fact she had taken Philippe with her eyes open. She did not pretend to love him, but his drawbacks as a husband were she felt more than counterbalanced by the prospect of spending her life at the Court of France; for though by birth an English princess, France was her spiritual home, and England she regarded with a mixture of horror and contempt. She felt that she owed nothing to Philippe, and the stage was now set for a comedy *à trois* which the Court was to watch with considerable amusement.

Fontainebleau in high summer was the setting for the piece in which Louis played *jeune premier* to Henriette's misunderstood wife, with the indignant Monsieur in the rôle of *mari cocu:* a comedy staged regardless of expense, with bathing parties, suppers on the canal, amateur theatricals, pursuit in dim moonlit glades and dark masses of woodland starred with fairy lamps, while the orchestra sobbed out the tender music of Lulli.

Whilst Louis and Henriette chased each other through the alleys and thickets Philippe and the neglected little Queen would be in the almost deserted *château*, plaguing the harassed Anne with their very legitimate grievances. Though in point of fact neither of them had quite such serious cause for complaint as was imagined; Louis might spend all his time with Henriette, might come home with her at three in the morning in an unlit coach, but he was as far as ever from obtaining what his century would have described as "the last favours." For Henriette kept her head better than did Louis. Perhaps she still nourished a lingering grudge against him for his unfortunate remark about skinny little girls. At any rate it was generally believed that in her hour of triumph she merely tantalized the King with the hope of delights which she had no intention of granting him.

It was some time before it dawned upon the infatuated Louis that his mother was seriously annoyed with him, and his brother at the end of his patience: but when Henriette told him that Anne was sending complaints of her conduct to the Queen of England, the two felt that something would have to be done. It was Henriette who came out with a brilliant plot, which, if she had lived in the next century, one would suspect her of having borrowed from a da Ponte libretto for a Mozart opera; why, said Henriette, should not Louis pretend to be smitten with one of her Maids-of-Honour? Let him parade his new infatuation, and then what more natural than that he should be constantly seen in Madame's quarters? And when they were discovered *tête-à-tête*, let it be assumed that he was pleading with Madame to use her authority to overcome the girl's scruples. Well, but who? said Louis. Oh, little La Vallière, replied Madame carelessly, naming the one of her maids whom she considered least to the King's taste. And Louis agreed.

Madame's action turned out be a capital blunder; a more experienced woman would have foreseen the danger of throwing Louis into the company of a girl so unlike any he had ever met before. For in Louise de La Vallière (1644–1710) the King was for the first time brought into contact with a daughter of his poor provincial *noblesse*, newly come to Court and dazzled by its unexpected glare. This shy and gentle girl, with her delicate pale beauty and silvery golden hair, her blue eyes and her sweet voice which no one ever forgot, made an instant impression on Louis;

an appeal which was in no wise lessened by her adoration of himself, which was as obvious as it was disinterested. The siege was swift, the defence feeble, and before summer had shortened into autumn, Louise de La Vallière was openly and avowedly the mistress of Louis XIV. Madame raged, Anne spoke sternly of sin and judgment, but society on the whole approved of the King's conduct. La Fare voices the general sentiment pretty accurately when he notes in his memoirs that the summer closed happily with the King choosing a mistress who was in every way worthy of him.

And meanwhile, what of the Queen? Whatever may have been Louis' shortcomings as a husband, he never ceased to treat Marie Thérèse with courtesy, and to show her a certain routine and perfunctory tenderness; once a fortnight she could always rely upon being the wife of the King of France. And when on the 1st November she bore him a son, his conduct left nothing to be desired in the eyes of a critical audience. Throughout her difficult and dangerous labour he sat holding her hand, "sensibly penetrated with grief" and, as a spectator said, "leaving no room for doubt that his love for the Queen held a greater place in his heart than any other." This may be an overstatement, but it contains an element of truth; with all his infidelity and selfishness Louis had come to feel an affection for his wife, and the feeling was to grow stronger as time went on, though he did nothing to mend his ways. From the Queen he would turn to Louise, and from Louise to more than one passing *amourette* before Mme. de Montespan crossed his path.

Françoise Athenais de Rochechouart Mortemart, Mlle. Tonnay-Charente (1641–1707), and afterwards Marquise de Montespan, was a very different person from Louise de La Vallière. Some seven hundred years had passed since a Rochechouart, even then described as "of a noble and ancient family," had first emerged from provincial obscurity, and the family tree had perhaps laboured for a thousand years to produce this exquisite blossom, Athenais.

Whether she threw herself deliberately in Louis XIV's way, or whether she drifted into her subsequent relations with him, is not even now clear; but it is significant that it was she who made overtures to Louise de La Vallière, and not La Vallière to her; overtures which were accepted with pathetic eagerness by the lonely mistress, who was growing ever lonelier. For satiety was creeping upon Louis without his being aware of it. Silvery blondes do not wear well under the most favourable circumstances, and life had been very hard to Louise; childbearing under conditions of cruel concealment, the terrible solitude of isolation in a crowd, and a conscience never at rest had played havoc with the shy loveliness which had won the King's heart. Then came the fatal day when Louis noticed how much less beautiful she was growing, and from then onwards he began to look forward to finding the witty, fascinating Mme. de Montespan in his mistress' rooms. This slim, arrogant daughter of a great house challenged his attention by her contrast to Louise; here was no awe of his divinity, no bashful shrinking from the rays of the Sun of France. Nor was Athenais playing a part. Why should she shrink? Was she not a Mortemart, and who after all were the Bourbons when compared with the Mortemarts?

The affair moved swiftly to its inevitable and sordid conclusion. Mme. de Montespan's was not a nature to inspire love, and Louis had hardened and coarsened with the years. As a shrewd contemporary remarked, he merely felt it due to his position to have the most beautiful woman in France for his mistress. Gay, haughty challenge, provoking the lust for possession, seems to have been the history of a liaison which broke poor La Vallière's heart. It was perhaps almost against his better judgment that Louis allowed himself to be enticed by Athenais' hard self-assurance, the sparkle, the wit, the mimicry which drew an audience whenever she spoke; but if he felt any qualms he stifled them in the thought that the seduction of a Mortemart was a feather in the cap of even a King of France.

For his subsequent treatment of Louise it is hard to find any excuse; he had broken her heart, he might have refrained from crucifying her. He might have allowed her to disappear into the obscurity of her newly acquired Duchy of Vaujours. But this did not harmonize with his plans. Mme. de Montespan was a married woman with a troublesome husband, who did not see eye to eye with the King about the honour which he proposed to do him; it would on all counts be desirable that the Court in general and M. de Montespan in particular should think that La Vallière was still his mistress and Mme. de Montespan their confidante. And thus was Louise's new life arranged for her.

While the King spent his afternoon in Athenais' bedroom,

Louise, who still loved Louis, and whom Louis knew still to love him, sat alone with her thoughts in the ante-room. Small wonder that when at last she summoned up courage to enter religion, the unsentimental Carmelites said that she had done much to expiate her sins in the last five years she had spent at Court. How could Louis have treated her with such callous brutality? "Frenchmen," says R. L. Stevenson, "on the whole are not very nice to women"; and we must leave it at that.

It is a remarkable fact, and sets us wondering about the supposed female talent for intrigue, that Madame, La Vallière, and Montespan were each in turn the engineers of their own downfall; Madame, by her absurd plot over La Vallière, La Vallière by her too ready acceptance of the treacherous friendship of Mme. de Montespan, and Montespan by her solution of the problem of the care of her bastards. Indeed, Mme. de Montespan, for all her wit, showed very little intelligence in her dealings with this business of the children. Children bored and irritated her, and she was so stupid as not to hide the fact from Louis, though she must have known that one of the pleasanter features of his character was his love for children in general, and for his own bastards in particular. She was even unwise enough to sneer at his affection for them, which she openly characterized as a *bourgeois* trait which he had inherited from Marie de Médicis, his grandmother. It was the beginning of the final rift in a liaison which had for long been showing signs of wear and tear; for Louis was not finding his beloved Athenais any easier to live with as time went on. He was becoming increasingly aware that what is wit in public is apt to take a sharper edge in private. To see his brilliant mistress' triumphant rapier play in public was one thing; to encounter it himself in his inner penetralia, where he must stand or fall as Louis de Bourbon, was quite another. With such thoughts in his mind it was hardly surprising that Louis should have shown a certain lack of enthusiasm when Mme. de Montespan suggested the widow Scarron as the ideal governess for the children; he must see a good deal of whoever filled the post, and the widow had a reputation for wit, a commodity of which the King felt he already had as much as he required. It was with considerable misgiving and reluctance that he sanctioned the appointment.

The life of Françoise d'Aubigné, Mme. Scarron (1635–1719), better known as Mme. de Maintenon, had up to this point been that of the heroine of a picaresque romance. Born in a jail, poultry keeper in a mouldering provincial manor, alternately Huguenot and Catholic according to the whim of her protectresses, nominal wife of a struggling man of letters, she emerges into the daylight as governess to Louis XIV's bastards at the age of thirty-five, already one of the most complex and enigmatical figures of the age. Charming she was, according to testimony that cannot be set aside. But, unlike her great contemporary, Mme. de Sévigné, she has not been able to communicate that volatile and evanescent quality to her equally voluminous correspondence. Mme. de Sévigné was a virtuous woman, but she is not constantly telling us so; Mme. de Maintenon is as obsessed with her own chastity as an Elizabethan heroine. To charm and to be virtuous, these are her twin ambitions, and the attainment of the second came very easily to her, for she was of an exceptionally cold temperament.[1] She herself tells us in speaking of her youth: "I have seen something of everything, but always in such a way as to gain a blameless reputation. The liking I inspired was rather a general affection than one of love. I did not desire to be loved in particular by anybody. I wished my name to be uttered with admiration and respect."

Even in this short passage there is something one feels a little priggish, something of the schoolroom, a kind of bloodlessness which prejudices us against her. Above all, there is that wariness which is ever present—and worse still ever evident—in all she writes. It is difficult to quarrel either with the sentiment or the mode of its expression, but how much she leaves unsaid. Her every word seems to have been selected, weighed, considered in its relation to every other word before it is allowed to escape from her pen. We never catch her off her guard, for she has a wonderful power of not giving herself away. "I have," says Mme. du Deffand after reading her letters, "a high opinion of her intelligence, little esteem for her heart, and no liking for her person." Had we something of the huge mass of letters which was addressed to Mme. de Maintenon, we should be in a better position to understand her; but she burnt them all in her old age. *Je veux rester une énigme pour*

---

[1] "Elle avait un dégoût marqué pour cet état (marriage). . . . Devenue la femme de Louis XIV, et malgré l'affection sincère qu'elle avait pour ce prince, elle garda ses repugnances: elle ne se soumettait qu'avec regret au devoir conjugal et . . . son directeur dût l'exorter à se vaincre dans *ces occasions pénibles.*" *Corres. Mme. de Maintenon,* edit. Lavallée, Paris, 1865, I, 85.

la postérité she said in answer to her secretary's protests. She has had her wish.

Whatever Mme. de Maintenon may have been, no one could deny that she was a devoted foster-mother to Mme. de Montespan's neglected children. Here lay a danger for Mme. de Montespan, but the first shiver of apprehension does not seem to have struck her until Louis' return from the deathbed of one of the children in 1672: a deathbed which the mother had not put herself to the trouble of visiting. "Mme. de Maintenon knows how to love," said the King heavily; "there would be great pleasure in being loved by her." It was the beginning of the end for the reigning favourite.

Whether Mme. de Maintenon deliberately set herself to win Louis' affections or whether Louis drifted into love with her through the common bond of the children, must forever remain uncertain. But it is at least obvious that the governess was an adept at biding her time. To Mme. de Montespan, long after her own position was seriously undermined, the rival still appeared in the light of an excellent upper servant who relieved her of the boredom of having to discuss the children's ailments and clever sayings with the King: and she remained fatally unaware of how deeply Louis was hurt by her neglect of their family, and how increasingly he turned to the governess for sympathy and understanding. Be the inner facts what they may, it was on the surface a slow deadly battle between the two women, fought in its early stages with smiles and curtseys, and one in which Mme. de Montespan lost round after round. In the middle of the struggle Louise de La Vallière at last found the peace which she desired in a convent, forgiven by the Queen, and leaving Louis in tears; for his heart was ever filled with a generous warmth of emotion at the sight of self-sacrifice in others.

The early weeks of 1673 found relations between Mmes. de Montespan and Maintenon approaching a crisis, and towards the end of February Louis surprised the two women in the midst of a furious quarrel: and it was Mme. de Maintenon who gained the King's ear. For not only was Louis tiring of Mme. de Montespan's tantrums, he was also growing seriously uneasy about the state of his soul, and about his personal reputation; Bossuet had disturbed him greatly with his outspoken rebukes, and there were hints and nuances in the tone of society which suggested that the continuance of the vices which had sat so gracefully on Louis in the 'sixties were becoming indecorous in a man who was nearing middle age. There was a rupture: reconciliation: a final rupture. And six months after the death of the Queen in 1683 came Mme. de Maintenon's triumph. She became the second wife of Louis XIV. And of a new Louis, whose reformation was to be lasting; there would be no more mistresses, no more dallying in the by-ways of love. That domesticity which he had cynically promised his dead Queen he would adopt at the age of thirty, descended upon him in his forty-sixth year. The King's amorous adventures were over.

Louis was not, and probably would not have claimed to be, a man of first rate intelligence, much less a man of genius, and his education had been deplorable. But to say that he had learnt nothing was an exaggeration; since Mazarin had reluctantly admitted him to the Council of State he had been brought into contact with the cleverest men in France, and he had not wasted his opportunities. All his life he was a good listener and a skilful questioner; he had early acquired the reputation of being a man with whom a secret was perfectly safe; and he rarely forgot a piece of information, or failed to arrive at a sound estimate of a man's character by listening to his conversation. *En conversant on achève sa pensée* was one of his favourite maxims, and about this time he writes:

A prince who can control his expression and his words in order to learn other men's views without betraying his own . . . should not avoid such occasions as offer to listen to talk on all kinds of topics, gambling, hunting and so forth . . . he must make up his mind to listen to a good deal of nonsense . . . but the man who says a worthless thing today may say a valuable one tomorrow.

Of book learning, Louis had next to nothing; he could speak Spanish and Italian, had somehow acquired a prose style which wins the approval of no less a judge than Ste. Beuve, and knew enough arithmetic to keep his own accounts, often worth inspection, if only to notice in what different perspective some of the famous men of the reign are seen by their contemporaries and by posterity. Thus in the pensions list for 1664 we find the following entries:

To the Sieur Racine, a French poet   40 louis d'or
To the Sieur Chapelain, the greatest
    French poet who has ever lived   150 louis d'or

But if his knowledge was scanty, Louis was well aware of his own deficiencies and made real efforts to remedy them: "I considered that it was very little consonant with my glory, holding the rank in the world which I do, not to know those things which the better part of the world knows; and that if it was painful to learn so late, it was shameful to remain ignorant always."

To the assets already noticed, we may add good-nature, a strong sense of justice, a taste for hard work, a determination to get to the bottom of any subject which presented itself, and a fund of common sense, which latter was however constantly at war with his over-weening arrogance, or stultified by his religious bigotry. And lastly he had a truly royal memory, even for trifles. In 1679, for instance, at a review of the Household Troops, he stopped in front of a certain trooper, remarked that he was riding a horse captured at Valenciennes three years earlier, and told him that it was time that he had a fresh mount.

To his fairness and good-nature even St. Simon bears witness. A Maid-of-Honour whose lover was in the Bastille could rate him like a fishwife, and even threaten to scratch his face without drawing from him anything but apologetic compliments. He orders a wedding dress for the Duchess of Burgundy, and the tailor assures the King that all other orders will wait until he has executed His Majesty's; certainly not, says Louis, the orders must be executed in strict rotation. On the same occasion we find him going out of his way to obtain justice for the Duc de Rohan, though he disliked him more than any man in France, and took no trouble to hide the fact. There is some hitch at the royal *lever*, and the throng try to pay their court by abusing the valet who has made the blunder: "Let us remember," says Louis, "that he is much more upset about it than I am." At Marly he is going hunting, but on seeing the wetness of the ground and reflecting how much damage he must do his neighbour's corn, he cancels the hunt.

Nor was his sense of fair play confined to trifles and matters of compliment. In 1666 he is investigating naval affairs, and tells us:

They (the lower deck) complained that their captains kept back a portion of their pay, and petitioned for another mode of payment than by the captains. The captains on the other hand maintained that to pay their men was one of the privileges of their appointments . . . but I, seeing that justice was on the side of the sailors, whose complaints appeared to be well founded . . . ordered that they should be paid at the bank.

His ready acceptance of the unspectacular drudgery of kingship, the humdrum office routine, is the more to his credit in that no man was less naturally inclined to desk work than was Louis XIV. But as time goes on, the uncongenial labour brings its own reward:

There is another thing, my son, which I hope experience will never teach you; you would find that there is no harder work than idleness, if you had the misfortune to fall into such a way of life; bored first with business, then with pleasure, and lastly with yourself, hunting everywhere for what is not to be found, that is to say the comfort of rest and leisure without the toil and fatigue which must precede it.

And he goes on to warn his heir that no pressure of work or amusement must render him inaccessible to those who really have business with him—Ambassadors always excepted, for these should never be seen without self-preparation; for they sometimes find, if one receives them too familiarly, a favourable opportunity either to obtain their desires or penetrate the King's designs. It was not a danger to which Louis himself was ever exposed, and he was well aware of the fact, for he goes on to say: "However alert one may be to surprise my plans, I think I don't deceive myself in saying that those who are always at the Louvre know no more than those who never come near me."

Nothing shows more clearly his determination to get to the root of a matter than his personal examination of the *placets*, petitions to the Crown, which poured in in such numbers, and the common sense with which he reviewed them:

They came in great numbers, but I did not allow that to put me off . . . many of them were concerned with lawsuits, which I neither could nor should have evoked from the courts (i.e., withdrawn from the ordinary courts to be dealt with by the royal council). But even in this work, at first sight useless, I found much of value to me. By these *placets* I was able to instruct myself in the details of the state of my people . . . I could quote instances of oppression to my judges and demand further information in such cases, and seek a general remedy. One or two examples of this kind were sufficient to put a stop to a thousand similar ills.

Care in such matters was to grow into a habit. In 1687 Mme. de Maintenon replies to Mme. de Caylus who has asked for a *lettre de câchet* to send a relative into a convent: "The King won't do that without first writing to your provincial Intendant to ask what it is all about, and that will create no end of a hullabaloo. Reflect whether in these circumstances you still want me to speak to the King."

One fortuitous but valuable asset Louis had when he began to reign, namely, the universal hatred felt towards his predecessor the Cardinal, or rather towards the two Cardinals, Richelieu and Mazarin. Fifty-one years had passed since Ravaillac made an end of the last French King who had both reigned and governed, and public opinion passionately desired an end of the régime of Mayors of the Palace. About Richelieu there had at least been something imposing, and he had done much for the glory of France. So for that matter had Mazarin, but Court and public saw in him only the detested Signor Pantaleone, the shabby tricky comedian of an Italian farce. France has rarely been grateful to those who have expanded her influence by unspectacular methods, and more rarely still forgives the man like Mazarin who shows an open contempt for *la gloire*. Louis, they rightly surmised, would take a very different line, and the ring of arrogance in his earliest utterances was received with an almost hysterical joy by Frenchman who were sick to death of the old Court and all its works. Louis was to give them their bellyful of *la gloire* before they were done with him, but this they naturally could not foresee, and the young captain at the head of his magnificent team of generals, statesmen and diplomats was adulated in a way that might pardonably have turned the head of a much older man.

But the most lasting and important of Louis' assets was his own deep conviction that as King of France he stood in a peculiar personal relationship with God: a conviction which was strengthened and sustained by the narrowness and rigidity of his own religious beliefs. Many of his contemporaries would indeed rather have described them as inadequate; the Bishop of Chartres for instance complains that the King is inclined to confound all that is austere and distasteful with virtuous living, and goes on to give Mme. de Maintenon the following advice: "I think you would do the King a great service if you could persuade him to join you in prayer occasionally. Such prayers should be short, very simple, and proportioned to his state of inapplication."

Mme. de Maintenon herself, who understood Louis better than anyone, says on the same subject:

He wants to accommodate religion to himself, not himself to religion; he wishes to observe all its externals, but not its spirit. He will never miss a station or a penance, but he will never understand that it is necessary to humiliate himself and enter into the true spirit of penitence. . . . He understands perfectly that he must confess in all good faith, and be scrupulous in fasting, almsgiving and so forth; but he doesn't in the least understand that what he needs is conversion.

About the same time his sister-in-law, Madame Palatine, writes to a friend in Germany: "It is inconceivable how naïf he is in matters of religion . . . the reason is that he has never made any study of it, has never read his Bible, and believes whatever he is told . . . he doesn't wish to have the fatigue of finding out for himself what religion really is." Finally, Bossuet, in an unguarded moment, asserted that the King's degree of religious enlightenment was on a par with that of a charcoal burner.

On the whole, however, these opinions seem to be unfair, or at least exaggerated. When we turn to Louis' memoirs we find that he had in fact given the matter some thought, and was perfectly capable of giving a reason for the faith that was in him:

In the first place I have allowed great weight to the general consent of all nations and of all centuries, and more particularly to the fact that nearly all the celebrated men of whom I have heard have reverenced piety . . . if, in the most important thing in the world . . . human reason was deceived in all times and in all natures into making us accept a chimera and always the same chimera, it would not be reason at all which is an extravagance which no reasonable person can maintain.

Then follows a passage on "machines, buildings, and a thousand other things" in which he anticipates Paley's watch, after which he goes on to consider the diversity of religions: "They have all at bottom so much in common . . . that their very diversity visibly confirms the existence of a true religion of which all the others are imperfect or falsified copies, conserving the most striking characteristics of the original."

And he proceeds to establish the existence of Christianity as that true religion with an argument very characteristic of his century: "All clever and enlightened men surrendered themselves to it as soon as it appeared, and today it is followed, not like all other religions by barbarous ignorant and gross nations, but by all those where good sense and *savoir vivre* are most cultivated."

And the whole concludes with an exordium on the duties and responsibilities of one who is to bear the title of *Rex Christianissimus*.

What Louis understood to be the position of the bearer of that title is made perfectly clear in other parts of the memoirs:

As he (the king) is of a rank superior to all other men, he sees things more perfectly than they do, and he ought to trust rather to the inner light than to information which reaches him from outside . . . occupying, so to speak, the place of God, we seem to be sharers of His knowledge as well as of His authority.

Exercising as we do the Divine functions here below. . . .

Kings, whom God appoints the sole guardians of the public weal. . . .

It is for kings to make their own decisions, for no one else either dares or is able to suggest any that are as good or as royal as those which we make ourselves.

Holding such maxims as he did, Louis' conception of his duties towards his subjects was a perfectly logical one. He had inherited France, just as any other French gentleman might inherit an estate; it was his property, always under God, and it was his duty to conduct himself as a virtuous and enlightened *seigneur*. But the idea that his tenants and domestics should have any say in the management of the estate would have struck him as fantastic. He asserts his position in so many words: "Kings, being absolute rulers, have naturally full and free liberty to dispose of all property, whether in the hands of the clergy or of the laity." And in another place he underlines this dictum by assuring his son that all the money in France belongs to the King, even that portion of it which he leaves in the hands of his commercial classes for the purposes of trade; in other words, the merchant class are simply the servants in the Parable of the Talents.

Louis often speaks of a king's duties, but nearly always we find that he means by that his duties towards God. True, he tells us that it is the duty of a king to rule justly, to refrain from oppression, and to ease the burdens of his people; but he goes on to add that if a king rules unjustly, this gives the subject no shadow of a right to complain, much less to rebel. The unjust king's rights remain unaffected, and his offence is not one against his people but against God.

And let us be fair to Louis XIV. His enumeration of a king's duties towards his people is no mere rhetorical flourish: if he was singularly unsuccessful in easing his subject's burdens, he at least never abandoned the hope and intention of doing so. As late as 1692 Mme. de Maintenon writes: "The King knows the sufferings of his people, nothing is hidden from him there, and he seeks all means of relieving them."

And again the following year: "The King wishes at all costs to see his people happier."

Where a king holds the views of a Louis XIV, the subject has but two courses open to him: he may accept the king's premiss, or he may try to chop off his head. The one thing which he cannot do is to attempt to argue with him, for the man who asserts that he is the recipient of a personal revelation is in a dialectically unassailable position. France chose to accept the personal revelation theory, with results which have not yet fully worked themselves out.

Louis has been accused both of choosing his ministers badly, and of being led by the nose by them when chosen; he had, say his detractors, all France to choose from, and he selects Pontchartrains and Chamillarts. But had he? With his usual good sense he points out for the benefit of the Dauphin that this nation-wide field of choice is illusory: kings are in fact restricted to choosing from the circle of men whose qualifications are already known to them. To hunt for new talent in the provinces is simply to saddle oneself with another man's protégé instead of one's own. And indeed, had Louis made any attempt to comb France for talent, there is no reason to suppose that the result would have been any more satisfactory than his own system of selection. We boast today of having replaced the narrow educational ladder of former times by a wide and expensive staircase, but it does not seem to produce Colberts and Le Telliers in any greater numbers than did the methods of the seventeenth century.

As to the charge that Louis was led by the nose, one indisputable fact seems to refute it. Where a king is a rubber stamp in the hands of his ministers, a change of ministry more often than not produces a change of policy. But where is the change in the fundamentals of French policy between 1661 and 1715? Ministers come and go, but policy remains unaltered. If the King himself was not the director of policy, then who was? And why is there a startling *volte face* and a complete domestic reorganization as soon as Louis XIV is dead?

Much ridicule has been cast on the punctilio, not to say braggadocio, of etiquette whereby Louis was always on the alert to exact the uttermost farthing of respect from his neighbours, and indeed some of his battles for European precedence now strike us as sufficiently ridiculous. But Louis has his defence ready. Subjects, he tells us, being ignorant of the inner working of the state, can found their judgments only on externals; and it is by the precedence accorded to his sovereign that the subject estimates his international standing. Therefore, so far from giving way in the most trifling points of precedence, it is the duty of a king to be ever on the *qui vive* to assert his position at the expense of his rivals. For, as he remarks elsewhere, a king who is not advancing is a king who is going backwards.

It is in the military portion of his own memoirs that we get the most interesting insight into Louis' character; for, like so many of us, it is not on the thing that he can really do, but on that which he imagines he can do, that his mind rests with most satisfaction. He was a very able foreign minister, and is indeed quite aware of the fact, but the memoirs appeal to posterity in every line to recognize the greatness of Louis the General. And Louis the General is an illusion born of his own vanity, and kept alive by the tongue-in-cheek praise of his Marshals. Victories indeed he had, of the kind which are always within the grasp of the absolute ruler of a powerful military state, but Louis never even looked like forcing his way into the inner ring of great commanders: admission to that circle of the elect does not come by striving, however earnest. And in the military section of his memoirs Louis exposes with pitiless clarity his own lack of qualification for high command. Not that we find here any carpet knight, or unmasked sham hero. The picture which emerges is that of a brave, hard working, conscientious, accurate, rather pedestrian junior staff officer, of the type invaluable in subordinate posts, who will in due course retire on a colonel's pension. There is initiative and foresight in matters of detail, no appreciation of the larger issues of a campaign. Always he has his eyes on the trees, never on the wood, and indeed he is often concerned with saplings rather than trees: "I entered into the smallest details, and kept myself informed of even trifles in order to do everything well."

Indeed, yes. What are we to make of a Commander-in-Chief who himself drafts such orders as these: "When the assembly sounds, the officers will turn their men out of the tents as quickly as possible. . . . It is forbidden to leave the ranks without permission. . . . One officer and twenty troopers per brigade will be detached daily for forage escort." And at times he becomes flatly ridiculous, as when he draws up a directive for the use of regimental officers on l'enterrement des ordures; here he is no longer usurping the functions of his junior staff officers, but those of the regimental doctor. Small wonder if, across their respective lines, the Imperial Marshals smiled with complete understanding when the Marshals of France winked and jerked their thumbs at Louis XIV caracoling under the guns of a besieged fortress. Whilst the King fondly imagined himself to be holding the stage, professional interest on both sides was centred on the performance of the commandant of the fortress, and as regarded Louis, the enemy generals merely pigeonholed the fact in their memories that his presence was a considerable handicap to the French Higher Command. Even if his own generals saw the King as he really was, they were none the less compelled by the whole social structure to give outward adherence to the doctrine that he was a great commander: so in the race for promotion and pensions—especially pensions—they outvied each other in comparing his exploits with those of Caesar and Alexander.

With disastrous results. The years of easy victory bred in Louis the conviction that, controlling everything as he did, his own whereabouts was a matter of indifference. Given efficient lieutenants in the field, he felt himself competent to conduct a campaign from Versailles, which was all very well so long as the lieutenants were really efficient, and only pretended to take their orders from Louis. But there came a day when the supply of efficient men failed, and their successors really did demand the King's instructions before executing any manoeuvre, which in due course produced the battles of Ramillies and Oudenarde, and very nearly cost Louis his Crown.

But if Louis the General was a nuisance to his Higher Command, Louis the Foreign Minister was a genuine national asset; that is, if we allow that territorial expansion is the only logical and legitimate object of foreign policy. In the dexterity with which he isolated his victims, the skill with which he sowed dissension among his opponents, and in his complete lack of scruples, he showed himself a pupil of whom Mazarin might well have been proud. Let us hear him on the sanctity of treaties, writing sometime about 1669; he is referring particularly at the moment to treaties between the Houses of Bourbon and Hapsburg, but there is nothing in his remarks which conflicts with his general practice regarding the keeping of treaties with any power. Having explained that Europe is so constituted that a Hapsburg gain must be a Bourbon loss, he goes on:

This causes between us a jealousy which . . . is essential, a sort of permanent hostility which treaties may plaster over but cannot extinguish. . . . And, to tell the truth, it is in this spirit that we enter into all treaties. Whatever specious articles one may include about union, friendship, and the seeking of common advantages, the real meaning, which each party understands quite well . . . is that we shall abstain from all overt hostilities and public demonstrations of bad faith; for as regards secret infractions . . . these are expected by each party. . . . So one may say that in dispensing with the obligation to observe a treaty in all its rigour, one does not contravene its terms, because no one has taken its words literally, although it is necessary to use such words, just as in society one uses expressions of compliment, absolutely necessary if we are to live politely, but which really have no particular significance.

And yet we are apt to think of the "cold war" as a twentieth-century invention. But what roused even more resentment against Louis XIV than his cold wars, or even his open and brutal aggressions, was his infuriating assumption that he was divinely ap-

pointed to stand *in loco parentis* to all members of the European
ruling caste. Not even Louis had the assurance to adopt a paternal attitude towards the Emperor, and with Charles II of England he completely failed in his attempt to do so; for his astute
and cynical cousin was always more than a match for him, largely
by reason of the fact that whilst Louis had many irons in the fire,
Charles's whole energies were concentrated on remaining King of
England. And though Louis held the purse strings, the result of
his foreign policy was to make it always a seller's market for Charles.
And Louis was a most gullible buyer.

But things were very different for the unhappy Dutch, the Rhine
princes, the Italian soverigns, and even for the Spaniards, when
they had the insolence to revolt against Louis' despotism. His dealings with Victor Amadeus II, fourteenth Duke of Savoy (1666–
1732), may be taken as typical of his way of treating the weaker
princes on his perimeter. In 1684 this prince had been forced into
a marriage with Louis XIV's niece, Mlle. de Valois (1669–1728),
and the Duke was not long in discovering what was the rôle expected from a sovereign who had had the honour of marrying into
the House of Bourbon.

Shortly after the marriage Louis calls the Duke's attention to
the existence of a heretic Savoyard population in the Waldensian
valleys, and goes on to say that he counts on their speedy extermination; the Duke replied evasively, seeking to escape on the ground
of expense. No expense at all, says Louis kindly, he himself will
lend troops and a general for the purpose. To liquidate a peaceful
and industrious section of his people was the last thing the Duke
desired to do, but his quibbles and cunctations were useless;
Catinat with a French army invaded the valleys—there was no
longer a Cromwell to intervene—and dealt with the inhabitants in
a manner which sickened even the French Ambassador at Turin.
To his credit, the Ambassador protested to Versailles, but received
only the pitiless reply: "It is fortunate for the Duke of Savoy that
illness is saving him a great deal of trouble with the rebels ('rebels' is good) of the valleys, and I have no doubt that he will easily
console himself for the loss of subjects who can be replaced by
others far more dependable."

Loathing the part he had been forced to play, the Duke announces that he is going to seek distraction and consolation at the
Venice Carnival; the fact is reported to Versailles, and Louis writes

to his Ambassador to put a peremptory veto on the proposed excursion, adding that if the Duke is disobedient, seven thousand French troops will enter Savoy to show that Louis means to be obeyed. Nothing remains for the unfortunate Duke but to assure the French Ambassador that he has been misled by rumour, and that he would not think of leaving his capital without first obtaining the permission of the Most Christian King.

Louis' treatment of the Duke of Savoy is perhaps an extreme case, but his manner of procedure elsewhere was much the same in essentials. "It will be necessary," Louvois used to say joyfully of some recalcitrant prince, "to show him the rods": or in other words send a powerful punitive expedition to his frontier. If the troublesome prince made instant submission, well and good: if not, a *blitzkrieg* was launched upon him with every possible attendant circumstance of horror. But Louis bore no malice; he might have applied to himself the words of a very different man, Ruskin— "my native disposition, though I say it, is extremely amiable when I'm not bothered." As the chastised prince looked across his ruined land, there over the western horizon loomed the colossal figure of the Sun-King with outstretched, pleading arms; all he asked of the culprit was that he should fling himself at his feet, and Louis would raise him up, kiss him on both cheeks, and assure him that the past should be forgotten and forgiven. Some princes adopted the rôle of prodigal son lest worse things should befall them. But not all. It was for instance singularly unfortunate from the French point of view that the incorrigibles should include William of Orange.

One feels that one should hate Louis XIV, and yet, somehow, it is not easy to do so; we are in the same quandary as those hostile contemporaries who set out to blacken him and finish by according him an exasperated and reluctant admiration. We remember, not that he brought his last war upon his own head, but the magnificent courage with which he faced its disasters; the years when even St. Simon admits that he showed himself really worthy of the title of *Louis Le Grand* which had been so prematurely bestowed upon him. Consider him in the spring of 1712, when Villars (1653–1734) waits upon him at Marly for his farewell audience before starting for the Flanders front to assume command of the last hope of France: the hungry, ragged army behind which are no reinforcements except the palace guard at Versailles. Louis,

says Villars, had shown himself unmoved before the courtiers, but
when he led the Marshal into his private room, the tears were running down his face. His first words to Villars were: "It happens to
few men to lose within a week a grandson, a grand-daughter and
a great grandson, all of much promise, and all of whom I loved
tenderly. God has punished me, and I have deserved it. . . . But
enough of this. . . . If disaster overtakes your army, how would
you advise me to act personally?"

Even the imperturbable Villars was considerably taken aback by
such an unexpected question: and as he hesitated to answer it, the
King continued, "While you are thinking I'll give you my own
views." His Ministers, said Louis, were unanimous that he should
move the seat of government to Blois: but he refused to consider a
step which he clearly saw would be the preliminary act to his ab-
dication.

"I know that an army of this size cannot be so cut up that the
bulk of it will be unable to fall back on the Somme. . . . What
I shall do is to go to Peronne or St. Quentin, scrape up what troops
I can, join you, and we will make one last effort, in which we
will either die together or save the state." It is easy to belittle
Louis XIV, and yet it is no small achievement to have held the
centre of the stage for over fifty years: and how many other kings
have imposed their name upon a century?

Eugène of Savoy (1663–1736) disliked Louis, and had everything to justify him in doing so; yet nothing of it appears in his
memoirs for 1715: "When I heard of the death of Louis XIV, I
admit it had the same effect upon me as if I had heard of a splendid old oak uprooted and laid flat upon the ground by a storm.
He had stood upright for so long! Death, before it effaces great
memories, recalls them for a moment in a flash of time."

But in this case death has not effaced great memories; in the historical sense Louis still lives, and not even yet have we arrived at
a definitive evaluation of the man and his work. Was he perhaps
after all a square peg in a round hole? One of nature's Orientals,
who would have been better placed as a benevolent Eastern despot
than as *Rex Christianissimus?* The idea is not entirely fanciful,
whether we look at his private life or at his domestic policy; Louis
the man rolls through France in his great coach with the Queen,
La Vallière and Montespan, unperturbed by the *naïveté* of his
excited peasantry who crowd around at halting places, calling to

each other to "come and see the three Queens." And Louis the politician is emphatically a leveller; he frankly dislikes a graduated hierarchy, and does his best, if not to abolish, at least to ignore it; King and subjects, these according to Louis should be the only two classes in the state. The *noblesse* is thrust aside and its place taken by *bourgeois viziers* whom the King has raised from nothing, and can dismiss to their original nothingness at a wave of his hand. Thus he endeavours to create a world in which he only shall stand out above the dead level of twenty million subjects.

In his lifetime Louis XIV undoubtedly appeared bigger than he was: even physically bigger. Hébert, parish priest of Versailles, who knew him well, says: "He is a very tall man, and very well proportioned, he is six feet tall as near as makes no matter, big in proportion to his height, with large shoulders and well-shaped legs." As a matter of fact Louis was about five foot five, but Hébert, if physically inaccurate, is symbolically correct in his description of him. Through his diary we look, not at the real Louis, but, which is much more interesting, at the Louis whom all France saw. And if we are no longer prepared to accept him as a six footer, we are still as far as ever from having decided that his real height was only five foot five.

II

The Court

Versailles, says the modern historian, was not seventeenth-century France; and he has spent much ink in endeavouring to refocus the age in the light of that assertion. But popular opinion remains unshaken by the modern view, and not unjustly. For if Versailles was not all France, it was at least the place to which all French eyes were turned, the concretion in stone and marble of the apocryphal dictum *l'état c'est moi*, a theory of life made visible. Regularity, dignity, magnificence, a bleak and comfortless splendour brooded throughout the huge *château* and the well-disciplined gardens, whose cost remains unknown to this day; for even Louis XIV blenched at the figures, and burnt Mansart's accounts.

We must not, however, reproach Versailles with its lack of comfort, for the idea of making it comfortable never entered the head of either builder or owner. By Louis and his contemporaries comfort was held in contempt, as an aspiration unworthy of a gentleman; the mark of the man of quality, as the King once said, is indifference to heat, cold, hunger and thirst. And if in the interior of the palace there was little indifference shown to hunger and thirst, there was at any rate ample opportunity for a stoic endurance of other discomforts. When the royal architect pointed out to his master that if certain chimneys were not raised, the fires would smoke, Louis replied that it was a matter of indifference to him whether they smoked or not, so long as the chimneys were not visible from the gardens. Mme. de Maintenon complains bitterly of the discomfort of her room at Fontainebleau where there is a window the size of an arcade, to which she is not allowed to fit a shutter because it would mar the external symmetry of the façade, with the result that the room was freezing in winter, and baking hot in summer. Magnificence was what was aimed at in a seventeenth-century house, not comfort.

The enormous *château* of Versailles, with its ten thousand inhabitants, in which was spent six out of every ten francs collected in taxes, was something more than a mere seat of government. To the man or woman of ambition it was a lottery in which the prizes were dazzling, and in which few could resist the temptation to take a ticket. The country gentleman, sulking in enforced idleness in his manor house, did not stop to consider how long were the odds against his drawing a prize; had not X, no whit better bred than himself, got a regiment, and little Y, the joke of the province, a Court office? And who was Z that his wife should be *au mieux* with a Princess of the Blood? Look at the d'Estrées family: obscure country gentlemen until Gabrielle had taken the fancy of Henri IV: and what were the d'Estrées now? In four generations they had produced two ecclesiastical and five lay peers, a cardinal, a Grandee of Spain, three Marshals of France, five Knights of the Order, a Minister of State, three Ambassadors and two Vice-Admirals. So yet another squire would mortgage his estate, mount his horse, and set off on the road to Versailles, confident in his ability to make his way under the eye of the King and with the assistance of his patron. For the great man of his province was almost certain to be his distant relative, and the *grand seigneur* would reluctantly admit his country cousin's claim to his assistance: probably not in cash, of which the great man himself would be uncommonly short, but he would feed him, perhaps find him a free garret to sleep in, and would have no objection to the newcomer using his name to obtain credit with the Court tradespeople.

And so a new courtier has arrived at Versailles. Not of course to live in the *château*, for many weary years will have to pass before he is even considered for a vacant attic; unless some lucky accident befall him such as happened to the Marquis de Dangeau when impromptu verse making was in fashion. The King one day jokingly offered him a room if he could fill in a set of verses on the spot; Dangeau did so, and Louis, who never broke a promise, gave him the coveted room. But this sort of thing came to few, and our newly fledged courtier could resign himself to an expensive lodging in the town, which he would never see by daylight in the winter months; to a life of rising in the shivering night to hurry to his patron's *lever* and to follow him to the King's, of standing all day in the ante-rooms, and of returning with aching feet to his bed in the small hours of the next morning.

But greater than his material sufferings would be those of a kind with which most of us are familiar, the embarrassments and agonies of a new boy at school; for there is a remarkable resemblance between the life of old Versailles and that of a public school. At Versailles was the same complex unwritten law, the same struggle for trivial distinctions, an intricate and illogical code of privilege, with public shame and biting rebuke for the man who transgressed against its provisions. Even the most unpleasing of public school vices, though abhorred by the King, flourished in that section of the Court which was under the influence of his depraved brother, *Monsieur*, the Duc d'Orléans.

Court etiquette was a life study. Who for instance could guess that at Versailles it was the height of bad manners to knock at a door? You must scratch it with the little finger of the left hand, growing the finger nail long for that purpose. Or could know that you must not *tutoyer* an intimate friend in any place where the King was present? That if the lackey of a social superior brought you a message, you had to receive him standing, and bare-headed? You have mastered the fact that you must not knock on a door, so when you go to make your first round of calls in the great houses in the town, you scratch: wrong again, you should have knocked. Next time you rattle the knocker, and a passing exquisite asks you contemptuously if you are so ignorant as not to know that you give one blow of the knocker on the door of a lady of quality? Who could guess that if you encounter the royal dinner on its way from the kitchens to the table, you must bow as to the King himself, sweep the ground with the plume of your hat, and say in a low, reverent, but distinct voice, *La viande du Roi?* Many times must the apprentice courtier have echoed the psalmist's lament, "Who can tell how oft he offendeth?" And it behoved you not to offend, for the King had an eye like a hawk, or shall we say, like a school prefect, for any breach of etiquette, and not even the most exalted were safe from his reproof. One night at supper his chatterbox of a brother put his hand in a dish before Louis had helped himself: "I perceive," said the King icily, "that you are no better able to control your hands than your tongue." Once at Marly, Mme. de Torcy, wife of a minister, took a seat above a duchess at supper. Louis, to her extreme discomfort, regarded her steadfastly throughout the meal, and when he reached Mme. de Maintenon's room, the storm broke; he had, he said, witnessed a piece of insolence so intolerable that the sight of it had prevented him from eating: a piece of presumption which would have been unendurable in a woman of quality. It took the combined efforts of Mme. de Maintenon and the Duchess of Burgundy the rest of the evening to pacify him. Decidedly not a king with whom to take liberties, or even make mistakes. This is Louis, or one side of Louis, at the height of his arrogance and prosperity: the *Grand Monarque* of the middle 'eighties, now forty-five or so, and in reluctant transition from Prince Charming to the impenetrably dignified King who struck Visconti as having the *gravité d'un roi de Théâtre*. Louis and Louis' Court had both been very different twenty years earlier, when the King's ambition had been to be the smartest of the smart set, *homme à bonnes fortunes* in his own right, owing his successes not to his crown but to his own graces. The King who climbed about the roofs of the Louvre at night to find an unbarred window in the quarters of the Maids-of-Honour was a very different man from the King who married Mme. de Maintenon; and for old courtiers it must have been difficult to realize that the new Louis was the same man who, when pinched *a tergo* by a pretty girl in full Court, sprang upwards with a shout of "Damn the bitch!" Villeroi was perhaps the only man left who could venture to remind the King of those old days, in this new Court in which a freezing but superficial decorum and a rigid etiquette had become the rule.

Of all branches of etiquette none caused more continuous and bitter quarrelling than the vexed matter of precedence; its minute and intricate ramifications entangled every waking action from the most intimate to the most public, and affected the daily lives of every inhabitant of the *château* from the Sun-King to the junior washer-up in the Fifth Kitchen. Precedence was a rumbling volcano which could be relied upon to erupt at every wedding, birth, funeral and public ceremony, and every encounter with a distinguished foreigner; and of course at any contact with the Magistracy. Not that the rules of precedence were ill-defined: it was the exceptions, glosses of time, place and circumstance, to say nothing of skilled encroachment, that made the trouble.

But before going into details, let us see the Versailles hierarchy as it was now constituted.

First, of course, came the King, followed by the Dauphin, *Monseigneur* as he was called at Court. Next in seniority came the *Children of France*, that is to say the King's brother, whose Court title was *Monsieur*, and the children and grandchildren of *Monseigneur*. The *Grandchildren of France* was in the later part of the reign a small class, consisting of Louis' first cousin, the Duchesse de Montpensier, known at Court as *Mademoiselle*, *Mademoiselle's* half-sisters, and *Monsieur's* children, the nephews and nieces of the King. Next came the *Princes of the Blood*, a more numerous class, consisting of Bourbons of collateral branches, having a reversionary right to the Crown; its chief members at this time were the Prince de Condé, *M. le Prince* to the Court, his eldest son, the Duc de Bourbon, called *M. le Duc*, the children of *Grandchildren of France*, and the King's bastards. The senior of them held the title of *First Prince of the Blood*; and we may note in passing that for purposes of precedence, a cardinal ranked as a Prince of the Blood. Following the Princes of the Blood came the six ecclesiastical Peers of France, the Count-Bishops of Rheims, Laon, Langres, Beauvais, Noyon, and Châlons, not a little confusion arising here for the modern reader owing to the fact that some of these dignitaries happened to be also dukes and arch-bishops, whilst the Cardinal-Arch-Bishop of Paris, though not an ecclesiastical peer, was a duke. Next in seniority came the lay peers, the dukes. And here let us beware of thinking of a French duke and peer as holding a position identical with, or even closely resembling, that of a duke in England. To begin with, although contemporaries of Louis XIV, and even the King himself, speak of "making" a man a duke, this is merely a convenient way of describing a more complex process. What in fact happened was that the King decided to elevate a certain estate into a duchy-peerage; and it was then for the owner of that estate to get his title ratified by the Parlement of Paris. If the Parlement was not satisfied that the estate could support the dignity, it could, and even under Louis XIV did, refuse to ratify the erection, and Louis on at least one occasion had to give a noble a sum of money to buy an estate which the Parlement would agree to ratify before he could get him made a duke. Once the transaction had been completed, the holder of the new duchy took his seat in the Parlement, not as a duke, but as a peer, and a piece of formal business was brought before the assembly in order that the new peer might vote upon it. The theory was that the dukes were the descendants of the Twelve Peers of Charlemagne, a representative committee of the *noblesse*, sitting as legislators under the King, and assisted by the chief men of the gown as technical advisors. The fact that it was the estate that held the legal position and not the man, explains what must otherwise seem so odd to us, the frequent resignation of a dukedom by an elderly peer in favour of his heir; the transaction is simple enough when we realize that it was merely the legal transfer of an estate, with the retention by the former holder of the life-rent as pension. A French duke naturally never sold his ducal estate, for the obvious reason that, if he had done so, he would have ceased to be a duke, the title being vested in the land. On the other hand, the acquisition of a duchy-peerage estate did not confer a dukedom on the new proprietor, in the way in which the purchase of a countship or marquisate transferred the title to the new owner. In the case of most dukedoms, the original patent limited inheritance to heirs male of the body of the man for whom the estate had originally been erected into a duchy-peerage. Its acquisition by a mere heir-at-law gave no claim to dual rank. The Duc de Chevreuse, for instance, was the heir of the last Duc de Chaulnes; but he became, not Duc de Chevreuse and de Chaulnes, but Duc de Chevreuse Seigneur of the Duchy of Chaulnes.

After the dukes came a small class, the life dukes or *ducs à Brevet*, whose rank was not recognized by the Parlement; they were not peers, and their privileges were limited to certain advantages at Court.

Counts, marquises, and barons must, one imagines, have originally been part of a graduated hierarchy as in the English peerage, but if so, all trace of differentiation had vanished by the seventeenth century, and no one of these titles yields precedence to another. They were all territorial, that is they were attached to the land and not to the individual, but, unlike the duchy-peerages, when one of these estates was sold, the buyer, if noble, could use the title; it is, for instance, by the purchase of an estate that Mme. Scarron was transformed into the Marquise de Maintenon. But so little importance had these titles at Court that their holders were technically untitled; *gens titrés* invariably means the dukes and their wives.

Ranking as the equals of the dukes were the *Foreign Princes*, the most ingeniously usurpative class at Court, and the cause of nine-tenths of the more notorious precedence squabbles. These so-called princes were mainly members of sundry foreign ruling houses domiciled in France, who, although they enjoyed Court parity with the dukes, had no legal status at all. The Lorraine princes were the most formidable and self-assertive members of a group which also included a branch of the House of Savoy, the Italian Gonzaguas, and finally the French Houses of La Tour d'Auvergne and Rohan. Naturally the French dukes resented the pretensions of the two latter houses even more than they did that of the foreigners, and indeed the Frenchmen's status of foreign prince was always as shaky as their claims were shadowy.

Finally, a Grandee of Spain ranked as a duke in France, and a French duke was received as a Grandee of Spain at Madrid.

Looking at this glittering pyramid, it needs little imagination to realize its unstable equilibrium; only the King and Monseigneur rode serenely above the storm level. Grandchildren of France galled the kibes of Children of France, Princes of the Blood attacked the privileges of the Grandchildren of France on the one hand and fought off the dukes on the other, while the Foreign Princes infiltrated where they could.

Who could sit down in the presence of whom, and on what, was perhaps the most fruitful source of bickering, the unending Battle of the Three Chairs: the arm-chair, the chair without arms, and the *tabouret*, or three-legged stool. So important was this matter considered that two prominent people could not meet without a preliminary skirmishing by messenger as to the type of chairs they were to sit upon. Madame, wife of a *Child of France*, proposes to visit her daughter, the Duchess of Lorraine; the Duke of Lorraine claims to sit in an arm-chair in her presence, and the matter at once becomes an affair of state. Long negotiations are conducted by the French and Lorraine Foreign Offices, a deadlock is reached, and the visit is cancelled. But Madame was an old lady who held strong views on the younger generation, and I suspect that the Duke of Lorraine was not so much concerned to claim equality with the Children of France as to ward off a visit from his mother-in-law.

Not even in chapel was there any truce to the war of etiquette; there it was the duty of the duchesses to make the collection in turn, and in 1703 the ladies of the House of Lorraine began to avoid this duty, in order to put themselves on the same footing as Princesses of the Blood. And Louis had to intervene in person to quell the storm which arose. In the following year neither Princes of the Blood nor dukes were able to attend the Adoration of the Cross on Good Friday, because the King had found their quarrel about precedence at the service insoluble. In 1709 the Princesse de Soubise lay dying; how did her husband, a Rohan, react to the blow? He hurriedly arranges for her burial at the church across the street, in order that as soon as she is dead, she may be taken there instead of to the Parish Church: a thing, says St. Simon indignantly, which is never done except in the case of a Prince or Princess of the Blood. On a morning in 1711 the fifteen-year-old Duchesse de Berri, by marriage a *Grand-daughter of France*, is seated at her toilet when the usher on duty throws open both leaves of the door to admit the Duchess' mother, a legitimated *Princess of the Blood*, who is entitled to have only one-half of the door opened for her when visiting her seniors in rank. The Duchesse de Berri, transported with rage, demands the instant dismissal of the usher, regardless of the fact that he happens to be the King's servant and not her own; when her lady-in-waiting refuses to give any such order, she "weeps and storms." But this is nothing to the fury of that same Duchesse de Berri when a few days later she finds it impossible to evade her own duty of handing the chemise to her sister-in-law, the Dauphine, at her *lever*.

But enough of precedence for the moment; books could be written on the subject, and indeed have been. For most contemporary memoirs make it clear that to their writers, precedence is the one serious subject in life; and we can but stand amazed at their childishness.

And now what was the daily life of the courtier, this man who has taken a ticket in the great gamble, the envied of his country relations? How did he live, and what did he do? The answer is simple: he watched the King as a dog does its master whenever permitted to do so, and when the King was invisible, he talked about him to his fellow courtiers.

This, however, does not argue so great a degree of fatuity on the part of the courtiers as one might imagine; for there was no surer way of getting into the King's bad books than to be caught discussing affairs of state. Even the members of his own family were severely snubbed if they attempted to do so, and it is therefore hardly surprising to find that as early as 1680 the only topic of conversation for the men was hunting and horses, whilst the women talked scandal and frocks. A fact more to the King's credit, is that debauchery, drunkenness, vice, and even obscene language, will ruin you as surely as will talking politics.

Let us take a day at this Court, already so alien, so remote from us. If, as we have said before, the courtier was very lucky, he would have a room or rooms in Versailles itself; but what sort of rooms? Happily for us, St. Simon had the best set in the *château*, which gives us a standard of criticism. His quarters consisted of three small rooms, looking out on a stinking courtyard, an entrance hall, very dark and low, and two little closets without windows; in the hall and closets you could just stand upright, these spaces having been cut in two horizontally, to provide servants' cubicles. In addition, in the courtyard outside he had the use of a kitchen which was, he tells us, a very rare convenience in the *château*. As the three best rooms were required for social purposes, St. Simon's study was one of the windowless dens in which candles were needed all day; and yet so appreciated was this suite that a royal duchess once begged the loan of it for a wedding reception which threatened to be too large for her own rooms. It does not sound to us very magnificent, but it was luxury itself as compared with the quarters of the less-favoured courtier. He thought himself happy to be the possessor of a couple of matchboard cabins under the roof, hot in summer, cold in winter, in which he could not speak above a whisper without being overheard by his neighbours, and permanently foetid with the stench of the neighbouring latrines. And if he had so chosen, the fool might have been living the life of a gentleman farmer in God's fresh air!

It was perhaps as well that the courtier had no inducement to linger abed of a morning, for it behoved him to make an early start if he was to be at his post in the ante-room when the King was awakened at eight o'clock. (We are inclined at this time of the day to envy the ladies, who are still in bed, and will not be making a move until nine.) The courtier had had his own toilet to make, which, even if it did not include washing, meant an elaborate powdering and prinking, before attending his patron's *lever* and following him to that of the King.

In the King's room the day began at about a quarter to eight, when the First Valet de Chambre, who had slept in the room, would dismantle and put away his folding bed; if it was winter, the two *porte-buchon du roi*, the royal faggot bearers, would next make their appearance to light the King's fire, followed a minute or two later by the King's watchmaker to wind up the royal watch. From a side door would enter the royal wigmaker, coming from the room in which the King's wigs reposed, each on its pedestal, in glass-fronted wardrobes—hunting wigs, council wigs, evening wigs, walking wigs, an endless array of wigs. But at the moment the wigmaker carries two only, the short wig which the King wears whilst dressing, and the first wig of the day.

All this time Louis would be in bed asleep, or pretending to be so, with the bedclothes turned down to his hips, as is his uncomfortable custom, winter and summer. On the first stroke of eight his valet would wake him, and the exciting news that His Majesty was awake would pass into the closely packed ante-room to set the courtiers rustling like a field of ripe corn in a summer breeze. At the same moment the First Physician and the First Surgeon entered the room, together with the King's old nurse, who went up to the bed, kissed him, and asked how he had slept, whilst the two medical men rubbed the King down and changed his shirt. At a quarter-past eight the Grand Chamberlain was admitted, together with those courtiers who had the coveted *grandes entreés*, and Louis was presented with Holy Water. Now was the time to ask the King a favour, we are told, which suggests that in this, as in so many other respects, his psychology differed considerably from that of ordinary mortals.

Had I been Louis, with Louis' day in prospect, it would certainly have been no propitious moment to approach me. The *Grande Entreé* now withdrew, while the King recited the Office of the

Holy Ghost, after which they were re-admitted for the treat of seeing him put on his dressing gown and wig; and a few minutes
later the common herd of the nobility swarmed in and packed the
room to watch Louis dress. We are grateful to one of them for
having recorded the fact that they found him putting on his
breeches, "which he did very cleverly and gracefully." When the
moment came for him to put on his shirt, that garment would be
handed to the senior person present by the First Valet, and the
man so favoured would then hand it to the King. So far, we notice
that there has been no mention of washing, much less of taking a
bath, in spite of the fact that so long ago as 1640 the well-bred
person is recommended to wash his hands every day "and his face
nearly as often." Not of course in water, which was considered a
dangerous proceeding, but by rubbing the face with cotton soaked
in diluted and scented alcohol. Perhaps Louis confined his washing
to those occasions on which he was shaved, that is every other day.
After that operation, during which the valet held a mirror in front
of him, he washed in water mixed with spirits of wine, and then
dried his own face without any assistance from his entourage. The
barber, we may note in passing, was one of the King's five hundred
attendants who had free board and lodging at Court. Perhaps it
was in the evening that Louis had his bath, for we know that he
sometimes took one; and that it was a rare event may perhaps be
inferred from the fact that when he did so, an official of the Fifth
Section of the First Kitchen stood by with perfume burning on a
red-hot shovel to keep the air sweet. This section of the kitchen
department, some forty-five strong, also included the two *porte-
chaise d'affaires*, gentlemen in black velvet and swords, who had
the exclusive privilege of emptying the royal *chaise percée*, at
what stage in the *lever* is not stated. By this time the first awe of
the King's presence had worn off a trifle, and some conversation
was got up, more often than not about hunting. If Lent was drawing near, Louis would invariably take this opportunity of remind-
ing his Court that he would find it *fort mauvais* if he heard of anyone eating meat without a dispensation, which by the way could
only be obtained on a doctor's certificate, except for those under
twenty-one or over seventy, who had an automatic dispensation.

While Louis finished dressing he would drink a cup of wine and
water, or possibly of hippocras, a distillation of white wine, sugar
and spices, scented with *musc* or amber; but in later life he took to

a sort of sage tea. Having dressed, the King then knelt down at his bed and said his prayers, all ecclesiastics in attendance kneeling down at the same time, but the lay courtiers remaining standing; after which he went into his private room, followed by the most exalted of the Court only. Here Louis gave out his orders and programme for the rest of the day, after which all left the room except the inner ring of the inner ring, with whom the King would chat until it was time to go to Mass, to which he was naturally followed by the whole Court. And woe betide the man who shirked, for Louis, though his religion was formal and not very enlightened, was both assiduous and devout in the performance of its duties; his five annual Communions were made with a gravity which is described as edifying; in Lent he fasted strictly and heard three sermons a week, and only once in his long life did he ever miss attendance at Mass. All of which makes the behaviour which was tolerated at Divine service in the chapel surprising. St. Simon, in 1715, was very anxious to avoid any intimacy with Maréchal de Villeroi; but found it impossible to do so at Mass, where the Marshal would have his hassock put beside St. Simon's, and would persist throughout the service in discussing topics which the diarist did not wish to discuss. In 1705 the same Villeroi arrived at Versailles from the front during matins on Christmas Eve; his entrance into the chapel caused a great stir, and we are told that he passed the remainder of the service in making gallant speeches to the ladies, receiving the compliments of the men, and in beating time to the music with great elegance. Next year it is the turn of the Maréchal de Boufflers to distinguish himself, and this, too, at Mass, by bursting out laughing at a funny story told him by a neighbour, and that so loudly that the King "turned round in astonishment."

Chapel over, the King got to work with his Council, unless it was a Thursday or a Friday; Thursday mornings were reserved for private audiences, whilst on Fridays he spent the time between chapel and dinner closeted with his confessor. If you had an audience of the King on Thursday morning, you saw the great actor so to speak, in his dressing-room; St. Simon on a memorable occasion discovered Louis sitting on the table swinging his legs, and found that it was possible to interrupt him without Louis' resenting it. It is not the only illustration of the fact that in public Louis was always consciously playing the King; another observer tells us that when he was with his familiar circle, if someone entered the room, he changed in a flash from the first gentleman in France to the King.

An engraving of a Council meeting survives; at the head of the table sits Louis XIV in his arm-chair, wearing a mantle and plumed hat, a vast window to his right. Round the table in two rows, also in mantles and hats, sit some thirty or forty people watching the King, who is addressing the meeting. Our chief impression, as with all Versailles interiors, is one of draughtiness and formality, though Torcy's diary in fact shows that the proceedings were informal rather than otherwise. On 10th November 1709, for instance, Louis interrupts a discussion on relations with the Vatican to retail a story of a miracle at Amiens which has just reached him. And Louis in council was clearly more human than the imperturbable demi-god of the Salle des Glaces; on 27th January 1710 Torcy was urging the immediate despatch of a courier to The Hague; perhaps with too much insistance, for *le roi s'emporta*, and rounding on his Foreign Minister, told him that he was a nice man to urge haste, seeing that he is the most dilatory negotiator in the country.

Whilst these winds were blowing in Olympus, the courtier would be thinking about where he was to get a dinner. The usual dinner hour of the period was noon, but there were less fashionable people who dined at eleven, so the thrifty noble was in a position to spend a full hour drawing the covers of his acquaintance, dine, and be back at Court for the King's dinner at one. For the average poor courtier was, in the slang of the time, an incorrigible *cherchemidi*, a cadger of free dinners. If he had no luck in town there was always his patron's table to fall back upon, or he might insinuate himself into a seat at that of the King's gentleman-servitors, who were among the five-hundred-odd people who ate at Versailles daily at the King's expense, and for whom he kept a special kitchen, the *cuisine de commun*. We may feel that perhaps Louis might have done more for the unhappy *cherchemidis* who formed so large a proportion of his Court, but after all, what could he do? Many of them were unfitted to be anything better, and even when they were men of parts, there were ten competitors for every piece of patronage in his gift. Remember, he wrote for the Dauphin's guidance, that every time you confer a favour, you render nine men discontented and one ungrateful. Hence his cleverness in building up a complex ritual of etiquette in which worthless trifles became in the eyes of their recipients valuable favours. Nor were the trifles of King Louis always worthless; he well understood that a simple comment on the weather to a courtier whose fortunes were tottering, would, such was the royal prestige, stave off the man's creditors for another six months. And he was not niggardly in the distribution of such favours.

When the Council broke up, Louis had the Dutch newspapers read to him by his Foreign Secretary, an amusement which must frequently have administered a salutary rebuke to his overweening pride, and may have had not a little to do with his lasting dislike of the Dutch.

After this came the solemn business of the King's dinner, which could be *au petit couvert, au grand couvert,* or *au public*. Dinner *au grand couvert* was virtually limited to state banquets, and on these occasions the King's table was served with an extravagance which seems to us as vulgar as it was reprehensible; for instance, at the wedding feast given for his eldest daughter, the bill for ortolans alone came to more than 600 louis d'or. If Louis was dining *au public*, any decently dressed person could witness him doing so, and to drive out from Paris to Versailles to see the King eat was a popular form of entertainment. But, unlike the more favoured courtier, you could not stand and stare at him; the public was admitted at one door and let out at another, in a queue which was kept moving past the royal dinner table. But Louis rarely dined in public, nearly always *au petit couvert*. Indeed, in the last few years of his life he showed signs of rebellion against even the modified etiquette of the *petit couvert*, and took to dining twice a week in Mme. de Maintenon's rooms. At these meals none of the King's servants were admitted, not even the *maître d'hôtel* on duty; the dishes were handed in at the door to Mme. de Maintenon's own servants, who served both her and the King. Madame, less brave than the King, continued to endure the constraint of a formal dinner, even when dining alone, though she complains bitterly of the unpleasantness of having twenty servants watching every bite she puts in her mouth. Even when the King dined *au petit couvert*, the ceremony was a lengthy and impressive one. First, the *maître d'hôtel* on duty repaired to the kitchen in the rue de la Surintendance, accompanied by a gentleman-servant and the Clerk of Office. There, having washed their hands, the *maître d'hôtel* received from the Equerry of the

Kitchen, two pieces of bread, which he dipped in the first dish, ate one himself, and handed the other to the Equerry, who did likewise. The process was continued until every dish had been tasted, and as there might be thirty or forty of them, proceedings must have begun about half-past eleven. This business completed, the *cortège de la viande de Sa Majesté* was assembled; first came two Life Guards, and an usher with his wand of office, then the *maître d'hôtel* with his *bâton*, followed by a gentleman-servant of the pantler's department, and the Controller-General of the King's Household. It is a little difficult to understand the presence of the Controller-General, who was the King's domestic accountant, and therefore only remotely connected with the actual service of the table. Possibly he was there to see that neither the food nor the plate was stolen in transit, a by no means impossible catastrophe, for the policing of Versailles left much to be desired. Towards the end of the century thieves succeeded in removing the gold bullion fringes from the curtains in one of the principal *salons*, and at about the same period a sacrilegious scoundrel, who was never caught, stole a solid silver receptacle from under the King's own bed. One summer night in 1699, harness and hammer cloths to the value of about 10,000 louis d'or were stolen from the *Grand Ecurie*, and there again, the thieves were never discovered.

After the Controller-General came the dinner itself. And the dinner was followed by the Equerry of the Kitchen, an official of the butler's department, and three more Life Guards. So escorted, the dinner crossed the street, entered the courtyard of the *château*, traversed several rooms, and finally arrived at the square table in front of the bedroom window at which the King dined. Did Louis ever in his life taste hot food? It seems improbable, except perhaps when taking pot luck with his Generals on active service, even allowing for the fact that in the room where he ate there were primitive hotplates, consisting of bowls filled with red embers.

Even when dining *au petit couvert* the King would have a considerable number of people about him; if his brother was one of them, he would be asked to join him, but the Dauphin would not even be offered a chair, much less would the cardinals and Princes of the Blood. There would be no women present, and conversation was dull; for the King was a famous trencherman, and preferred to do his talking between meals. Here we should note in passing that Louis wiped his hands on a damp cloth before and after dinner. As soon as dinner was over, and if the Council was not going to meet in the afternoon, the King went off to his private room to feed his dogs and change his clothes as a preliminary to going out for a drive, or shooting in the park, or hunting; the best time of the day for Louis, who was an open air man, indifferent to the weather, never happier than when out of doors, and in the house insisting on open windows, to the dismay of his Court. When at Versailles, Louis hunted once a week, apparently the whole year round, for there does not seem to have been any close season. On Sundays and Fasts there was no hunting, in order that the hunt servants should not be robbed of their holidays. Louis' common-sense views on hunting must have been a great relief to the nervous horseman; the King was really a sportsman, and the spectacle of an agonized sycophant clinging precariously to his saddle in the hope of winning the royal favour, was to him an irritation. If you liked hunting, well and good; but if not, you were given a hint to stop at home.

Hunting was conducted on a magnificent scale under Louis XIV; between his own staghounds, Monseigneur's wolf-hounds and the packs of the Duc du Maine and the Comte de Toulouse, the royal family kept something like five hundred couple of hounds and hunted nearly every day in the week. By modern standards, hounds were very riotous; the Comte de Toulouse's pack, for instance, was known as the "no-quarter" because his hounds would hunt anything, and if they could not find a wolf or stag, would settle down to kill rabbits, apparently to the complete satisfaction of the field.

Louis was not only a good man to hounds, but an excellent shot, and no pains were spared with the Versailles shooting; birds were turned down in such enormous numbers that they were put up in thousands at a time. When the King was out with any of the royal packs, an official, called a *wine-runner*, followed the hunt with a cold collation carried on a pack-horse; but Louis does not seem to have made much use of his services. The King retained his love of hunting to the end of his life, and when he grew too old to ride to hounds, followed the hunt in a light open carriage with four horses, which he drove himself.

If it was a non-hunting afternoon, and there was no shooting, the King went for a walk after dinner, only those who had been invited accompanying him; but if he merely strolled in the garden, anyone who pleased could follow him. A walking afternoon must have been a severe trial to the invited courtiers, assuming that Madame is speaking more or less the truth when she says that the King, Mme. de Chevreuse and herself are the only three people in France who can walk twenty paces without puffing and sweating. Louis rarely strolled at Versailles, for even he seems to have felt the oppression of those vast formal spaces in which the gravel burnt through the shoes in summer, and through which oozed black mud in winter. As St. Simon says of the gardens, "One admired and avoided them."

On returning from his afternoon's exercise the King disappeared into his private room to work with one or more of his Ministers, or to chat with Mme. de Maintenon, with whom, if the weather was exceptionally bad, he would spend the afternoon. But information as to the King's private life is tantalizingly scanty. Mme. de Maintenon is our only source, and that discreet lady gives us but fleeting glimpses of the King at ease. We know that he hated reading, and that he was often bored and difficult to amuse; and that he was apt to be irritable in ill-health. Here and there we have a skeleton of a conversation; on a December evening in 1695 he listened with apparent pleasure whilst Mme. de Maintenon told him of the life of St. Augustine, but evaded her suggestion that they should undertake a regular course of religious reading together. In the course of a long chat in 1696 he gently refused to yield to Mme. de Maintenon's appeal that he should increase his private charities, pointing out with his usual good sense that a King's charities were simply an additional burden on his subjects. Often the talk seems to have turned on the filling of vacant benefices, the only branch of politics in which Mme. de Maintenon cared to exert any direct influence. But as we read her letters, we cannot help wishing that either Louis had married Mme. de Sévigné, or that Mme. de Maintenon had had some fraction of Mme. de Sévigné's *abandon* in her correspondence.

One of Louis' evening interviews with a Minister sheds a curious light on the habits of the time; Pontchartrain had just left the King when the Duchess of Burgundy came in, to find the floor covered with snuff and spittle. "How disgusting," she cried, "that must be that nasty one-eyed man of yours; nobody else would be capable of such a thing." One hardly knows whether to be more surprised at the tolerance of the King or at the boldness of the Duchess.

On three evenings a week at Versailles there was what was called an *appartement*, or as we should put it, Louis was "At Home" to his Court from seven to ten. The entertainment began with a concert, which was followed by cards and billiards, and a formal informality was the note of the party. The Draconian laws about sitting down in the presence of one's superiors were relaxed, anyone could cut in at any card table as the fancy took him, or adjourn to the refreshment room when he thought fit. But it was as well not to miss an *appartement*, for the King had the faculty of being able to see at a glance who was absent, and if you absented yourself without good reason, enquiries were apt to be made. Especially if you were suspected of having slipped off to Paris for an evening's recreation; for Louis hated his good town of Paris, and had no patience with those who showed a liking for it. In the latter years of his reign the King himself no longer put in an appearance at an *appartement*, but spent the time from seven to ten working in Mme. de Maintenon's room with a succession of Ministers. It does not strike us as a very comfortable retreat, being a large room with two doors, one leading into the ante-room, and the other into a big *salon*. Between the door of the ante-room and the fireplace stood Louis' arm-chair and desk, with a *tabouret* by it for the Minister in attendance; Mme. de Maintenon's arm-chair was in a niche on the other side of the fire, and near the other door was her bed, in a recess. At about nine o'clock Mme. de Maintenon would have a light supper brought in for herself, and soon afterwards would be undressed by her maid and put to bed. One presumes that the Minister left the room whilst she was undressing, but we are not told so; perhaps he merely pretended not to notice what was going on.

At an *appartement* gambling was heavy, and if Louis did nothing to restrain it, he at least gave it no encouragement; his attitude to card playing was the same as his attitude towards hunting. If people liked to gamble, well and good; but you acquired no kudos by playing. Even in the King's presence, cards were played with what would today strike us as a very odd lack of decorum; oaths, curses, shouts of joy, banging of clenched fists on the table, were the usual accompaniments of deep play, and passed as unnoticed as did even less pleasant habits. St. Simon mentions, for instance, the ill-breeding of the Marquis d'Heudicourt, who at the card table would spit over his shoulder without first looking to make sure that there was no one standing behind him. The vivacity of the players is, however, understandable when we consider the sums at stake; Mme. de Montespan once lost about 160,000 louis d'or in an evening, and won it all back again during the night. This is, of course, exceptional, for few people were, like her, in the position of being able to gamble with the taxpayer's money; but her legitimate son, d'Antin, confessed to having won 28,000 louis d'or at cards, and was believed to have made considerably more. There has been much moralizing, much shaking of heads, over the recklessness with which Louis XIV's Court sat down to the card table night after night, and no doubt many of them did so from a genuine love of gambling; but I suspect that there was also a large number to whom the attraction must have been that here at last was a chance to *sit down*. But in order to enjoy this rare boon, it was necessary that you should be actually playing, or at least backing a player: and sharp eyes were watching you. Madame once went up to a seated duchess in the card room and asked her if she was playing: the duchess said "No." "Is it then permitted to enquire why you are seated?" said Madame. The duchess rose, made a deep curtsey, left the room, and never entered the palace again.

A less ruinous opportunity for sitting down was offered the courtier on the other three nights of the week, when there was a comedy or an opera, which, as Madame says candidly, had at least the merit of being free. Louis seems to have kept a sharper eye on his theatre than he did on his evening parties, and in 1688 we find him warning the Italian comedians to cut out of their script all *mots à double entendre qui sont trop libres*.

The King's supper hour was nominally ten o'clock, but if he had had a heavy evening it might be much later, and Madame, whose attendance at the meal was compulsory, complains that the King often did not sup before half-past eleven.

Louis enjoyed his dinner, but supper was to him the crown of the day, and his performances at that meal filled his courtiers with respectful amazement. One night in 1708, when in bed on invalid diet, and being then seventy years of age, he consumed a *potage*, followed by four wings, a leg, and all the white meat off three chickens. And do not hastily assume that *potage* means soup, for it does not; in the seventeenth century a *potage* was ordinarily a large dish of meat or fish, boiled with vegetables. There were over a hundred and fifty *potage* recipes, from which let us take *Potage à la Jacobine* as a sample: bone, boil, and mince as many partridges and chickens as required, and serve hot with almond sauce on a layer of cheese.

But Louis in good health was a very different performer; then his supper was known to consist of, say, four plates of soup, a whole pheasant, a whole partridge, two slices of ham and a salad, some mutton with garlic, followed by pastry, and finishing off with fruit and hard-boiled eggs. Nor did this exhaust the gastronomic possibilities of his day, for on reaching his bedroom he would find there his *en cas de nuit*, a snack to see him through the dark hours, and which consisted of three loaves, two bottles of wine, a decanter of water, and three cold dishes. In extenuation of what we can only call the gluttony of Louis, it must be remembered that he never ate anything between meals, and that his *post-mortem* revealed the fact that his stomach had double the capacity of that of the normal man of his size. Supper was always eaten *au grand couvert*, that is to say in the presence of the full Court, and with all those seated at the King's table who were entitled to the honour; it was in fact Louis *en père de famille*, surrounded by his family and his dependents, a sumptuous version of the evening gathering for the last meal of the day, which was taking place under every roof in the kingdom. But, let us hope, not with equal tedium, for the royal supper was a dull business. Madame tells us that the table was as silent as in a refectory, and that one had barely the courage to murmur a word in one's neighbour's ear.

When supper was finished, the King went into his bedroom and stood for a few minutes leaning against the balustrade which shut in his bed, where he received the curtseys of the ladies; when all had thus bidden him good night, Louis made his world-famous bow, gave the parole and countersign to the officer of the guard, and passed into his private room, where the family awaited him. The King and his brother sat in arm-chairs, the princesses on *ta-bourets*, while all the men stood: that is to say, the Dauphin, his sons, and the royal bastards. On each side of the room, doors—left open—gave entrance, one to the Council Chamber where the Ladies-of-Honour awaited the departure of the Princesses, and the other to the dogs' room, in which were assembled those who were going to attend the King's *coucher*. After an hour's somewhat laboured conversation, the King gave the signal for the breakup of the party by going into the next room to feed his dogs, and then went into his bedroom, where he found the courtiers waiting for the *grand coucher*. Having said his prayers, the King arose and glanced around the circle to select the recipient of the most distinguished favour of the day, that of holding the candlestick which had up to this been in the keeping of the Almoner. The lucky courtier singled out received the candlestick from the First Valet de Chambre, and had the privilege of holding it for the remainder of the *coucher*. Louis then undressed and dismissed his Court with a bow. Was he relieved to know that only the ceremony of the *petit coucher* separated him from his bed? We don't know, but may at least suspect that the *petit coucher* was one of the more tiresome ordeals of the day. For it was then that those who had the *entrée* were entitled to speak confidentially to the King; and he knew by long experience that a courtier's confidences would most certainly take the form of an application for money or money's worth. And let it be remembered to Louis' credit that to every petitioner he listened with patience, kindliness, and an obvious desire to master the substance of the petition.

The *petit coucher* closed with a ceremony which only the inner circle of the elect witnessed, and which is too characteristic of the age to be passed over in silence; Louis has now got himself into his nightshirt and dressing gown, and is installed on his *chaise percée*. Happy the Gentlemen of the Bedchamber, who for a trifling outlay of some 15,000 louis d'or apiece have the honour and pleasure of assisting at this performance every night of their lives. A happiness marred only by the fact that the business is a mere formality; for the King is *fort honnête*, and puts himself in this posture at the *coucher*, not from necessity, but as part of the nightly ritual.

The cup of pleasure is now drained to the dregs, the lights begin to go out, another Versailles day is over; and as the great clock booms the stroke of half-past one, the courtier may start climbing the stairs to his bed.

There was little variation in the splendid routine which, if Mme. de Maintenon is to be believed, brought the pleasure seekers nothing but sadness, fatigue, and boredom. If the King had taken medicine, which happened once a month, he heard Mass in bed in the presence of the Court, spent the morning with Mme. de Maintenon, and rose at three. Occasionally a traditional feast broke the monotony, and we get a momentary impression of the Court really enjoying itself. Chief of these was the Day of the Kings, the eve of the Epiphany, when a cake containing a bean was served at every supper table, and the one who got the slice containing it was king or queen of the evening. In 1684, Mlle. de Rambures gets the lucky slice at Louis' own table, and is waited on by the King, napkin in hand, for the rest of the meal: after which she makes the round of the Court, Louis following her as *chevalier d'honneur*. Sometimes even Louis rebelled against the intolerable burden of the etiquette in which he had imprisoned himself, and kicked over the traces; at Marly he was known to flip bread pellets at the ladies during dinner, and to enjoy their doing the same to him. But Marly was not Versailles; had in fact been planned by Louis as a mere country box where *Le Roi Soleil* could become Louis de Bourbon the country gentleman, entertaining a few friends without fuss or ceremony. If the little country box eventually grew into the Marly which cost his subjects some 530,000 louis d'or, he was at least successful in there avoiding the stranglehold of Court etiquette. To be invited to Marly was the highest sign of favour, but those ladies who made the journey in the King's own coach paid dearly for the honour. Louis, as we have seen, never ate between meals; but he liked to see other people do so, and his coach was always filled with picnic baskets. The ladies were expected to feel hungry on a journey whatever the hour of the day, and to eat heartily. The King, in his favourite phrase would have found it *fort mauvais* if they had not done so. There were two further sources of discomfort: firstly, the royal carriage stopped between stages only for the King's convenience, and had any lady requested that it be stopped for hers, this would have been found in the highest degree *mauvais*. Secondly, whatever the weather, Louis insisted on having all the windows of the coach wide open, so that the unfortunate women sat in driving rain and splashes of mud thrown in by the Life Guard escort's horses, or else smothered in clouds of evil smelling dust. Let us hope that Marly made amends for the discomforts of reaching it. One more anxiety preoccupied the guest during the journey. Would the Court Quartermaster have chalked your name alone on the door of your room, or would it be preceded by the coveted "for." A grave matter this, for the omission of the word "for" was enough to poison all your pleasure in the visit, a source of mortification to you, and of unconcealed gratification to your rivals.

Marly seems to have been a charming spot, on the evidence of Madame, usually so severe a critic of the royal residences; woods, fountains, lakes, statues were there in abundance, all indeed that the century admired; "one would say that the fairies are at work here," is Madame's exclamation on a visit in 1702. Mme. de Maintenon, however, not at any time addicted to poetry, and regarding Marly with a housewifely eye, merely remarks that the place is turning into a second Versailles. When completed, Marly was a small white *château*, perched on a terrace excavated from the side of a wooded valley, and approached by an avenue upon which fronted twelve pavilions or bungalows containing the guest rooms. Everywhere was a studied simplicity, or what passed for such at Court, and even the King's suite consisted of one large and one small room only. But in all these royal houses, life seems to have been cramped and overcrowded; Mme. de Maintenon, writing from St. Germain in 1678, apologizes for the badness of her letter by explaining that it is written in a room containing twenty women, three children, and seven dogs. The King and Monseigneur positively roughed it at Marly, both dining in the same room and at the same time, though at separate tables. In the Marly ante-room there was no question of *tabourets*, one sat where one could, and if there were no seats vacant, you were at liberty to sit on the floor, a privilege of which many of the women availed themselves. Fancy dress balls were often given, at which old Louis, to show that he was with the revellers in spirit though his dancing days were over, would appear in the ball-room with a gauze robe over his clothes. Of an afternoon there would be hunting, as at Versailles, and often in the evening a lottery in Mme. de Maintenon's room, in which every ticket drew a prize. Marly life produced amusing contretemps which would have been impossible at Versailles; as for instance, on the evening when a raw Swiss footman entered the room in which Louis was playing cards, and going up to one of the ladies, said in a loud voice, "Matam, go to ped; your husband iss in ped and wants you." Even practical jokes were admitted, and you were apt to have a squib let off under your chair, or to be abruptly wakened from your first sleep with volleys of snowballs flung by a troupe of high-spirited princesses, for which favour you were no doubt becomingly grateful.

Fontainebleau, loveliest of the royal residences, had a stricter etiquette than had Marly, but something of the holiday spirit prevailed there, too. It was a favourite place with Madame, that tireless rider, for there was hunting with one of the royal packs seven days a week, and twice weekly she got her other favourite diversion, the theatre. "This," she says in October 1714, "is the last letter I shall write to you from my dear Fontainebleau."

Trianon seems to have been a pleasant summer resort, at least for the more exalted guests. "I am very well lodged," writes Madame in June 1705; "I have four rooms and a cabinet, in which I am writing . . . the trees almost come in at my windows." Except for the specially invited, Trianon was out of bounds to the courtiers until after dinner, when they trooped over from Versailles to stroll amid the streams and fountains, or to take a hand at cards in the *salon*. Often the Court did not go into residence at Trianon at all, but merely came over to the little palace of a summer evening to dance and have supper. It would have been a delightful place but for a typical example of that magnificence so closely resembling bad taste which Louis often displayed; the immense garden was filled with tuberoses, all of which were changed every day, and their scent was so strong as to render the grounds oppressive.

In addition to the King's own palaces, he and his more favoured courtiers would from time to time be the guests of Monseigneur at Meudun, of M. le Prince at Chantilly, of Monsieur at St. Cloud, or of the Duc du Maine at Sceaux. More rarely some wealthy courtier would be allowed the honour of entertaining his Sovereign, and would eagerly pour out the revenues of a couple of years in as many nights. Most adroit at tickling the King's jaded appetite was d'Antin, the successful gambler. Louis, on his first visit to d'Antin's country house, Petit Bourg, was strolling in the grounds with his host; the King remarked that if Petit Bourg was his, he thought he would remove a certain avenue of chestnut trees, which in his opinion spoilt the view. D'Antin said nothing at the time, but on the following day brought the King back to the same spot. Not only was there not a chestnut tree to be seen, but even the roots had been grubbed up and the excavations filled in and turfed. There is an Oriental magnificence about this stupendous piece of folly which one cannot but admire. Flattery can hardly be pushed further. D'Antin's perfection of courtly servility is an episode with which we may well close this attempt to recreate something of the atmosphere of Louis XIV's Court.

III

The Base of the Pyramid

Few periods are more difficult to focus than the age of Louis XIV. On the Court shines a beam so brilliant, so intense, the concentrated light of a score of vivid memoirs, that in reading them we cheat ourselves into believing that we ourselves have made our bow to the *Grand Monarque*, and have chatted with the courtiers in his ante-rooms. A diffused light sheds itself even over the great towns. But when we come to consider the peasant, we enter upon a realm of conjecture. As we contemplate that dim mass which made up the largest section of the population, we are sharply aware that when St. Simon speaks of *all France*, he means some fifty or sixty thousand people: and that when he begins a sentence with *even the common people*, he is talking of what we should call the middle classes. How from such material can we gain any idea of the life of that dumb and elusive creature, the French peasant?

As we examine what evidence exists, the first fact that strikes us is that we are in a France which had forgotten that the peasant, whether farm owner, tenant, or labourer, was the creator of the national wealth; *la lie du peuple,* the dregs of the nation, is the term usually applied to him, not only in private, but sometimes in official correspondence. The second is that the structure of the *ancien régime* renders any generalization about the submerged tenth exceedingly difficult; for monarchical France may be compared to a heavily bombed town in which the inhabitants have evolved a makeshift way of life amidst the ruins of the old. Everywhere is the rubble of feudalism, blocking every street, here by-passed by an improvised route, there dragged aside where its presence had become intolerable, and everywhere forming a barrier to reconstruction.

Whether he lived in considerable poverty or comparative comfort was decided for the seventeenth-century peasant by the accident of his birthplace; for hardly any two provinces, or even two parishes, enjoyed the same type and weight of taxation. And the whole fiscal system was in itself radically and incurably vicious; as a contemporary remarks, if the Devil himself had been given a free hand to plan the ruin of France, he could not have invented any scheme more likely to achieve that object than the system of taxation in vogue, a system which would seem to have been designed with the sole object of ensuring a minimum return to the King at a maximum price to his subjects, with the heaviest share falling on the poorest section of the population.

How was this ingenious result achieved? In the first place, the *noblesse,* the clergy, and a vast horde of government officials enjoyed total exemption from all forms of direct taxation. And how vast was the latter class may be seen from a memorandum of Colbert's in 1664 in which he points out that in the departments of justice and finance alone, there were 46,000 persons enjoying tax exemption: and that of those 46,000, at least 40,000 were in his opinion unnecessary, were in fact employed by the Crown only because they had purchased sinecures in order to evade their taxes. That all well-to-do citizens should escape direct taxation was in itself bad enough, but there is worse to follow. Let us go into the operation of the chief direct tax, the *Taille,* in some detail. We have just said that the prudent peasant would choose his birthplace with care, and from no point of view was this more important than when it came to paying the *Taille.* For old France consisted of two classes of province having entirely different administrative systems: the *Pays d'Etat* and the *Pays d'Election*. The former enjoyed a certain measure of autonomy, being to some extent ruled by their own "Estates," or provincial parliament, to which all three orders sent delegates, and in which the annual provincial taxation was assessed. The *Pays d'Etat* had, therefore, some machinery for bargaining with the central government, and for protesting against a more than ordinary rapacity on the part of the financiers. Further, such provinces paid the *Taille Réelle* as it was called, which was based, not on the collector's guess as to what a man should pay, but on a percentage of the value of his property. The *Pays d'Election* enjoyed no such privileges; in an *Election* province the *Taille* was fixed arbitrarily by the Council of State, no accounts were ever published, and it was ruled to be not in the public interest to disclose how the assessment was arrived at, for the very good reason that there was no scale or principle behind the assessment. To augment the *Taille* was simply the most convenient method of attempting to bridge the ever widening gap between revenue and expenditure. An additional drawback to living in a *Pays d'Election* was that the *Taille* was not "real," as in the *Pays d'Etat*, but was simply the government's estimate of how much tax the province would stand without revolting; sometimes the government guessed wrongly, and there would be a revolt, as was the case in Normandy in 1658. Such being the system, or rather lack of system, of assessment, the peasant lived in uncertainty, not knowing what sum might be demanded from him from year to year: except, of course, that each year's assessment would be heavier than that for the past year. And finally, the tax was collected not annually, but quarterly, so that its collection exacerbated an improverished village from one year's end to another. It is not difficult to see how exquisitely adapted the system was for throwing the whole burden on those least able to bear it.

As soon as the Council of State had communicated the gross figure for the year to the Controller-General in Paris, that overworked and harassed man would be besieged by great landowners and influential ladies, who naturally wanted a light assessment in those provinces from which they drew their rents: and this kind of pressure was generally successful. In other words, collection of the tax began by the wealthy *noblesse* transferring the bulk of the obligation from the shoulders of their own farmers to those of their poorer brethren. The heaviest assessment would then go out to the poorest province, where the same lobbying and intrigue took place around the Intendant, with probably the same result; the poorest *generality* received the lion's share of the tax, passed on as much of it as it could to the least influential *élection*, which in turn saddled the worst represented, that is to say the poorest, parish with the heaviest share.

At last the tax has reached Jacques Bonhomme, and let us see how he dealt with it. After sermon the *curé* would read out the unwelcome news that the year's assessment had arrived in the parish, and the village elders, more usually called the communal council, would meet to discuss the matter of raising the money. This council is by the way unique in being the only legally recognized democratic body in Louis XIV's France; though its powers were strictly limited, and tended to become more so, it was sometimes an elective body, more often the whole of the village, with the *seigneur* and the *curé* as *ex officio* members, and the *syndic* as man of business. The usual place of meeting was the churchyard, or, if the weather was wet, inside the church itself. "Every man over the age of fourteen" had a right to vote, but the elders did most of the talking. In some districts, women were voting members of the village assembly. Ten members formed a quorum, and absentees were in some districts fined a quart of wine to each member present, and a quart of wax for the Church. The proceedings of the meeting needed the approval of the seigneurial judge, and, after the grip of the central government had tightened, that of the Intendant. But in this, as in all other matters in the France of those days, there was no uniformity of procedure. In the meeting which we are imagining, the first item on the agenda would be the appointment of a collector of the *Taille*, a hateful and dreaded office, in spite of the fact that the collector was entitled to retain a percentage of the amount raised as compensation for his trouble. It would have been in keeping with the whole vicious system if the poorest and stupidest man in the village had invariably been chosen for this office, but as a matter of fact this was not the case; the post went around the village by election annually. Upon the appointed man now fell the preliminary duty of splitting up the assessment, and we need hardly describe how he set about it; firstly, there would be a swinging assessment on A, the previous year's collector, against whom he had nourished a grudge for the last twelve months; then he would consider the remainder of the village. B, the wealthiest farmer in the parish, must be let off very lightly; for did he not employ six of their number, including the collector himself? It would be madness to assess him at anything like his fair tax. C's brother-in-law is a minor official in the Salt Gabelle; it would be very dangerous to make an enemy of C. In fact, assessment at the bottom of the scale was conducted in exactly the same manner as it had been at the top, and with the same result. The poorest landowner and the poorest villager could count on paying the heaviest taxes. But it was one thing to make an assessment, and quite another thing to collect the money; the unfortunate collector, himself both tyrant and victim, would be met with threats, evasions, and passive resistance. Such villagers as paid would do so a sou at a time, involving him in endless journeys to outlying farms, and while he tramped the commune, his own little farm might be going to wrack and ruin. Fear made him merciless, for he was responsible in his own person for the transmission of the whole sum to the Subdelegate, the lowest salaried officer in the tax collecting army. If he failed to collect the total, the Subdelegate would most infallibly clap him up in the nearest jail, probably a cellar at the manor house, though we must not think of such a place as the horrid pit in which peasants of an earlier generation had been confined. The seigneurial cellar was probably no more uncomfortable than his own cottage, he was allowed visitors, and once a week he was visited by a government official who asked him if he had any complaints. There, however, he would remain until finally the Intendant of the province would protest to the Controller-General that he had several hundred imprisoned collectors in his Intendancy, not one of whom had the slightest prospect of paying, and whose imprisonment and consequent neglect of their holdings was reducing the tax-paying capacity of his government for the following year; whereupon the Controller would order a jail delivery, and the collector would return to his neglected farm. If, however, the village was fairly well-to-do, it was not necessary for the collector to go to jail at all; the Subdelegate, who tended to be a dissolute city clerk of the shyster lawyer school, was always bribable, and for a consideration would imprison the collector in his own cottage, which meant that it was merely necessary for him to be indoors when that man of business happened to visit the village.

The dishonesty of the whole proceedings worried the Subdelegate not at all. He had bought his office, and his only desire was to leave the hated countryside as soon as possible, and to settle down in his beloved Paris on the competence which he had filched from the country bumpkins.

The evil inflicted on the country by this absurd tax had ramifications which even its inventors can hardly have foreseen. Firstly, it meant the destruction of much good feeling over the countryside, by making every man a spy on his neighbour; the smallest sign of increasing prosperity was jealously watched for, and the man who was rash enough to let it be seen that he was rising above the subsistence level would certainly find his *Taille* doubled at the next assessment. In consequence, deliberate bad farming became the rule rather than the exception in the *Pays d'Elections*. For who would buy more stock, or manure his fields to get a richer yield for the benefit of the tax-farmer? Families who could have bought good clothes went in rags, for the same reason, which in turn reacted unfavourably on the taxable capacity of tradesmen in the neighbouring town, who, as the *Taille* increased, found their profits diminishing. Even more serious, the system produced a constant drain of population from country to town, where, for a variety of reasons, taxation was less onerous; the dream of every ambitious peasant was to save enough to buy a small government post carrying exemption from the *Taille*, and to settle in the nearest town. Many accomplished it by dint of savage thrift and heartbreaking toil, so that every year there were so many less villagers, and those the least capable, left to pay a heavier *Taille*. Finally, the tax cost twenty-five per cent of its total to collect. It seems to have been everything that a direct tax ought not to have been.

As we have already noticed, the *Taille* was by no means uniform in the manner of its assessment, and in some favoured localities, life seems to have been very tolerable: notably in those districts allowed to raise what was called the *Taille en Tarif*, that is to say the right of producing the sum required by taxing consumption in the area concerned. But the greatest privilege was to live in a *Pays d'Etat*, and be liable for the *Taille Réelle*. Boisguillebert, who published his *Détail de La France* in 1697, was a native of Montauban, holding a government appointment in Rouen, and he draws a striking contrast between the two generalities. That of Montauban, a poor, hilly district, pays the "real"

Taille, and there you find no peasant who does not wear a good linen smock, and consume bread, meat, and wine in his own well built tiled cottage. Rouen pays the *Pays d'Election Taille*. At Rouen land should be worth about six times as much as at Montauban, but around Rouen meat and wine are unknown luxuries, most peasants' cottages are ruinous, and the villagers consider themselves fortunate when they have a sufficiency of bread and water. Land is rapidly going out of cultivation. And yet Rouen yields the Crown only double the *Taille* of Montauban.

Louis XIV and his ministers were not blind to the disturbing implications of the decline of farming in a corn exporting nation; the problem had their most serious consideration, and edict after edict was promulgated in an effort to revitalize the life of the countryside. In 1665 Louis formed the first stud farm in France, where peasants' mares could be served free of charge. In 1667 he forbade the seizure of peasants' beasts, carts, and implements for debt, even for debts due to the Crown. By 1679 every Intendant was being plagued with *questionnaires* demanding information on the minutest details of economic conditions in the country districts. Some years later Louis offers four years' exemption from the *Taille* to any peasant who restored abandoned land to cultivation, and prohibits hunting over sown fields. But these and many other expedients were mere empirical remedies applied to a deepseated disease. Louis was at the mercy of his own town-bred and overcentralized bureaucracy, whose members never realized that nature cannot be controlled by edicts. Neither King nor minister had the wit to see that the cure for the sickness of agricultural France was not more controls, but a root and branch reorganization of the whole fiscal system.

Of the other forms of direct taxation, the *Gabelle*, or salt tax, was probably the most onerous, and certainly one of the most expensive to collect; and, as everywhere in *ancien régime* finance, we find here, too, a complete lack of uniformity. For purposes of *Gabelle*, the country was divided into five classes, ranging from the *Grande Gabelle* generalities, where every inhabitant was compelled every year to buy an excessive quantity of bad salt at an exorbitant price, to the *Pays de Salines*, or salt-producing areas, where he was not allowed to buy sufficient for his own domestic consumption. The latter restriction was imposed in a fruitless attempt to check salt smuggling, one of the major industries of old

France, which involved Louis in the maintenance of a sort of Customs army, the *Maréchaussée*, which not infrequently fought regular pitched battles with the smugglers. Ferocious penalties were, of course, enacted against smugglers, the *Faux Saulniers* as they are called, but under the *ancien régime* it was considerably easier to promulgate a law than to get it obeyed; especially when, as in this case, public sympathy was on the side of the law breaker. Perhaps even a degree of official sympathy, if we are to judge from one recorded case. The local smugglers were camped in a wood on the outskirts of a certain village, when the *Maréchaussée* entered the village; a quick-witted villager sounded the parish bell, the smugglers decamped, and the *Maréchaussée* lost its prey. The obstructive villagers had rendered themselves liable to exemplary punishment. The Customs complained to the Intendant, and he in due course gave sentence. The village bell was to be dismounted, placed in the street, and there flogged by the hangman in the presence of the whole village. And this when Voltaire has already written *Oedipe*, and over in Staffordshire, Sam Johnson is an unpromising lad of eight! It is difficult to believe that the Intendant did not write with his tongue in his cheek. And parenthetically, the further we explore the reign, the more we are struck with the limitations imposed on Louis' supposed absolutism by the actions of his government officials and the stubborn passive resistance of the common people. Had the King heard of this matter of the bell, he would not, I think, have been amused; but what would he have said about the conduct of the Intendant of Normandy a few years earlier? Boisguillebert was exiled to the south of France in 1707 for publishing a supplement to the book from which we have already quoted; the execution of the *Lettre de Cachet* was entrusted to the Intendant of his province, who takes it upon himself to say that if the erring Boisguillebert makes a *journey* to the place of his exile and then returns, nothing more will be heard of the matter: and so far as we know, nothing more *was* heard of the matter. Even with the peasantry, Louis often seems to be powerless to enforce his will; in 1666 a number of saints' days were suppressed as public holidays in the hope of stimulating agricultural output. The peasant, having considered the matter, decided that it was safer to offend the King than the saints, and continued to celebrate the prohibited festivals: and the central government took no action.

The chief indirect tax, the *Aides*, was at least as inept as the *Taille*, and rather more exasperating. Farmed, like all the other taxes, and controlled by the *Cour des Aides* in Paris, it was a complicated type of liquor tax, embracing the whole process from growth of the primary material, grapes, apples and so forth, through manufacture, distribution, and wholesaling, down to the retail trade; and this intricate business was in the hands of an army of officials who were, if anything, more corrupt than their brethren of the *Taille* office. The modern Englishman will learn without surprise that under their fostering care, the Frenchman's bottle of wine showed a progressive increase in price and decline in quality as the reign advanced. And indeed, when the bad war years came, the revenue from the *Aides* became subject to the law of diminishing returns. Just as today in England none but the rich can afford to drink spirits, so by the end of the century few people could afford wine or cider. This in its turn, of course, brought about an increasing scarcity of these articles; landowners ploughed up their vines and cut down their apple trees for fuel as the demand fell off, and the state endeavoured to make good its falling revenue by still further raising the price. The vicious circle was complete.

But there will always be wine drinkers, however high the price of wine, and the French excise system continued to function somehow. When the tax on the vines, the tax on the grape harvest, the tax on the manufacture, and the tax on transportation of the finished product had all been paid, the article at last reached the distributor; at each stage of the proceedings the *Aides* had collected a legal revenue, and its agents an illegal one. But for the happy *employé* of the *Aides*, the real perquisites had not yet begun. By the time the wine reached the innkeeper the price was so high that there were endless ingenuities of fraud practised on the one hand, and of blackmail on the other. Every day the *Aides* clerk would take stock of the liquor in every bar, and every night each innkeeper would surreptitiously replenish his bar stock from his cellar. It was only a matter of time until the official caught him, but this caused little anxiety; it was merely one more bribe to be paid, and the amount was, of course, passed on to the consumer in the ordinary way. Under such a system it is not to be wondered at that the number of public houses in France was small and their sales low; Vauban estimates that in 1707 there were 36,000 parishes in France, sharing between them 40,000 licensed premises; the average house sold about 4,500 pints of wine in a year, or rather more than twelve pints a day. But the figure does not seem to include what are now known as "off licence" sales.

The chief perquisite of the *Aides* official was the facilities which his post gave him for entering the wholesale wine trade on his own account; he alone was in a position to get a permit for the transit of wine without encountering endless difficulties. And he could make it almost impossible for the grower at the one end to sell to anyone except the official's man of straw, and at the other end, could ensure that the publican who did not deal with him, went short of supplies; in other words, "innkeepers tended to become, in effect, the unpaid employees of the Customs clerk." For the traveller, this fraudulent system produced exasperating consequences; deprived of his legitimate profit on the sale of his wines, the innkeeper indemnified himself by extorting a four hundred per cent profit on food, accommodation and forage.

On the long-term view, the policy of the *Cour des Aides* defeated its own purpose even more decisively than did the administration of the *Taille*; in Normandy, for instance, in 1697, the *Aides* was bringing in 80,000 livres a year, but owing to the destruction of the vines of that province, and the land thus thrown out of cultivation, the *Taille* had to be reduced by 150,000 livres. In passing we notice with some surprise that the publican of the *ancien régime*, in addition to the troubles peculiar to his period, was faced with the same anxieties which confront his English colleagues of today; his house had to be closed during Mass hours, he had to eject his clientele at 8:00 P.M. in winter and 9:00 P.M. in summer; and he was heavily fined for permitting drunkenness on his premises. The publican's lot, like that of his persecutor, the policeman, was even then not a happy one.

Next in the list of obstacles set in the path of the farmer was the *Douane*, an internal customs service, a mass of ill-understood, undigested, and confused legislation, the object of which seems to have been to prevent goods from circulating within the kingdom. In addition to the usual anomalies and complications of the whole fiscal system, we here find one peculiar to itself, namely, that some dues (*droits de Traite*) were payable to the state, and others (*droits de Péage*) to the towns and *seigneuries* through which the goods passed. The result was to make long-distance transport of goods a financial impossibility, and a risk which no one would undertake: for at each town *en route* there was a fresh Customs examination, and, of course, fresh dues to be paid. The merchant had to await the convenience of the Customs officers, who, if not suitably bribed, would keep him waiting for days before examining his wares: and the slightest irregularity in the completion of one of an interminable series of forms led to the confiscation, not only of the merchandise, but of the wagon and horses into the bargain. There are actually cases on record in which the tax on the internal movement of produce was estimated at four times the salable value of the commodity transported; and a measure of wine, selling in Bordeaux at a sou, could not be retailed in Normandy for less than twenty-four sous. Often the farmer preferred to let his produce rot in the ground instead of facing the vexation and danger of transporting it; and it not only could but did happen from time to time that there was acute shortage of corn in one province, whilst its neighbour's barns were full of unsalable grain. It is perhaps unnecessary to add that the privileged classes could secure permits exempting them from all transit taxes, and indeed from almost every tax, and that the only people who really benefited from the *Douane* were the financiers who had bought the right of collection: unless we include as beneficiaries the smugglers, who flourished in large numbers all over the kingdom.

The remaining tax, the *Capitation*, was a poll tax invented in 1695 as a comprehensive substitute for all existing direct taxation; but it was quietly added to the existing taxes as a new impost. Having paid this, the peasant was now at liberty to satisfy the claims of the Church and of his feudal overlord; but the latter taxes we can more conveniently look into when we come to deal with the position of the *seigneur*. Ecclesiastical taxation was the most modest of the peasant's burdens, and the only one of which we do not hear frequent complaints; called the *Dîme* or tenth, it, in fact, never seems to have attained that figure, but to have varied between a thirteenth and a fortieth. It was a logical and understandable tax, not an arbitary assessment, but levied in kind on the actual produce of the year's farming—the tenth sheaf, the tenth barrel of wine, the tenth pig, and so on. Its collection seems to have been made in nearly all districts and at nearly all times, without any friction.

But the peasant was by no means quit of the central government when he had paid his taxes, for there were various body services which he was required to render, as for instance the *Corvée*. By this enactment every villager under the age of sixty was liable for forced labour on a number of days in the year, usually being employed at road making, repairs, bridge building, and generally speaking, maintenance of communications; unless, of course, he lived in a *Pays d'Etat*, for in those isles of the blest the *Corvée* was unknown, and all public works were executed by the provincial Estates. In the *Pays d'Election* the *Corvée*, though compulsory, was paid labour, but the rate of payment was low, and insufficient to indemnify the farmer for his absence from home, especially if he had to lie out overnight, which was often the case. It is hardly surprising to learn in the circumstances that *Corvée* works were always expensive and slowly executed. It produced excellent first-class roads, but the second class, being under village management, became impassable.

Oddly enough, it was not the *Corvée* but the comparatively mild innovation of compulsory militia service which caused most resentment amongst the village populations. The reasons for this resentment are not easy to understand, but it must be remembered that there was no conscription in Louis' France, and it is possible that the peasantry saw in the militia service, the thin end of the wedge of conscription for the Regular Army. To us it seems that service in the militia, which Louvois had introduced in 1688, was not devoid of attraction. The strength of the force was about 60,000, so that even had the militia been drawn exclusively from the countryside, the quota required was considerably under two per parish. The recruit had to be a bachelor, not less than five feet high, and was provided by a drawing of lots in the village assembly; service was for six years, and except in time of war the militia rarely moved from the district in which it was raised; nor were the units permanently mobilized. Their conditions of service were, in fact, not unlike those prevailing in the British Territorial Army of today: were in fact lighter, for the French militiaman attended no annual camp. The recruit received a free outfit, a bounty from the village chest, and lower taxation during his six years' service; and on discharge, a year's total exemption from the *Taille*. But whatever the reason, the innovation was extremely unpopular, Intendants were deluged with petitions for exemption from service, and desertion was common.

The seventeenth century (like all other centuries, by the way) was an age of transition, an age of which the chief event, so far as the peasant was concerned, was the steadily decreasing influence and power of the *seigneur* whose duties were gradually taken over by the central government; or it might perhaps be put in the form that the government became the universal *seigneur*. From the people's point of view this change had both its advantages and disadvantages, the disadvantages being perhaps more in evidence than the advantages. For centralized government brought in its train the militia, the state *Corvée*, and a heavier taxation; but on the other hand, it brought protection from a tyrannous and irresponsible overlord, and a less costly and cumbersome administration. During the civil war, which had been the prelude of Louis XIV's personal reign, many villages had bankrupted themselves by alienation of property and extravagant borrowing, and by 1667 the King found that many communities could not even pay the interest on their debts, a state of affairs with which Louis dealt vigorously. He declared such communities to be minors, wrote off the more iniquitous of their loans, reduced the rate of interest on others, and forbade villages to alienate or borrow without his consent. And, so sharply did the Intendant watch over the villager's finance, that by 1683 the majority of the communities were again solvent. But even before the 'sixties had run out, the village fathers had sorrowfully realized that the days of meeting current expenditure by borrowing from the benevolent banker in the nearest town were gone for ever; responsibility was being taken out of their hands by the Intendant. If the parish wished either to sell or purchase the land, the Intendant's permission was required, and it was by no means easy to get that permission. Eventually, even the treasurership of the village funds was taken over by a paternal government, which, when asked to allow the village a sum of its own money, usually replied in an official minute which boiled down to "but if we give you some of your own money, you'll only spend it."

The new régime was not inaugurated without some protest: noisy protest under the village elms, which brought the deliberation of the village assembly to a standstill. Whereupon the Intendant quietly substituted an elective assembly for the old meeting of the whole village: and he was the man who supervised the elections. But the most startled people in the village must have been the *seigneur* and the *curé*, who woke up to find that the Intendant had not only assessed them for communal expenses, but also expected them to pay their assessment. Village officers continued to be elected by the parish, but as the grip of the government tightened, they tended to become rather the delegates of the Intendant than the representatives of their fellows. The post of *Syndic* is a case in point; his duty, theoretically, was to carry out the mandate entrusted to him by the village, but in fact he had to try to serve three masters, the village, the *seigneur*, and the Intendant. It is not surprising that, though the post was a salaried one, a situation gradually arose in which it was regarded as yet another *Corvée*, and less than half-way through the reign fines had to be imposed on those who refused to accept the office.

But even in spite of the governess-like attitude of the central government, the everyday affairs of the village continued to be conducted by the villagers themselves, and through the surviving minutes of assembly meetings we get some dim picture of village life as it was under Louis XIV. Appointments and salaries of the village officers—the schoolmaster, the *va-pied* or village postman, the shepherd—provision for the repair of the church and presbytery, the upkeep of the courthouse—all these, though subject to the Intendant's supervision, were parish preoccupations. And here again we come up against the limitations of Louis' absolutism. Until 1673 the itinerant seigneurial judge had held his court wherever convenient, more often than not in the open air; but in that year an edict was issued ordering the construction of village courthouses. Little notice was taken of it, and justice continued to be done under the village elms, as had been done from time immemorial. And, let us note, this means that it was the Intendants who ignored the King's orders, not the villagers.

Next in importance to the *seigneur* in the hierarchy of the commune came the *curé*, and a great deal of parish business is concerned with the upkeep of the presbytery and of the church. An edict of 1695 decrees that the presbytery must be a four-roomed house, with two fireplaces, a barn, cellar, and the "usual offices"; which building had to be both erected and maintained by the parish, always subject to the parishioners' right of appeal to the Intendant if the *curé's* demands seemed unreasonable. Often the parish did appeal, and the Intendant would rule that the proposed tithe barn was too large, or point out that the plans made no provision for a pigsty. And let us at this point transfer a little of our sympathy from the peasant to the Intendant; he had perhaps twelve hundred parishes in his Intendancy, each plaguing him with similar questions. Having dealt with the portentous matter of the incumbent's pigsty, he would turn to what are, in the jargon of the day, known as top level decisions, and would turn back again to the matter of the *seigneur's* precedence in a village procession. Small wonder that an Intendant who could keep abreast of current affairs by working fourteen hours a day, was considered to be a lucky man.

On the whole, the standard of village priests during the reign seems to have been high, and an enormous improvement on what would have been thought adequate in the reign of Louis XIII; but the whole Church, from village to archbishopric, was under the curse of absenteeism. In the case of a bishop, or the head of a religious house, absenteeism was of no great financial importance to anyone, but it was very different in the case of the absentee *curé*. The holder of the living rarely paid his substitute a living wage, and the necessary additional stipend had to be contributed by the parish. As his right-hand man, the *curé* had a *marguillier* or treasurer, elected by the village, and whose functions were much the same as those of the vicar's warden in the Church of England. In some provinces, for instance, Auvergne, the *marguillier* might be a woman, which must have been strongly resented by those incumbents who found themselves saddled with a Mrs. Proudie invested with legal rights of interference in the conduct of the parish: for the absolutism of the parish priest proves on investigation to be as much of a myth as that of Louis XIV himself. At least one incumbent complains to his ecclesiastical superiors that he finds himself nothing but a spiritual *chargé d'affaires* in the hands of his *marguillier* and his parishioners. In many ways the *curé* tended to become the agent of the central government, notably in the collection of statistical data and the dissemination of news. Few of his parishioners could read, and the Intendant generally furnished the priest with a short résumé of events in the great world, which was read from the pulpit after sermon.

The maintenance of the church was a dual responsibility, an

unsatisfactory system which led to much controversy and recrimination; the nave, which was often the village store, schoolroom, and public hall, had to be kept in repair by the village, whilst the choir, which was never used for profane purposes, was maintained by the *curé* out of his tithes. Naturally there were ambiguities; if, as was sometimes the case, the bell hung over the nave, who had to pay for new bell ropes? A small thing as seen from Paris, but enough to throw a village into a ferment.

Next to the *curé* in standing came the schoolmaster, whose position in the life of the village became more prominent after 1698, in which year primary education was made compulsory and the salaries of schoolmasters were increased. The leaving age was fixed at fourteen, and the school was to be open throughout the winter months. The school had to be built and maintained by the parish, but the schoolmaster seems to have had to fend for himself as regards accommodation. Now for the first time a schoolmaster had to give proof of his fitness for his post by appearing before the bishop, who examined him in reading, writing, arithmetic, plain song, the duties òf religion, and divinity; but a very slight knowledge of divinity must have sufficed, judging from Mme. de Sévigné's examination on her Brittany estate, where the peasant children told her that the Virgin was the creator of Heaven and Earth. Mixed schools were forbidden by an edict in which we seem to trace Mme. de Maintenon's hand, but this prohibition was ignored for financial reasons, as was the obligation to keep children at school until they were fourteen. The schoolmaster, in addition to keeping school, was usually the village sacristan, and in that capacity was responsible for the behaviour of the village clock, and for ringing the bell to ward off thunderstorms in harvest time.

In most villages there was no doctor, but there would be a primitive attempt at a health service, and even a kind of cottage hospital. Poor relief was administered by the village assembly, and when in 1686 beggary was declared to be an illegal profession, the government introduced a series of measures for the employment of beggars, which was also administered by the village. Two more salaried posts in the gifts of the community were that of village midwife and village shepherd. It throws an ominous sidelight on one aspect of seventeenth-century life when we discover that the only qualification required of the midwife was that she should know how to baptize. A communal shepherd would, of course, only be found in villages in the sheep-rearing districts. Often the shepherd and the schoolmaster shared a house. Pasture land in all grazing villages was the property not of the *seigneur* but of the village, though the *seigneur* had grazing rights over the common land. In one community arose the momentous question—referred of course to the Intendant—whether the *seigneur* had abused his common rights by turning loose his geese as well as his sheep on the village common. For villages were always of a litigious disposition; one official, taking over an Intendancy in 1670, found his local court with 2,400 community lawsuits on hand. He appears to have settled them summarily himself, and after that chastening experience, to have got an edict promulgated, by which communities were forbidden to go to law without the permission of the Intendant.

It is inevitable but misleading to visualize the life of the French peasant as not only continuously bleak, but always grim; inevitable because so much of the material from which we collect our picture is in the nature of special pleading. Even Vauban, whose case depends on denigrating the existing régime, is betrayed into a grumble that on Sundays and fête days every public house is full of drinking peasants. The façade of poverty raised by the peasantry as a protection against augmented taxation often concealed a degree of secret comfort which was unsuspected, even by the neighbours. Even more misleading are the Intendant's reports, from which the bulk of the evidence is drawn; for the Intendant was not an ogre, the heir of the bad Baron, more wicked because he was more powerful. Here and there there was, of course, a bad Intendant, but broadly speaking, he was a humane and enlightened man, anxious to do the best for his subjects, and to act as their advocate at Versailles. Even when he was moved by no higher motive, professional pride, a desire to boast of getting the better of the neighbouring Intendants, spurred him on to keep his Intendancy flourishing and its taxes as low as possible. We must, therefore, read his reports with caution and even scepticism; a report depicting the misery of a province, written with the express object of reducing the provincial taxes, and based on material furnished by peasants and *curés* who were aware of the writer's intention, can hardly be called an objective document.

On the whole, I feel we must reject La Bruyère's famous purple passage on the French peasant. Country life was not totally lacking in cakes and ale; not even in the poorest districts was the peasant without a decent suit for Sundays and feast days. On her Brittany estate in 1680, Mme. de Sévigné meets a pretty farmeress, whose dress of Holland, cut over taffeta, arouses her admiration; but she goes on to say, that she wishes the woman would pay some of that eight thousand francs she owes the estate. The size of the debt argues a substantial holding.

In some ways the French peasant was actually better off than his German or English contemporary, and no worse off than his descendant in France today. At least a very large minority of Louis XIV's peasants owned their own holdings, at a time when such tenures were rare in England and unknown across the Rhine. And we have Boulenger's opinion that the seventeenth-century French peasant was not more heavily taxed than the peasant of 1920. There was an unbreakable resilience about Jacques Bonhomme's spirit which seems to have set all hardship at defiance. Taxes might be impending and debts unpaid, but he is still to be found dancing with violins and hautboys in public places of a Sunday, and on any day following the fiddles to a village marriage feast. Each year brings with it the election of the village king and queen, and the feast of the Prince of Youth, who takes precedence over the *seigneur* in starting the village ball. There is dancing on the lawns of the *château* in summer, the harvest home dinner in the *château* barn in autumn, and a cup of smuggled wine by the cottage fireside when the night is black with frost. And when we consider his condition, let us be under no illusions as to the way of life of his English contemporary. Let us turn to Evelyn, who had visited France during the worst years of the civil war, and had then visited rural England in the comparatively prosperous year of 1654. Listen to him: "7. Aug. Went to . . . Rutland . . . where most of the rural parishes are but mud, and the people living as wretchedly as the most impoverish'd parts of France, wh. they much resemble, being idle and sluttish."

It seems that we must rid ourselves of the picture of the French peasant as something but little above the beasts. If he was the devitalized and hunger-crushed animal of La Bruyère's etching, whence came the man who fought under Villars at Malplaquet in 1709?

IV

The Church

Seventeenth-century France offered Bossuet a poor background against which to present the Protestant world with his picture of the Roman Catholic Church as the only *dépôt* of a corpus of authoritative doctrine which had been received with unquestioning submission by the faithful from the earliest times up to the present day. We strain our ears to catch the words of his resonant exposition of the variations in the Protestant Church, too often drowned in the tumult and the shouting of that internecine doctrinal warfare which was the contemporary Church of France.

But the story goes back a long way before Bossuet's time, or rather the stories, for there are four of them: four hurricanes which devastated the Church of Louis XIV: Jansenism, Quietism, The War of Gallican versus Ultramontane, and the attempt to extirpate Protestantism. To disentangle the main threads is no easy task, for these struggles not only overlap in time, but are further complicated by divided allegiances; we cannot equate Jan-

senism with Gallicanism, nor what, for lack of a better term, may
be called Jesuitism with the Ultramontane party. Indeed we cannot even talk, except loosely, of the Ultramontane party, for
here we find a perplexing differentiation between theological and
political values. It was, for instance, both practicable and logical
to be a political Gallican and an ecclesiastical Ultramontane.
The four subjects do not fall into convenient water-tight com-
partments of themselves, either chronologically or as regards the
protagonists, but only by their arbitary isolation can any clear
outline be attempted.

Let us begin with the Jansenist controversy.

Cornelis Jansen (1585–1638) was a pupil of the Jesuits who
took orders, was refused admission to the Society, and ultimately
became Bishop of Ypres, where he devoted the rest of his life
to writing, with the assistance of his intimate friend the Abbé de
St. Cyran (1581-1643), a commentary on the works of St. Augustine called *Augustinus*. For both men St. Augustine was the
Father *par excellence*, and indeed the bishop goes so far as to call
him "the only authoritative Father."

In 1636 St. Cyran was appointed *directeur* of Port-Royal, and
speedily inoculated the community with the enthusiastic Aug-
ustinianism, or as his enemies called it, Jansenism, of his old friend
the Bishop of Ypres. Chief amongst the so-called novelties introduced by St. Cyran at Port-Royal was the theory that it was
sinful to communicate without perfect contrition, that is, without
being in a state of perfect love towards God: a view which was
opposed by many contemporary theologians, who held that at-
trition, or penitence from fear of damnation was an adequate
state in which to make a Communion. And one cannot but share
the view of the older school that if we waited for contrition, many
of us would never communicate at all. At this stage the Jesuits
entered the controversy with a shrewd enquiry as to how the
Jansenists explained away St. Augustine's advocacy of weekly
Communion?

In 1638 Richelieu, who probably understood very little of the
points at issue, but who regarded theological innovation as a specialized branch of civil revolt, imprisoned St. Cyran, who
remained in jail until the accession of Louis XIV in 1643: and
in the same year, 1638, Jansen died, leaving orders that the publication of his completed *Augustinus* should be subject to the ap-

proval of the Vatican. This for some reason does not appear to have been obtained, and in 1640 the book appeared with the *nihil obstat* of the Censors of Louvain University. The general thesis of the *Augustinus* leads logically to a denial of Free Will, but the book seems to have attracted little notice, though in 1641 the Pope forbade its perusal on the ground that it contained propositions of one Baius, which had already been stated to be heretical.

Here the matter might have rested had not the great Jansenist leader, Antoine Arnauld (1612–94), launched an attack on the Jesuits in 1643 with his *Frequent Communion*, in which the society was attacked for moral laxity in allowing its penitents to take the Sacrament when not in a proper state to do so. And here, in parentheses, let us put in a word in defence of the Jesuits; it should be pointed out that the heavily advertised charge of teaching a lax morality which was brought against them, rested, not on their instructions to their penitents, but on a small number of technical works written solely for the use of confessors.

Battle was now joined along the whole front, and the search for ammunition led to a revival of interest in Jansen's *Augustinus*, from which one Cornet in 1649 claimed to have extracted the famous *Five Propositions*, which were submitted to the Sorbonne, and in 1650 referred to Rome. It was not until 1653 that the Pope gave judgment: the Propositions were condemned as "false, temerarious, scandalous, derogatory to the Divine goodness," and especially the fifth—"It is semi-Pelagianism to say that Jesus Christ died or shed His Blood for all men without exception." It looked as if Arnauld's intervention had brought irreparable disaster upon the party, but he succeeded for the moment in parrying the blow. He accepted the condemnation of the *Five Propositions*, but denied that they were to be found in Jansen's book. The Pope, said Arnauld, was infallible in matters of faith, but liable to error in matters of fact. Richelieu would have made short work of Arnauld, but his successor, Mazarin, was a man of a very different temper. With his usual cynicism he fanned the flames of a controversy which he found distracted public attention from the precarious state of the country, and did his best to keep on good terms with the Vatican without declaring against the Jansenists.

Sixteen fifty-six was a black year for Jansenism. In January Arnauld was condemned by the Sorbonne for his doctrine of

Grace, which was labelled "temerarious," and in the following month he was deprived of his Doctorate. But in February the Jansenists struck back with the most famous blow of the campaign: Pascal began to publish his *Provincial Letters*. Unfair, according to some well qualified judges, and perhaps doing little ultimately for the Jansenist cause, they not only permanently enriched French literature, but for the moment aroused a considerable body of anti-Jesuit sentiment amongst the worldly. In March the Jansenists obtained some further relief from the Miracle of the Holy Thorn at Port-Royal, and before the end of the year more of the pressure was diverted from their front by a petition of the Paris and Rouen clergy for the condemnation of the Casuists. But these successes were more than offset by a Papal Bull fulminated in October, which declared that the Five Propositions were contained in the writings of Jansen, and were condemned in the sense in which Jansen had understood them.

By 1657 the state of the parties was roughly as follows: against the Jansenists were the King, most of the Court, and the Jesuits: for them were the Cardinal de Retz, and his henchmen the Grand Vicars of Paris, the Archbishop of Sens, and an important minority of bishops. That Louis should have been opposed to Jansenism was inevitable; not only was the religion which he had inherited from his Spanish mother the very antithesis of all that Jansenism stood for, but his first confessor, Father Paulin, S.J., boasts that he had successfully instilled a hatred of Jansenism into the boy King. But it is doubtful whether Father Paulin's training had much to do with the matter; for from his earliest years and for all his life, a hatred of innovation was a fundamental element in Louis' character. And further, Jansenism presented itself to the King not only as a novelty, and therefore objectionable, but as a pseudo-theological revolt against his own autocracy. Were the Jansenists not openly allied to that arch-rebel the Cardinal de Retz, and did not Port-Royal open its gates to malcontents who had withdrawn from Court? Of the theological implications of Jansenism Louis was no doubt entirely ignorant; but he was quite clear that there could be one king only in France, and from that there followed the, to him, logical deduction that there could be no other type of religious belief in France than his own.

The support of de Retz did the Jansenists perhaps more harm than any other single factor: with the King because he had been the power behind the Fronde, and with the devout because the cardinal, so far from being a Jansenist, did not even become a believer until chastened by old age and political frustration.

In December came the answer to the Jansenist prayer, "Oh that mine enemy would write a book!" One Father Pirot, S.J., plunged into the fray with his *Apology for the Casuists*, in which the delighted Jansenists found plausible evidence of the truth of Pascal's charges against the Society, and an apparent admission of the laxity of Jesuit morality, the whole couched in a tone which even to seventeenth-century ears, sounded inexcusably provocative and insulting. Pascal leapt to the opportunity, and after a skilful campaign of propaganda, secured the censure of Pirot's book by the French bishops and its subsequent condemnation at Rome: and Pirot disappears from the firing line into that obscurity which so well became him.

Sixteen sixty was a year for the Assembly of the Clergy, a semi-elective body not unlike the English House of Convocation, and dealing with the same type of business which met every five years. On this occasion it passed a resolution insisting on the acceptance by the whole Church of a compromise formula in the matter of the *Five Propositions* which had been drawn up four years earlier, but not put into effect. The nuns of Port-Royal refused to sign, on the ground that they could have no certainty of truth in the matter, and the convent was promptly forbidden to accept postulants. In 1664 Hardouin de Péréfixe (1605–71), Archbishop of Paris, attempted to close the long controversy with an instruction explaining that no one was expected to believe that the Pope was infallible in matters of unrevealed fact, and assuring his people that the Formulary made no such demands upon them. The instruction seems to have had some effect, but Port-Royal remained inflexible; Péréfixe, not one of the most enlightened of Louis' bishops, was badly worsted in a dialectical battle with the Abbess of Port-Royal, and retaliated by exiling twelve of the most recalcitrant nuns, excommunicating the rest, and handing over control of the convent to the Order of the Visitation; whilst Louis was reduced to asking the Pope to issue a more authoritative Formulary than that which had been produced in France.

That Louis took such action is a significant indication of the depth of his annoyance with the Jansenists, for by appealing to

Rome he played straight into the hands of the Ultramontanes, whom he disliked nearly as much. The Pope could well afford to gratify him, and must have smiled as he did so; for here was the Gallican champion, the aggressive exponent of the extrusion of the Papacy from domestic affairs in France, reduced to begging assistance from a power thus tacitly admitted to be superior to his own. On 15th February 1665 the Pope fulminated the stringent Bull which had been asked for; Louis had it registered by his Parlement, Port-Royal still refused its submission, and in July the troublesome nunnery was placed under military guard, its contacts with the outside world severed, and all courts in the kingdom forbidden to take cognizance of its affairs. Matters remained in this state until 1669, when a truce was arranged, known as *The Peace of the Church*, whereby a compromise Formula was introduced which should be acceptable to the still recalcitrant Port-Royalists. Ten years of uneasy quiet followed, until the death in 1679 of Anne de Bourbon, Duchesse de Longueville, the most powerful social force in Jansenism, when a spasmodic persecution broke out afresh and continued fitfully until 1709 when the King got to work in earnest.

In July Port-Royal-les-Champs, the inner shrine of Jansenism, was placed under the orders of Port-Royal-de-Paris, which had long ceased to have any Jansenist traditions. In October the remaining nuns of the Jansenist Port-Royal were arrested by the archers of the Provost of Paris, bundled into hackney coaches, and distributed among those convents notorious for their hostility to Jansenism, there to end their days in spiritual isolation amid petty persecutions. Even that section of society untainted with Jansenism murmured against the brutality of the proceedings; as one observer says, it suggested more a police raid on a disorderly house than the enforcement of a measure of ecclesiastical discipline. In 1710 the buildings of the convent were destroyed, and in the following year the graveyard was desecrated and the site of Port-Royal ploughed over.

Here we may end the story, for though the Bull *Unigenitus* was published in Louis XIV's lifetime (1713), the recrudescence of Jansenism, or more properly Quesnelism which it provoked, belongs rather to eighteenth than to seventeenth-century history.

Louis does not come well out of the Jansenist controversy.

There is something Oriental about his policy of vigorous attacks on the Port-Royalists alternating with long periods of inactivity, which is repugnant to the Western mind, and the brutality of the closing scene disgusts us. Moreover, the irrationality of such a policy did much to keep Jansenism alive: for there was for most of the reign a degree of persecution which, while it was insufficient to eradicate the heresy, was sufficiently severe to discredit the opponents of Jansenism in public opinion.

But this is not to condemn Louis' policy of extirpating Jansenism. On the whole, Jansenism has been sympathetically regarded by Protestantism, and that very fact should put us on our guard in judging its opponents. It is easy to distort the picture by a violent contrast between the prevalent conventual laxity and the austere and holy life of Port-Royal, where dowries were refused and a vocation was essential, and to conclude that, therefore, Jansenism was the leaven of the French Church. But unfortunately the religious fervour of Port-Royal is not the question, and its existence is admitted by those most hostile to the nuns. "As pure as angels and as disobedient as devils," was the verdict of the Archbishop of Paris on his rebellious nuns, and it touches the real point at issue: did the Port-Royal religious and solitaires hold heretical opinions, and had the nuns broken their vows of obedience? The Pope's decision on the matter makes it absolutely clear that, in spite of much skilful if unedifying quibbling, the Jansenists stand convicted on both counts. It was Louis' method, not his policy, which was blameworthy.

The Quietist controversy is shorter, sharper, more dramatic; and, being decisive, no doubt did less harm to the Church in the long run than the incurable ulcer of Jansenism. But on the short term view it was infinitely more damaging to the prestige of the Roman Church in the Protestant world.

In the Jansenist quarrel, Protestant sympathies were engaged; Protestants, however erroneously, saw Jansenism as a crypto-Protestant movement within the Roman Catholic Church which might ultimately lead to a reunion of Christendom on Protestant terms. While Jansenism produced a war, Quietism led to a duel; there was little to stir Protestant emotion in two rival interpretations of Roman Catholic doctrine, but much to raise sarcastic and malicious laughter in the spectacle of Bossuet, the apostle to the Protestants, and Fénelon, the shepherd of the "converted" Huguenots, locked in a savage and disingenuous struggle from which both men emerged with tarnished reputations.

The originator of the whole trouble was Father Miguel Molinos (1640–97), a fashionable confessor living in Rome, who in 1675 published a *Spiritual Guide* which, according to its defenders, was nothing more than a restatement of the mysticism of St. Theresa, but which in fact contained some very curious propositions, propositions which in the hands of Molinos' ignorant admirers were to be pushed to the point of absurdity. Molinism, or Quietism, as it came to be called, was in the words of St. Cyres, "a movement of the spiritual democracy, of ignorance against learning, of personal experience against the dogmas of the Church." Not for the Quietist is the painful narrow road to perfection; let him abandon himself utterly to that absorption in the Divine love where there is an utter annihilation, not only of his own will, but of all effort or desire for effort; let his soul become so lost in God that he ceases to hope for Heaven or dread Hell, no longer desires to do what is right, or feels any dread of sin. There must be, says Molinos, an entire cessation of self-consciousness. And much more to the same effect.

Then, oddly enough, nothing happened for the next twelve years, until 1687, when Molinos was tried by the Inquisition for certain moral offences and sentenced to imprisonment for life. This led to an examination, or presumably a re-examination, of his writings, and in the same year sixty-eight propositions from the *Spiritual Guide* were condemned by the Pope; Quietism had become a heresy. In France in the same year, Mme. Guyon (1648–1717), published her *Short Method of Prayer*, and Quietism breached the defences of the Gallican Church.

She was a remarkable woman, this Mme. Guyon. The daughter of rich parents, married very young to an elderly barrister, she found herself in 1676 a wealthy widow with no particular object in life. Intelligent, eccentric, and from her earliest years subject to religious hysteria, idleness reduced her to melancholia, and in an unhappy moment she turned to the writings of Molinos and the mystics, which certainly cured her melancholia, but at the price of reducing her permanently to a mental condition not far removed from insanity. Her obstinate and ill-regulated mind soon carried her far beyond the mystics, and even beyond Molinos: she had attained perfection: she practised all the virtues unconsciously: she could not mortify herself because she was beyond the reach of mortification: and, indeed, she could not sin, for sin is self, and she had rid herself of self.

In 1681 in Savoy she met a priest, one Father Lacombe, converted him to her tenets, and together they made a missionary journey through the Midi, teaching, preaching, performing miracles, and always being moved on by a succession of anxious bishops, until in 1687 the pair reached Paris. Before the year was out, Lacombe had been convicted of heresy and imprisoned for life, whilst Mme. Guyon herself was shut up in a convent, where she remained until the autumn of 1688. It is significant that she owed her release to the influence of a great lady, the Duchesse de Béthune, who introduced her into that exclusive group of *dévotes* led by herself, the Duchesse de Beauvilliers (1658–1734), and the latter's sister the Duchesse de Chevreuse (1650–1734), the notorious "little flock" of Fénelon.

Mme. Guyon may have lived on the borderland of insanity, but there must have been a most persuasive charm about the woman who could captivate, not only such a group, but also the brilliant Fénelon and the cold and cautious Mme. de Maintenon. For captivate them all she did; they capitulated to her almost at the first summons. That she should have made a capture of Fénelon was to Bossuet inexplicable, and to us, with the advantage of all the subsequent accumulation of evidence, it still remains so; d'Aguesseau was no doubt partly right when he explains the fact by saying that Mme. Guyon's congenial mysticism trapped Fénelon into believing himself to be a theologian when in fact he was merely a master of eloquence. But a further explanation must be looked for in the character of Fénelon himself.

Fénelon's spiritual life found its chief nourishment in mysticism, and his outstanding worldly characteristic was his unfailing charm of manner; we love him without quite knowing why, says Ste. Beuve, and even before we have fathomed him; one could not take one's eyes off him without an effort, says St. Simon. Like many charming people, Fénelon was quite aware of his own charm, and like many charming men, he delighted most to exercise his powers upon a little circle of devoted women. Such men, however, rarely give to one person that which they feel was meant for mankind; they instinctively recoil from the idea of a soul mate, preferring to move through life in an aroma of their own charm which affects all with whom they come in contact. And Fénelon was no exception. Is it after all an over-simplification to talk of his "capture" by Mme. Guyon? To imagine that he was in any sense a disciple like poor Father Lacombe would be absurd, and Fénelon's morals were irreproachable. We have not got Fénelon's letters to the lady, or hers to him, for these were destroyed when the storm broke; but no doubt he wrote to her charmingly, with just that intimate cosy flavour of an esoteric creed shared, which would be exactly calculated to capture Mme. Guyon. For I incline to the view that it was he who captured her, not she him; that he saw in her, under a coating of extravagance whose existence he ignored as far as possible, a fellow-mystic who would be a valuable recruit to the little flock; and then when the trouble came, he found his honour too far engaged to disown his *protégée*.

But whatever may have been Fénelon's exact attitude towards Mme. Guyon, there can be no doubt that Mme. de Maintenon was completely taken in by her; she liked the woman personally, as did nearly all who knew her; she relished the contrast between the worldly talk of Versailles and the enthusiastic hypnotic charm of the low voice which spoke to her of abandonment into the arms of God; and she allowed her new friend free access to the jealously guarded precincts of St. Cyr. This was the beginning of Mme. Guyon's downfall, and incidentally of that of her protector, Fénelon; Quietism ran like measles through the school, and was, of course, almost at once detected by Godet Desmarets, Bishop of Chartres, who was both *Directeur* of St. Cyr and Mme. de Maintenon's confessor. The alarm was sounded, Bourdaloue, the foremost preacher of the day supporting the bishop, and Mme. de Maintenon, badly frightened, turned Mme. Guyon adrift and invoked Louis XIV's aid. The King referred the *Short Method of Prayer* to Rome, and in 1689 the book was condemned by the Pope.

Here the matter might have rested, had it not been for Fénelon; but there was a streak of vanity in that complex character which forbade him to let well, or rather ill, alone. And in 1693 Bossuet was considerably surprised by a request from Mme. Guyon that he should examine her writings. He was very unwilling to interrupt his own work to do so, and would probably have refused had it not been revealed to him that the request really originated with Fénelon. Then he undertook the task with a view to clearing his friend of the charges of walking in perilous ways which were already being whispered against him in ecclesiastical circles.

Up to this time the relations between the two men had been cordial, even intimate; Bossuet was now sixty-six, and Fénelon forty-two; and the elder man had been struck with the ability of the younger since they first met at the *Little Council*, a club founded by Bossuet for Biblical and theological study in 1673. When Fénelon had been appointed tutor to the Duke of Burgundy in 1689, no one had congratulated him more warmly than Bossuet. It is clear that Bossuet entered upon the controversy, not only with no hostile feelings towards Fénelon, but with a determination to defend him up to the extreme limit imposed by orthodoxy.

But to draw Bossuet into the Quietist controversy was a fatal mistake, whether the action was prompted by Fénelon or taken by Mme. Guyon on her own initiative. Personally, I incline to the view that it was Mme. Guyon's doing, and that Fénelon found himself forced to acquiesce in a *fait accompli*. For it seems incredible that a man of Fénelon's *savoir faire*, who was moreover well acquainted with Bossuet's climate of theological thought, could have failed to realize that he was the last man in France likely to sympathize with or understand the delicacies of an exalted mysticism alien to his whole temperament. Fénelon, with his subtle, complex brain, is a man of nuances, an artist in chiaroscuro, whereas Bossuet's thought reminds us of an architect's drawings; it is a thing without shade or perspective, a matter of thin hard lines, beautifully drawn, each correct to a fraction of an inch, each dovetailing into a plan, clear, clean-cut, leaving no room for ambiguity. Bossuet is the Quartermaster of the Gallican regiment, who refutes our hesitations, not with argument, but by telling us that the answer to all possible questions is laid down in regulations: and, so far as he is concerned, that closes the matter. It would indeed have been surprising if he could have been drawn into mystical controversy with Fénelon without both men losing their tempers.

And, had Fénelon showed a little more foresight, or relied a little less on Mme. de Maintenon's friendship, he would have realized that the relationship subsisting between Bossuet and the

King was an added reason for keeping the bishop out of the dispute at all costs. For Bossuet was Louis' theological watchdog, his beau-ideal of a Gallican churchman, whilst to Bossuet, Louis was a visible assurance of the correctness of his own belief that government by an absolute ruler was a divinely appointed institution in France. Furthermore, Bossuet had a personal love, not to say adoration, for Louis which can have been of little assistance to him in taking an objective view of a question on which Louis must sooner or later be enlightened; and on which side Louis' sympathies would lie was certain. To him Quietism would present itself as an innovation, and after that there would be no more to be said. It would be most unjust to Bossuet to assume that he was capable of violating his conscience by adapting his theological convictions to suit the King's theories of Church government; he was no Court sycophant, and had shown both courage and dignity in his rebukes to Louis during his liaison with Mme. de Montespan. It was rather that the circumstances of his birth and upbringing had conditioned him to believe that the doctrines of the Gallican Church and the Louis XIV theory of monarchy were so indissolubly wedded that neither could be injured without doing fatal damage to the other; if Mme. Guyon was a Quietist, she was a heretic, and both King and bishop took the view that heresy was not only a theological offence, but also treason against the King. It was not difficult to foresee the verdict which Bossuet would inevitably arrive at.

From the outset Bossuet showed himself allergic to the charm which Mme. Guyon had exercised with success in so many unexpected quarters; the more he saw of her the less he liked her, and his indignation that such a woman should have dared to write on theological matters at all, was increased by his distaste for the language in which her enthusiasm was couched. But he treated her and her work with a laborious patience which perhaps neither deserved, and it was not until January 1694 that he pronounced the book "intolerable as well in matter as in form . . . and containing one positive heresy." Mme. Guyon appeared to accept the verdict, and in April retired to the country, having promised to preach or write no more. But nothing short of imprisonment could really suppress Mme. Guyon, and in June she returned to the charge with a request that a commission of clergy should be appointed to make a more formal examination of her works than had been made by Bossuet. Bossuet saw his chance and took it: Mme. Guyon should have her commission, which should in fact investigate the whole question of the new doctrine, define its orthodox limits, and embody the commissioner's findings in a code of rules binding on all *directeurs:* Fénelon should have a full opportunity to state both his and Mme. Guyon's case, and both of them should give a signed assent to the conclusions of the commission. Fénelon was still in high favour with Mme. de Maintenon at this time, and both she and Bossuet were determined that the real work of the commission should be, first a restraining, and then a public whitewashing of the overenthusiastic Abbé. No doubt with this object in view, Bossuet was appointed chairman, assisted by Noailles, Bishop of Châlons (1651–1729), and Tronson, Superior of St. Sulpice (1622–1700), an intimate personal friend of Fénelon's. The *Conference of Issy,* as it was called, began to sit in July 1694, and concluded its labours in March 1695. And in the meantime the Abbé de Fénelon had had a resounding personal triumph which immensely raised his ecclesiastical standing; on 4th February, with little more than a month to spare as it turned out, Mme. de Maintenon persuaded Louis, who still knew nothing of what was brewing, to appoint him Archbishop of Cambrai.

On 10th March Fénelon signed the articles of Issy in circumstances which are still obscure; Bossuet and Noailles both say that Fénelon signed the articles as they stood, but that he did it against his own conviction, and with great reluctance. Fénelon, on the other hand, maintains that he refused to sign until four additional articles, all in his favour, had been added to the original draft. However this may be, the conference broke up leaving Bossuet and Fénelon equally dissatisfied, and each determined to publish a gloss on the articles which should establish him victorious in the questions at issue.

Bossuet hoped to have the first word. In July 1696 he completed his *Sur les Etats d'Oraison,* plainly designed to give Quietism its deathblow, and sent the manuscript to Fénelon for his criticism and approval. Some three weeks later Fénelon returned the manuscript, apparently without having read it, and accompanied or followed it by a letter in which he attempted to reopen the whole subject with a disingenuous defence of Mme. Guyon.

Bossuet, highly indignant at what he not unreasonably regarded as an insult to himself, left Fénelon to his own devices and announced the publication of his new book for March 1697. But Fénelon too had been hard at work, and in February was first in the field with his own contribution to the controversy, the notorious *Maxims of the Saints,* the first copy of which was presented to the King at Versailles on the first of the month.

The whole business of the publication of the *Maxims* leaves a nasty taste in one's mouth; Fénelon had submitted his manuscript to Noailles, now Archbishop of Paris, in October 1696, and the archbishop, no very clear thinker, had asked him not to publish until after the appearance of Bossuet's work on the same topic. This Fénelon had promised to do, but when he went off to the country soon afterwards, he left his manuscript in the hands of one of his staunchest disciples, the Duc de Chevreuse (1646–1712), who not only handed it over to the printers, but established himself in the printing house to rush the book through the press. It turned out to be a capital blunder; the King was highly indignant when the news reached him that a duke and peer had acted as proofreader, printer's devil, midwife, or whatnot to Fénelon's book, and society refused to believe the archbishop's protestations that Chevreuse had acted entirely contrary to his instructions.

The book which purported to draw the distinction between true and false mysticism in the abstract was, as anyone could see, nothing more or less than a defence of the doctrines of Mme. Guyon, and therefore by inference, a retraction of Fénelon's signature to the articles of Issy; and its publication was Fénelon's Waterloo. Bossuet, not unnaturally, was infuriated both by the book itself and by the shady manner of its publication, and prepared himself for total war. Both he and Mme. de Maintenon, cuttingly taken to task by Louis XIV for their joint responsibility in the promotion to Cambrai of one who was little better than a heretic, were to be henceforth amongst his bitterest enemies. Mme. de Maintenon was too occupied in restoring her own credit with the King to take any active part in the quarrel, but there is apparent in Bossuet for the rest of his life a savage hatred of Fénelon which is as deplorable as is the consistent disingenuousness of Fénelon in his attacks on Bossuet; but let us do Bossuet this justice, that his hatred is not so much an expression of personal venom as the anger of the churchman who has found in an erstwhile ally a fifth columnist within the fortress.

Bossuet never forgave Fénelon, and his anger was not in the least cooled by the fact that his own book was a triumphant success, whilst Fénelon's was a complete failure. Theologians disliked it, and no one else could understand it.

I have spoken of the Quietist controversy as a duel, but it must not be supposed that either combatant was without seconds; behind Bossuet were ranged Louis and his Court, with the exception of that small but important minority, the "little flock"; whilst for Fénelon was a collection of miscellaneous allies and benevolent neutrals, most important of whom was Cardinal de Bouillon (1644–1715). The cardinal, a de La Tour d'Auvergne, had had little difficulty in choosing sides; of the doctrinal dispute he knew nothing, and wanted to know nothing; but he knew that Fénelon was a de La Mothe-Salignac, and that Bossuet was the descendant of a Burgundy shopkeeper. And he could afford to please himself in taking sides; he was a cardinal, Grand Almoner of France, a Commander of the Order of the Holy Ghost, and French Ambassador to the Vatican; Louis XIV could do nothing more for him, and he was a hot favourite for the Deanery of the Sacred College. His assistance to Fénelon at the Roman Court was invaluable.

The Jesuits, if not entirely favourable to Fénelon, were at least very hostile to his opponents; they detested Bossuet, who had outmanoeuvred them on sundry occasions, and they happened to have various grievances against those other prelates who opposed Fénelon. On the whole it may be said that the Jesuit attitude was to keep as aloof from the open controversy in France as possible, whilst giving the weight of their secret support to Fénelon's cause at Rome.

It is both tedious and saddening to follow the quarrel through all its stages, for there can be no pleasure which is not wholly bad in contemplating the spectacle of two zealous Christians, each convinced of his own rightness, steadily degenerating under the influence of what had become a personal quarrel. It is a question in which it is difficult for the layman to take sides, and almost certainly unprofitable for him to do so; and, if we must take sides, our decision is apt to be made, not on the merits of the case, but in accordance with the dictates of our own temperament. To me, there is a certain evasiveness, a slipperiness about Fénelon's dialectic which recalls the least admirable side of Newman. Both men protest too loudly that all they seek is an opportunity of stating their cases in words so clear that not even the most simple can have any excuse for misunderstanding them. Only read what I have to say, they cry, and judge for yourself. But, in the case of Fénelon at least, you do so at your peril; one follows, or attempts to follow, the easy simplicity of the *Maxims of the Saints* with the mounting exasperation of a man who has been beguiled into taking a short cut through the African bush on a sultry afternoon. And when you emerge from these entangling and exhausting thickets on to the track of Bossuet, you are prepared to give your full adherence to his cause. But only for a moment. If Fénelon exasperates you by his obscurity, Bossuet repels by his vindictiveness; and his nephew and lobbyist at the Vatican, the Abbé Bossuet, is an object of disgust.

It was in the summer of 1697 that Fénelon extorted a reluctant permission from the King to submit his case to Rome, and thus won what appeared to be a tactical success, for the climate of Rome was much more favourable to him than it was to Bossuet. But even at Rome he was to suffer defeat for a variety of reasons, least among which were his theological opinions. True, Bossuet was chiefly known to the Vatican as the foremost champion of the detestable doctrine of Gallicanism, but on the other hand the cardinals knew that the Pope was old and sick, and that France would exercise a preponderating influence in the election of his successor. The preoccupation of the cardinals was not the finding of a true bill for or against Fénelon, but the discovery of a *via media* which would let down the archbishop as lightly as possible without antagonizing Louis XIV. By nice judgment and very careful packing, a Roman committee of experts was constituted which managed to extricate Innocent XII from his difficulties without committing him too deeply on either side. On 12th March 1699 the Pope prohibited the circulation of the *Maxims* and condemned twenty-three of its propositions, but without declaring the book to be heretical; and there was nothing in the condemnation to signify Vatican approbation of Bossuet's tenets. Innocent had in fact decided to do as little as he could afford to, consistently with avoiding Louis' hostility.

Fénelon received the news on the morning of 25th March, as he was preparing to enter the pulpit at Cambrai. Instantly abandoning the sermon which he had written, he read the condemnation to his people, and then preached extempore, making the subject a text on which to hang a moving discourse on the duty of implicit submission to the Holy See. Fénelon had in a sense snatched victory from defeat; be his case good or bad, he played his enemy off the stage, and it is Fénelon not Bossuet who takes the curtain at the end of a deplorable drama.

The broad strategical outlines of the Gallican versus Ultramontane struggle are not difficult to follow. It is a war between irreconcilable claims to absolute autocracy. On the one hand we have the Pope claiming an infallible authority in matters of faith throughout France, and on the other the King claiming the undivided loyalty and obedience of all his subjects. In theory the competing claims were not incapable of adjustment, but in practice the discord could not be resolved; the Pope's claim could not be admitted without giving him constant opportunities to interfere in French domestic affairs, and in the eyes of the Vatican, an assent to Louis' propositions was the first step towards a schismatical France. Ultramontanes, for instance, held that it was within the competence of the Pope to interfere with the King's legislation if it trenched on faith or morals: whilst the Gallicans asserted that the French courts could take cognizance of ecclesiastical affairs if it was suspected that a Vatican decision prejudiced the law of the land. In practice the deadlock was complete. On the surface the problem, as opposed to its solution, was a simple one, but there were undertows and hidden currents which confused the issue considerably; it was inextricably tangled up with the usually unsatisfactory relations existing between the regular and secular clergy, and yet cannot be simplified by asserting that the regulars were Ultramontanes and the seculars Gallicans, for Gallicanism itself was split into ecclesiastical and political Gallicanism. The Jesuits, for instance, were popularly regarded as the shock troops of Ultramontanism, yet more than once we find the whole influence of the Society mobilized in support of political Gallicanism: and some seculars were Ultramontanes, either theologically, or politically, or both.

Then again, the struggle from time to time has a purely financial aspect, Louis striving to retain or extend Gallican privileges which benefited his exchequer, and the Pope struggling to wrest them from him for the benefit of the Holy See. And yet again, the theological, juridical, and financial aspects of the matter are frequently swamped in those purely political phases of the struggle which resulted from Louis' aggressive foreign policy. For Louis, Eldest Son of the Church though he was, was less inclined to see in the Pope the Father of Christendom than an Italian reigning prince whose peculiar status gave him a prestige and influence in Europe out of all proportion to his material resources. It is perhaps not unfair to say that Louis was perfectly prepared to be the obedient Eldest Son, on condition that the Pope never demanded his obedience in French domestic affairs and, in foreign policy, was prepared to act as a permanent ally of the French Crown. But if the Pope transgressed in either respect, or, as the French would put it, forgot the obligations of a spiritual father, Louis never had the slightest compunction about playing the unfilial son.

The famous *Gallican Liberties*, the Ark of the Covenant to the French Church, were as old as the Monarchy, and, according to Louis' lawyers, had never been granted by Pope or Council but had grown up out of the very root and nature of things, a view never admitted by the Vatican, though on the other hand never formally denounced, and whose application to ecclesiastical matters was usually tacitly allowed by the Pope.

These liberties were in brief:

(1) That permission of the Crown was needed before a Papal Bull could be fulminated in France.
(2) That no legal weight attached in France to decisions of the Roman Congregation.
(3) That no French subject could be summoned to appear before a Roman tribunal.
(4) That French courts could take cognizance of ecclesiastical matters in all cases where the law of the land was involved.

Such doctrines, even if strictly interpreted, could not fail to be offensive to Ultramontane ears, but as glossed and amplified by men like Richelieu and Louis XIV, they could have formed the articles of faith of a schismatical Church of France. What inference, for example, does Richelieu draw from the fact that the "French courts"—which at that time meant Richelieu himself—can take cognizance of ecclesiastical affairs? In 1637 Father Caussin, Louis XIII's confessor, refused to admit Richelieu's contention that he was confessor to Louis de Bourbon, but not to the King of France, and must therefore submit for Richelieu's approval a list of the questions which he proposed to ask the King in the confessional. On Caussin's refusal to do so, he was promptly exiled for "meddling in politics." Small wonder that the Ultramontanes accused Richelieu of plotting to become the Patriarch of a Gallican Church!

Louis XIV's first clash with the Pope was purely secular, but it not only threw a dazzling light on the young King's attitude towards the Papacy, but led to an enthusiastic outburst of Gallicanism. In 1662 the Duc de Créqui was French Ambassador at Rome; his swaggering insolence had made him intolerable to the whole city, and on 20th August his coach was fired upon by the Corsican Guard. Louis, who received the news at supper, left the table to give orders for the mobilization of an Italian expeditionary force, and was only with much difficulty induced to countermand them on condition that the Pope disbanded his Guards, raised a pyramid in Rome bearing an account of the crime and its expiation, surrendered Avignon to France, and sent his nephew, Cardinal Chigi, to Paris to read a full apology for the outrage in the presence of the whole Court.

The enthusiasm engendered in the French people by this rather cheap display of the mailed fist on the part of their extravagantly popular ruler infected even the Sorbonne, which in 1663 took advantage of the prevailing temper to lay down the *Six Articles*, a restatement of the Gallican position in terms even more dogmatic and objectionable to Ultramontane sentiment than the *Liberties* themselves. In 1665 there was further trouble; the Sorbonne censured a work written in defence of the Pope's authority, and when the Pope censured the censure, the Paris Parlement stepped in with an edict upholding the Sorbonne's censure and forbidding the dissemination of the Pope's. The "beautiful years," to use the French historians term, had set in in earnest, the years in which Louis rode roughshod over Europe, sowing that crop of hatred which was to bring him fifty years later to the very edge of complete disaster.

A short breathing space followed, but in 1673 Louis once more found himself at loggerheads with the Pope, this time over the question of *La Régale*, or rather Louis' interpretation of it, for the right itself was not in dispute. For some reason, long since forgotten, the Council of Orléans in A.D. 511, had granted the King of France the privilege of appropriating the revenues of all vacant Sees and of dispensing the patronage in the dead bishop's gift pending the final and formal installation of his successor. But as France extended, bishoprics in the newly acquired territories were not subjected to the *Régale,* for the original grant had apparently named as subject to it only those Sees that were in French territory in 511. Thus by 1673, much of the Midi was exempt.

In that year, Colbert, hard pressed for money as usual, persuaded the King to issue an edict announcing that henceforward he would exercise the right of *La Régale* over all French bishoprics, irrespective of their historical or geographical claims to exemption. It is a significant indication of the completeness of absolutism to which Louis had already attained that out of the twenty-nine bishops affected by his usurpation, only two refused to acquiesce in it. The two recusants were deprived of their revenues, and those members of their Chapters who supported them were exiled or put in prison. Both bishops had appealed to Rome, and the matter was still *sub judice* when in 1676 Odescalchi became Pope under the title of Innocent XI: an austere, upright, hot-headed man, no enemy to Jansenism, and with a strong personal dislike for Louis XIV. In fact, a bad Pope in French eyes. Two years later one of the recusants, Pavillon of Aleth, died, and in 1680 the other, Caulet of Pamiers, followed him to the tomb. Louis nominated to the two vacant Sees, and Innocent promptly retorted by excommunicating the King's nominees. It was an awkward situation; neither the Pope nor the King had envisaged it with sufficient clarity, and each suddenly found himself in a situation where deadlock meant chaos, and retreat a loss of face. Louis was the first to move, as indeed he had to be, for, in the language of chess, the Pope had taken the King's bishop and said check. In May 1681 Louis summoned a conference of bishops to consider the *Régale* impasse, and on its advice decided to submit the matter to the 1681 Assembly of the Clergy.

But the King, though he had, so to speak, moved out of check, was smarting under the necessity for doing so, and took care to choose such deputies to the Assembly as would give a strongly Gallican flavour to any decisions at which it might arrive. Amongst them Bossuet, who viewed the situation with dismay; he had in 1663 opposed any further definition of the Gallican liberties on the ground that such things were best left undefined, even in the interests of the Church itself, and had had no reason to alter his opinion; and he had now a personal objection to entering upon controversy for he was in the running for a cardinal's hat, and saw small hope of it if he identified himself with the proceedings to be expected from an Assembly led by Harlay, Archbishop of Paris (1625–95); for Harlay was a notorious evil liver, detested at Rome, and whose whole future depended upon pleasing the King.

All that Bossuet had feared happened. True, a conciliatory letter on the *Régale* question was sent to the Pope, but Maurice Le Tellier of Rheims (1642–1710), and Gilbert de Choiseul of Tournai (1613–89), probably egged on by Colbert, or even by the King himself, carried the Assembly with them in the proposal that this was an excellent opportunity for a final authoritative definition of the liberties of the Gallican Church, though a strong party led by Bossuet protested that a worse moment could hardly be chosen for a proceeding which at best could do no good, and at worst might do infinite harm. But all that Bossuet gained was permission to draft the Assembly's declaration himself, and in March 1862 the result, the famous *Four Articles*, appeared. They may be briefly summarized as follows:

(1) The Pope has no jurisdiction over the temporal affairs of kings.
(2) The authority of a General Council overrides that of the Pope.
(3) The Gallican Liberties are perpetual and irrefragable.
(4) The Pope has the chief authority in all matters of faith, but the decisions of the Pope in matters of faith require the concurrence of the Church.

On the 23rd of the same month Louis issued an edict commanding the acceptance of the *Four Articles* by all his subjects, and the Pope immediately retaliated with a condemnation, not only of what the Assembly had done, but of anything it might do in the future; and in June Louis prorogued the Assembly, in order, according to one account, to parry the Pope's threat of excommunicating every member of it. Open hostilities were, for a moment, at an end, but Pope and King settled down to a cold war which was to last for a further ten years. The Pope opened the second phase by blacklisting all clergy who had sat in the Assembly, and whenever the King appointed one of them to a bishopric, he refused to issue the indispensable Bull of institution. Louis' retort was to refuse to demand these Bulls on behalf of any priest who had not been a member of the Assembly, with the result that, so long as the quarrel lasted, no bishop, of whatever shade of opinion, was canonically instituted.

In 1687 the quarrel was further envenomed by the outbreak of a sudden dispute between Paris and Rome on a purely temporal matter, that of the *Franchises*. Franchises was the name given to those rights of extra-territoriality which all embassy premises enjoyed, and which at Rome had been abused by all the powers in many ways: criminals found sanctuary in the houses of ambassadors, and the embassy staffs exploited their immunity from Customs office control by indulging in large-scale commercial smuggling. The Pope, tired of this state of affairs, announced in this year that he was going to withdraw all franchises.

Louis was in no mood to humour His Holiness: he insisted upon the retention of the French franchises, and underlined his demand by sending the Marquis de Lavardin (1644–1701), a professional soldier, as Ambassador Extraordinary to Rome with an escort of a thousand picked troops. And Lavardin, entering into the spirit of the thing, took over the embassy, fortified and garrisoned it, and proceeded to exercise *de facto* the rights of franchise of which he had been deprived *de jure*. Such time as he could spare from fighting the Pope he devoted to fighting Cardinal d'Estrées (1628–1714), whom Louis had sent to Rome to discuss the *Régale* dispute with the Vatican secretaries. Towards the end of the year the Pope excommunicated Lavardin—a deprivation which he bore with admirable fortitude—and when the news reached Versailles, Louis caused his Parlement to declare the excommunication an abuse, and decorated Lavardin with the Order of the Holy Ghost.

Here the matter rested until 1689, when for reasons both of domestic and foreign policy Louis found himself compelled to seek a solution of the problem in earnest. At home, he already had thirty-five bishops who had no canonical title to their bishoprics, and the situation was drifting towards a point at which schism could be the outcome of the quarrel: and abroad, France confronted a very different Europe to that in which Louis had so light-heartedly chastised the Pope in 1662. Since then Louis' chickens had come home to roost; nearly thirty years of hot and cold wars, equivocations, usurpations, and above all, of intolerable arrogance, had convinced his neighbours that nothing short of his absolute defeat could give the world peace. And Louis now found himself engaged in his first defensive war, against a very dangerous coalition; somehow the Pope must be conciliated, and Louis took advantage of the death of Innocent XI and the accession of Alexander VIII (1610–91) to reopen negotiations. As a preliminary, the truculent Lavardin was recalled, and Louis fell into line with the other powers in abandoning his claims to the franchises. In the following year he restored Avignon to the Papacy; and in 1693 a reconciliation was effected on compromise terms. A letter from the Assembly to the Pope more or less withdrew or watered down the most offensive decisions of the meeting of 1682, and Louis himself let the Pope understand that the *Four Articles* would be interpreted in a manner to which no exception could be taken. The Pope for his part undertook to issue the Bulls of institution for the thirty-five Sees, and agreed to the *fait accompli* of the extension of the *Régale* to all France.

On the whole, the victory rested with Louis XIV, who kept his *Four Articles* as part of the law of the land, whilst concessions made by him to the Pope were contained in mere letters having behind them no legal authority.

The liquidation of the Huguenots is a story one would gladly leave untold were it possible to do so, a crime which stood preeminent in its vileness for over two hundred and fifty years, until a more advanced civilization produced the gas chamber and the concentration camp. But also a crime which called down a swift and dramatic vengeance, for the Revocation of the Edict of Nantes in 1685 is the beginning of Louis XIV's downfall; his realm never recovered from that self-inflicted wound. Louis' cup was nearly full before the Revocation, but that act filled it to overflowing; as the refugees swarmed into Holland and England with their pitiful tales, there arose in their hosts a cold, implacable anger, a determination which went far deeper than any merely political issue, to rid Europe of a monstrous and evil system.

Many efforts have been made to pin down the responsibility for the French government's treatment of the Huguenots, and everyone has his favourite scapegoat: Mme. de Maintenon, Louvois, the French Church, Louis XIV himself, have in turn been denounced with more or less plausibility. But the fact seems to be that there is no one villain to whom we can allot the blame; detestation of the Huguenots was in the very air of seventeenth-century France, and their extirpation was a national aspiration. The anti-Huguenot movement is the one case in the reign where a policy was initiated by the ordinary man, and imposed on the executive by pressure from below. Though, perhaps, "imposed" is hardly the right word to use, for it suggests a degree of unwillingness on the part of Louis and his advisors to meet the nation's wishes which certainly did not exist; it might be truer to say that for the first time in the reign, King, bureaucracy, and the three estates of the realm, found themselves moving in enthusiastic accord towards a commonly desired goal. But the push that set the stone rolling was given not at Versailles but by the inferior clergy, petty officialdom, and the people themselves. For the people had long memories, and had no trace of the modern tendency to picture the Huguenots as the harmless and helpless victims of persecution. Harmless and helpless they might be at the moment, but the peasants and townfolk remembered their father's stories of what had happened in the districts where the Huguenots had had the upper hand: flaming farmsteads, murders and rapes, the desecration of the Host, and the priest burnt alive in the ruins of the blazing parish church. And at their elbows was the *curé* to whisper that it might all happen again if France tired out God's patience by its failure to root out the deadly sin and scandal of heresy once and for ever.

And there was often a baser cause for the hatred which both the lower clergy and the common people felt for the Huguenot; only too often the way of life of the Protestant minister was a standing reproof to the neighbouring priests, both secular and religious; and to the people, the Huguenot was a very dangerous, and sometimes crushing, business rival. It is not clear why it should have been so, but the fact remains that, broadly speaking, the Huguenot was more intelligent, harder working, soberer, and a better man of business than his Roman Catholic neighbour; wherever Huguenots were to be found in any numbers, there the commerce of the town would be found mainly in their hands. So to an understandable religious antipathy was added that economic cause for hatred which in our time has been at the root of so much anti-Semitism; the Huguenot was, in a sense, the Jew of Louis XIV's kingdom.

The theory that Mme. de Maintenon was responsible for the

Huguenot persecution does not bear a moment's investigation; there is no evidence at all that she took any part in its initiation or development, and the worst that can be said of her is that she made no attempt to check it. And why should she have done so? She was a pious woman, sharing the delight of most of France that at last the King had realized his duties as *père de famille* of his country, and was about to save the souls of his heretic children by the exercise of a little fatherly severity. And throughout the whole sad business neither she nor the King had any true idea of the grim interpretation placed on the words *compelle intrare* by a host of minor officials; she saw only the steady stream of conversions which preceded the Revocation of the edict, and rejoiced to think that the whole structure of Protestantism was collapsing under its own inherent rottenness. Why not give the final push that would bring it to the ground?

Louvois, at first sight a more plausible candidate, was in reality the last man in France likely to interest himself in the problem; if he had any religion at all, which is doubtful, it certainly was not of the kind that runs to missionary zeal, and then, as always, his chief concern was with the efficiency of the French army: an efficiency which could not fail to be lowered by any drastic action against the Huguenots. What in fact happened was simply that Louvois, as War Minister, was partly responsible for administering a policy which he did not initiate, that of forcing Huguenot conversions by the billeting of troops upon them, the infamous *Dragonnades*; and when the Huguenots in desperation resisted his dragoons, Louvois saw in their act a revolt against the King's authority, which he punished with the brutality which was his normal method of procedure. But his letters furnish much evidence that he was opposed to, rather than in favour of, extreme measures; Intendants who overstep the limit in the employment of troops sent to their districts, like Marillac in Poitou, and his successor Foucault, receive constant reprimands, and at the height of the *Dragonnades* in 1685, he warns military commanders against allowing themselves to be led away by the inconsiderate zeal of the local clergy. On the whole, in spite of his occasional outbursts of ferocity, his letters urge caution and moderation.

It remains to consider Louis XIV's personal responsibility in the matter, and him we can hear speak for himself in his memoirs for the instruction of the Dauphin, which, if they do nothing else, throw doubt on the theory that the converted Louis of 1685 suddenly decided to offer up the Huguenots as a vicarious sacrifice for the sins of his own earlier life. On the contrary the memoirs make it clear that the problem of his heretic subjects was exercising his mind from the beginning of the personal reign. Here is Louis writing certainly not later than 1670, and probably earlier, of the year 1661 when he was twenty-three:

And as for the large number of my subjects of the so-called reformed religion, which is an evil that I have always regarded, and still regard, with grief . . . I settled a plan of conduct towards them . . . that the best means to reduce them gradually . . . was in the first place not to oppress them at all by any new measures against them, and to maintain all that had been granted to them by my predecessors; but to grant them nothing further, and to confine the execution of the Edict within the strictest limits that justice and *bienséance* permitted. . . . But as for favour which depended on my own will, I resolved, and have carefully observed my rule, to show them none, and that through kindness . . . so that they may consider from time to time if they have any good reason to deprive themselves voluntarily of those advantages which should be shared by all my subjects . . . and I also resolved . . . to stir up the Bishops as much as I could to work for their instruction, and to suppress all scandals which alienate the so-called reformed church from us.

His correspondence shows his attitude even more clearly. In 1666 he writes to the governor of Le Hâvre:

Those who profess the so-called reformed religion, being no less faithful than my other subjects, must not be treated with less consideration and kindness; your vigilance should be the same over all, and if you find any thing being done by any (Huguenot) which cannot be allowed, you must take great care not to make a general matter of it, but to take the necessary action against individuals only.

In fact the evidence of the memoirs and correspondence reveals Louis, not as the inaugurator of a persecution, but as marching in step with a universal trend of public opinion, and sometimes even lagging behind it; for instance, sometime probably in the 'seventies, he received a project for a reunion of the Churches which suggests the bribing of some fifty Protestant ministers to enter into conference with a representative body of the clergy, that this joint assembly should vote in favour of reunion, that the Edict of Nantes should then be suppressed as useless, and that the Pope should issue a dispensation from certain Catholic practices to overscrupulous Huguenots. Louis took no action beyond filing the project with the note *memoire à garder*.

In fact, as we have said before, there is no villain in the piece, or if one prefers to put it in another way, all France was the villain.

There is a horrid fascination in watching the tide of persecution creep in to overwhelm the doomed Huguenots, rising higher at every meeting of the Assembly of the Clergy. In that of 1655, three years after the confirmation of the edict, the Assembly calls for a stricter interpretation of its provisions, six years ahead of the King's acceptance of the idea, we notice, and ten years before he gave the policy his sanction. In 1660 the Assembly recommendations include the exclusion of all Huguenots from government appointments, and the closing of all Huguenot colleges and hospitals. In 1665 begins the "interpretation" of the edict in real earnest, conducted with a base cynicism perhaps more revolting than the subsequent revocation. For its effect was to hand over the whole Huguenot population, bound hand and foot, to venal lawyers and corrupt underlings.

The contention of the Crown lawyers, breathtaking in its effrontery, was simply this: that any activity for which specific provision was not made in the edict, was by implication and intention, illegal. Did the edict, for instance, lay it down that a Huguenot could be a midwife? Of course a general instrument of toleration had nothing to say on such a point, and therefore it was illegal for a Protestant to practice midwifery. Where was the paragraph in the edict authorizing a Huguenot to be a shoemaker, a tailor, a wholesale merchant, or what you like? Nowhere. Then all these activities were illegal. And the victims had no redress, for by the middle 'sixties it was already only too evident that in no civil or criminal court in the land could a Huguenot hope to find justice. As early as 1666 the stream of emigration which was to drain away the strength of France had already begun, and in 1669 very large numbers of shrewd and industrious Picards quietly disappeared into England and Holland. In 1670 the Assembly returned to the charge with the further recommendations that Huguenots be forbidden to teach anything beyond the three R's, and that Huguenot children of the age of seven be deemed capable of abjuring their faith of their own free will: and that those who do so be removed from the custody of their parents to guard against the risk of their incurring the penalties for relapsed heretics. Five years later the clergy call for legislation which foreshadows Hitler's Nuremberg laws; mixed marriages are to be declared null, and the children of them to be considered bastards.

Along with this open persecution went the more insidious attack of wholesale bribery; in 1677 were established the *bureaux of conversion*, where any Huguenot who produced a certificate that he had been received into the Roman Church, was paid a cash gratuity, which varied according to the size of his family, but seems to have averaged about twelve livres a head for each convert. The scheme was fatally successful. The bishops, in reporting to Versailles the steadily increasing flow of conversions in their diocese, were either themselves ignorant of the secret activities of the conversion bureaux, or else, not unnaturally, soft-pedalled them; and Louis and his Court, as we have said before, were generally deceived into thinking the work of extirpating heresy already as good as done. For it is distressing to notice throughout the whole business the number of men, and good men, too, not excepting even some highly placed ecclesiastics, who viewed the matter as one of externals only. Efforts at effecting genuine conversions were spasmodic and never uniform; let the Huguenots abjure, attend Mass, keep their mouths shut, and believe what they please, seems to have been a common attitude towards the problem. Even a man of Bossuet's standing seems to have thought that a forced conversion to Rome was perfectly justified, in that it must infallibly lead to a sincere love of the true Church as its beauties and consolations unfolded themselves to the unwilling proselyte.

In 1681 the tide of persecution rose higher, and again the impulsion came from below and not from above. Bribery and brutality still go hand in hand in the suggestion of Marillac, Intendant of Poitou, who proposes that the Huguenots be forbidden to act as postmasters, doctors, surgeons, or druggists, that an unjust burden in the distribution of troop billeting be thrown on Huguenot households, and that Huguenots who abjure their faith be granted a two years' exemption from billeting. And, not content with making his proposals, Marillac proceeded to institute a reign of terror in his Intendancy, paying no heed to the reiterated and infuriated orders of Louvois, who had considerable difficulty in putting a stop to the Intendant's unauthorized *Dragonnades*. Had Louis had eyes to see, the most significant events of this year were the large-scale emigration of his northern subjects, and the speed with which the Lord Mayor of London collected £25,000 for the distressed Huguenots in England.

Probably by now there was nothing that the Huguenots could have done which would have averted or even greatly delayed their fate, but any chance they had vanished when in 1682 they reacted to the cancellation of the *Dragonnade* by adopting an intransigent attitude whenever opportunity served, and even by opening fire on the royal troops. Louvois, as we have said, took little interest in the controversy, but at this news his fury boiled over; no mercy was henceforward to be shown to any Huguenot anywhere, and the Protestant provinces were given over to fire and sword. The purely incidental missionary results of Louvois' devastations were hailed at Court as a miracle: whole towns abjured *en masse*, and in the outlying districts the machine ran so efficiently that a Huguenot who had been beaten up at dawn, before the day was out, could find himself a Roman convert who had already made his first communion.

Simultaneously, with this military activity, the Chancellor turned his attention to the wholesale bribery of the Huguenot gentry, bribery after dark, conducted in whispers between the needy gentleman and the local Intendant, who was told to do the thing regardless of expense. And indeed so handsome was the treatment of renegades that in the closing years of the persecution, the *Nouveau Converti* became the spoilt child of the administration and an object of considerable jealousy to the real Catholics. Pensions, regiments, sinecures, Court offices, magistracies, all the good things of life were to be had practically for the asking by any gentleman who would abjure.

But it was left to the unscrupulous Basville (1648–1724), Intendant of Languedoc, to strike the most deadly blow at the Huguenots, through their nobility; in 1685 he put forward the idea of a general verification of all titles of nobility throughout the kingdom. The plan was adopted, and there was hardly any attempt made to conceal the fact that the "verification" would actually take the form of leaving Catholics unmolested, whilst Huguenots would be deprived of their rank. There was a shoal of fresh conversions: for, whilst a gentleman must be prepared to suffer ex-

ile, imprisonment, or even death itself for his faith, it was not to
be expected that he should face the certainty of being reduced to
the social level of his own peasantry.

In the same year the Assembly of the Clergy struck its last blow
in the campaign with a recommendation that Huguenots be de-
barred from carrying on business as lawyers, librarians, printers,
or hotel keepers. But the Assembly was really in action after the
cease fire had sounded; on 22nd October 1685 Louis issued an
edict in which it was stated that there were now so few Huguenots left in the kingdom that the Edict of Nantes had lost its *raison d'être*, and was therefore revoked, and the practice of the so-
called Reformed Religion was thenceforth declared to be illegal
in France. Protestant ministers were given fifteen days in which to
leave the kingdom, and all other Huguenots were forbidden to do
so under pain of a life sentence in the galleys.

But no edict of Louis XIV's could stem the steady flow of emigration, even though, with that stupid brutality which at times
characterizes all governments, persecution of the remaining Huguenots was intensified in an effort to break their hearts. Louis,
with his long coastal frontiers, was in no position to let down an
Iron Curtain, and merely wasted money and men badly needed
elsewhere in endeavouring to picket his borders. Peasants were
offered about thirty-six livres a head for the capture of an escaping
Huguenot, and the penalty of the galleys was extended to all who
should assist a Huguenot to escape, even if it were only to offer
him food or shelter on his way. But it was all labour lost. Huguenots escaped somehow, on foot through the bitter nights, in open
and unprovisioned boats, sometimes packed up in bales of goods,
disguised as Roman priests or Catholic Huguenot-hunters, or by
fighting their way, sword in hand, through the frontier guards.
And these flights continued until the end of the reign.

There is only one feature of the miserable story on which one
can dwell with any satisfaction, and that is the discovery that, as
usual, individuals behave better than peoples, and peoples better
than their governments. Much furtive assistance was rendered to
fleeing Huguenots by the frontier peasantry, and more than one
Roman Catholic gentleman went to the galleys for his share in
smuggling a Huguenot neighbour across the border. Many bishops
showed true charity in their dealings with the persecuted remnant,
and some who breathed threatenings and slaughter proved that

their practice was better than their principles. We look in vain for any trace of toleration in Bossuet's utterances, but we notice that in his diocese, Huguenots, especially poor Huguenots, were more humanely treated than elsewhere, and that he instructed his clergy that reasonableness and gentleness, not violence, were the weapons with which a priest must fight heresy. It is to his everlasting credit that he was accused of inconsistency by a merciless civil service, and indeed not unjustly; for he was, in theory, an exterminator.

He comes much better out of the tragedy than Fénelon, who for some curious reason, has a reputation for tolerance which seems to be completely undeserved. Those who believe in a Fénelon born out of his time, the tolerant man of a later age, should read an account of his missionary activities at La Rochelle in 1685 and 1686: bribery, forgery, the employment of spies, enforced attendance at Mass, all these weapons he cheerfully made use of, and he wholeheartedly approved Louis' extermination policy. His missionary tour leaves an unpleasant impression on us.

The rest of the story belongs rather to the political than to the Church history of the period. By the end of 1686 the government had at last realized the futility of its endeavours to prevent escapes from the country and these were henceforward winked at; at the same time, the policy of mass deportations to America were also abandoned.

Louis XIV was now in a position to draw up a balance sheet. On the credit side he could show several thousands of embittered subjects, nominally reconciled to his Church, and a further demonstration of the fact that the King's will was the only law in France. On the debit, a loss of a hundred thousand of his most industrious people, 50,000 louis d'or in cash smuggled out of the realm, and many secret trade processes communicated to his commercial rivals: a loss of nine thousand of his best sailors, six hundred army officers with twelve thousand first-class troops, and irreparable damage done to the whole structure of France. And what of the invisible items which appeared in no balance sheet, yet were of infinitely greater moment? Loss of honour and good faith on the part of the Crown, misery, fear, hatred, delations, bribery, savagery, the enmity of all Europe, the disapproval of the Pope—who shall say at what price these were estimated when the account finally came up for audit?

(11)

The normal method of recruitment of both higher clergy and religious under Louis XIV was an unpromising one, but when we come to examine the personnel of the French Church we are surprised rather by its goodness than its badness. It would be an exaggeration to say that the Church was a branch of the civil service, distinguished from it only by being mainly an aristocratic preserve; and indeed not so much an exaggeration as an untruth, for lack of birth was no bar to a bishopric, though it increased the difficulty of obtaining one. Bossuet, for instance, was a *bourgeois*, as was Godet Desmarets, Bishop of Chartres; nor were genuine vocations lacking amongst the great nobles who entered the priesthood. Fénelon was a noble, and the saintly Noailles, Cardinal-Archbishop of Paris, was a son of one of the greatest houses in France. But it would be misleading to assume that a vocation was regarded as even one of the qualifications necessary for the priesthood or the cloister.

The reason is not far to seek. Louis' policy of depriving the nobles of all share in the government, together with other factors outlined elsewhere, tended to throw the burden of maintaining the nobility on the Crown: and the King's revenues were insufficient for this purpose. Given the retention of the nobles as a privileged class, something had to be done to supplement from, other than Crown revenue, the grants and pensions on which the nobility lived, and the patrimony of the Church was an obvious source upon which to draw. Society assumed a pattern in which it was taken as a matter of course that younger sons and daughters should be forced into the Church, and should be brought up to the idea of such a destiny from earliest childhood. For every family in old France was a small totalitarian state in which the individual counted for nothing, the house for everything; to increase the wealth and glory of the house was accepted as each member's sole duty, and it was carried out with a heroism which compels our admiration. For the eldest son, the title and the wealth, for the next a bishopric; for the rest, regiments, abbeys or Knighthoods of Malta. For the eldest daughter a dowry; for the rest the veil. We find the same general plan in every family from the greatest down to that of the country squire, whose appeals to the King for financial assistance would often be met by an order to the Intendant to pay the dowry of one of his daughters in a neighbouring convent.

The younger sons of a great house, destined to be Knights of Malta, had indeed a method of escaping their fate which must have often been envied by elder brothers conscripted into the priesthood: they could always refuse, or at least fail, to learn to swim. And if you could not swim, you could not be a Knight of Malta. And why did your father so desire that you should become one? Simply because a Knight of Malta had to take a vow of celibacy. Here and there a strong-minded boy or girl would make an effort to escape the stranglehold of economic circumstances, but such attempts were always considered anti-social and were generally unsuccessful. The notorious de Retz, for instance, tells us himself that when he made his début in society he made a parade of debauchery in the hope that he would be refused Holy Orders; his conduct did not make the slightest difference, and, without any striking improvement in his morals, he became coadjutor to his uncle, the Archbishop of Paris, and a cardinal. But men like de Retz were in the minority, happily for the Church; most young nobles, once committed to a priestly career, developed into conscientious administrators of dioceses and abbeys, living lives which, if not particularly edifying, were at least not scandalous or even unseemly. Coislin, Bishop of Metz, may be cited as a typical example of the class. "Nothing," says St. Simon, "was ever said against his morals, though his life was by no means devout or constrained . . . but he was entirely devoted to the affairs of his diocese . . . and abounded in deeds of charity, some open, others concealed." Or Maurice Le Tellier (1642–1710), Archbishop of Rheims, *le cochon mitré* as he was called, who though a notorious gambler, was also famous for ruling over the best-managed diocese in the kingdom. A more amusing man of the same stamp was François de Clermont-Tonnerre (1629–1701), Count-Bishop of Noyon, the fine flower of the vanity of a vain house. The ceilings and floors of his palace, and even those of the sanctuary of his private chapel, were covered with the arms of Clermont-Tonnerre, whilst the walls held trees establishing his descent from the Emperors of the East and the West. To the delight of society and the indignation of the Vatican, he claimed to live on terms of complete equality with the Pope, whom he invariably referred to as "M. de Rome," and he died leaving several alternative versions of his own funeral eulogy. But St. Simon, who cannot be suspected of any partiality towards him, tells us that he was a learned, honourable, virtuous prelate, much regretted in his diocese.

Of course many of this curious assembly of conscripted priests fell far below these standards. There was, for instance, the Bishop of Agde (1633–1702), a friend of Mme. de Lyonne's, who greatly resented M. de Lyonne's ungentlemanly conduct in sleeping with his wife: the Abbé de Pompadour, whose conception of prayer was that he was responsible for periodical recitals of the Breviary, and therefore paid a servant to carry out this duty for him at stated intervals: Pardaillan, Archbishop of Sens (1620–74), who, apparently in all good faith, ordered prayers throughout his archbishopric for the conversion of the Jesuits: and the Bishop of Clermont, who concluded a dispute with his Chapter by smashing in the cathedral door with a battering ram.

But if such men as these existed among the higher clergy, let us not forget the types which were much more common. Motier of Limoges, for instance, praised equally for living *en grand seigneur,* for his learning, his charity, and his maintenance of ecclesiastical discipline: Nesmond of Bayeux (1629–1715), a true saint, we are told, whom one must reverence, but whose perfect innocence made him so embarrassing in conversation that Mme. de Lamoignon always used to turn her daughter out of the room when he was announced, but who, with a large fortune and a rich see, never had a penny in his pocket, for all was given to the poor. After his death, for instance, it was discovered that he had been making the exiled James II a secret allowance of 28,800 livres a year. Then there was Froulay of Avranches, who was so afraid of dying out of his diocese that he never left it at all: and Janson, Cardinal-Count-Bishop of Beauvais (1630–1713), unique in that his death was equally regretted by the King and by the poor of his diocese.

The system was even less satisfactory than it at first sight appears, for once a see or an abbey fell into the hands of a noble house, it tended to become an hereditary possession; no sooner had the King appointed to, say, a priory, than the head of the family immediately earmarked a son to step into Uncle Prior's shoes on his death. And when that event happened, every possible influence was brought to bear to have the priory given to the dead man's nephew, usually with success. Often indeed the ecclesiastical member of a well-known family would, by the death of uncles and brothers, become not only a prior, but a pluralist on a large scale; Victor Bouthillier, Bishop of Tours, for example, in addition to being a bishop, was a Canon of Nôtre Dame, the holder of three abbeys, and Almoner to Monsieur, which last post, of course, entailed permanent residence at Court: the Abbé de la Rochefoucauld (1687–1717) held abbeys worth about 60,000 livres a year, for, as we are told, "the abbeys held by his uncles and great-uncles were given to him one by one as they fell vacant": three generations of the de Retz family controlled the See of Paris between them for over a hundred years: and the House of Villeroi, while it could not produce a candidate to replace Camille de Villeroi as Archbishop of Lyons in 1698, recovered the see in 1714.

But it was for the maintenance of their daughters that the nobles leant most heavily upon the Church, and a cursory glance into the Debrett of the period gives us significant evidence of the numbers of girls who must have been forced into convents without any vocation. The Comte de La Feuillade, for instance, had five daughters, one an abbess, the other four nuns: the four daughters of the first Duc de Chaulnes were luckier than most, for three of them were abbesses and the youngest a prioress: three of the five daughters of the Marquis de Rambouillet were abbesses: and eight of the eleven daughters of the Duc de Beauvilliers were nuns. With such statistics before us, the abuse of the convent under Louis XIV is a point which need not be laboured; and indeed, to do contemporaries justice, there was little or no hypocrisy shown by them over the matter. We were told in the nursery, says one writer, that we must be nuns so that our eldest sister could have a dowry. Angélique Arnauld (1591–1661), afterwards the famous Abbess of Port-Royal, tells us how she herself entered religion:

I was only seven years old when my grandfather, observing that my father had five daughters, . . . resolved to make some of them nuns, and chose me . . . to be the first to enter a convent. With that object he made me come to him, and said, "My dear, would you like to be a nun . . . not a common nun, but an Abbess, over all the others?" I saw I should have to agree, and replied . . . "Yes, Grandfather, I should like it."

The reader may think that this is exceptional, but that is not the case.

Louise de Rouxel de Grancey (1593–1652) became not only a titular but an actual abbess at the age of nine, and, we are told, "her extreme youth did not prevent her from ruling her convent in an edifying manner." But then doubtless she had a wise and tactful coadjutrix.

The system may arouse our indignation, but not on account of the unhappiness of its victims; for in the main, and especially in the case of those who were caught young, we rarely find that beating against the bars of the cage which we might have expected. The girl's earliest recollections would be of visits to her aunt the abbess, of games in the convent garden, of being spoilt and petted by the nuns. Then would come a time when she lived permanently in the convent, picking up such education as was available, absorbed in the petty amusements and intrigues of the nuns, and so saturated with the atmosphere of the house that taking the veil meant little more than an exciting family reunion in which she was the chief figure, disturbing the monotony of the idle days. And a week or two later would follow the even more exciting ceremony of her installation as coadjutrix to her aunt the abbess. No, by no means a miserable life, always providing that the girl did not by some plaguey mischance develop a genuine vocation after her profession; for then the struggle against the contented tepidity of her sisters could be heartbreaking.

Too much sympathy has, I think, been given to the girls who made forced professions without vocations, and too little to those frustrated vocations which the seventeenth-century social structure also entailed. The most striking case of the reign is perhaps that of Mary of Modena, the Carmelite novice, who was in 1673 compelled to relinquish her vows to become the second wife of James, Duke of York. Here was a girl of deep religious feeling, with a genuine vocation, who had deliberately chosen the cloister in opposition to the wishes of her family, and who was, one would have imagined, safe in the haven of her own choosing. But *realpolitik* took little account of vocations; though Mary resisted the importunities of her mother and of Louis XIV's diplomats, she was forced to bow to the will of the Pope, who told her that God had chosen her to reconquer England for the Faith. It is true that, against all probability, her marriage ultimately turned out a happy one, but it was only after much agony of spirit.

Sadder, because there is no happy ending, is the case of Henriette d'Albert (1647–99), younger daughter of the second Duc de Luynes. The family had Jansenist leanings, and Henriette was sent to Port-Royal, where she early proved herself the ideal material from which to fashion the perfect religious, as perfection was understood in that convent. In 1661 came a fresh outbreak of anti-Jansenist persecution, in which all postulants and pupils were expelled from Port-Royal, and Henriette, already a model and a shining light of the ideas of that sombre and austere house, found herself homeless. She and her elder sister were then handed over to their aunt, the Abbess of Jouarre, worldliest of those great ladies who ruled over a little group of really fashionable convents inhabited only by the best people. For the unfortunate girl whose spiritual home was Port-Royal, the travesty of the religious life which obtained at Jouarre must have been at once a misery and a nightmare. She does not seem to have been persecuted or even ostracized, but merely to have been thought to be exceedingly odd; confessors of the Jouarre type could make nothing of her, her aunt the abbess, on the rare occasions when she visited the convent, must have found her a bore, and her aspirations to holiness must have struck her fellow religious as both uncomfortable and in very bad taste. She was already a middle-aged woman when Bossuet became her *directeur,* and brought some comfort to her closing years. But she remains a melancholy example of the victims of those mundane considerations which too often intervened to ruin the religious life in seventeenth-century France.

A great deal of nasty nonsense has been written about conventual life under the *ancien régime,* and one is pleased to find that most of this is, to say the least of it, of dubious authenticity, drawn from little books now catalogued as "Curious," and emanating from contemporary Dutch printing houses. Sexual scandals did from time to time undoubtedly occur, but they have been given a publicity out of all proportion to their frequency. Firstly, for the discreditable but very human reason that scandal always sells, whilst no one wishes to read about life in the interior of a pious and well-governed convent. And secondly, much of such writing proves on investigation to be primarily anti-French propaganda turned out in Holland during the war against France, and only secondarily pornography.

The real faults of a convent of the period were of quite a different complexion from those alleged in contemporary libels. The

Abbess of the Carmelite house of Val-de-Grâce—the Carmelites being, by the way, the fashionable order of those days—complains that the vows of obedience and poverty are totally neglected in easy-going convents, and that owing to the slackness with which the rule of enclosure is observed, a young nun has actually more freedom than an unmarried girl living at home. Val-de-Grâce itself had ever since the Fronde been a focus of political intrigue, and is strongly condemned on that ground, both by Louis XIV and Bossuet, in spite of the somewhat overpublicised but perfectly genuine austerity and mortification in which the nuns lived. Gabrielle de Rochechouart, Abbess of Fontevrault, complains that all the fruit of her nuns' austerities is cancelled by their spiteful quarrelling. And practically every thoughtful critic, ecclesiastic or lay, comments most unfavourably on the pettiness and puerility which is the prevailing tone in the average convent.

It is, of course, impossible to speak statistically in such a matter, but it seems safe to hazard the guess that a majority of seventeenth-century convents were neither hotbeds of vice nor enclaves of holy living, but simply residential clubs inhabited by virtuous single women endowed with a somewhat unenlightened and worldly piety; they probably had about them much more of the flavour of a Y.W.C.A. hostel than of those very different establishments to which they have been so unjustly compared. Perhaps the worst that can be said of them was that the centre of conventual life was the parlour rather than the chapel, and that conversations tended to concern itself with Court fashions rather than with things of the spirit. For the rest, there would be two, perhaps three, services a day, regular confession and Communion, and a mild but sincere piety. Cards, billiards, gardening and gossip filled in the blank spaces of the day when there were no visitors, and there was always the resource of letter writing to friends at Court, or even a little light reading. Often there would be exciting conversations with a Court lady doing what she imagined to be a retreat, or in disgrace, and detained in the convent. For convents, in addition to being religious houses and girls' boarding schools, also acted the part of prisons for female offenders of the highest quality. In the less objectionable but still cynical type of story, much is made of the parlour flirtations in easy-going convents, but in fact only the most worldly of abbesses would tolerate anything of that sort. One abbess, for instance, who did find a nephew in the Guards whispering compliments to one of her nuns, literally ran the youth out of the parlour, exclaiming, *Je t'apprendray de faire cocu le Bon Seigneur.*

Even after the middle of the reign the obligation of enclosure was interpreted with considerable latitude; sick leave to take the waters was easily obtained, nor was it difficult to find a pretext for paying long visits to other convents, or even to the houses of lay friends. And an abbess, of course, could spend much time at Court petitioning the King on matters of business concerning her house. Sometimes, indeed, she hardly pretended to have any business at Court at all, but merely became embedded in the King's household, as was the case with the last of the Guises, Henriette de Lorraine, Abbess of Jouarre (1631–94). Jouarre was a royal abbey, independent of the bishop of the diocese, and had been ruled by a succession of ladies whose rank put them in an unassailable position, a fact of which Henriette took the fullest advantage. She made no attempt to observe conventual rules, spent the revenues of her house to maintain herself at Court, and used Jouarre only as a country house to which to retire for a month or so at the fashionable time of the year. Finally, she was rash enough to quarrel with Bossuet, in whose diocese Jouarre was situated, and resigned in disgust when he, after a hard struggle, obtained recognition of his authority over her abbey.

Of a very different type, and quite the best of the worldlings, was Gabrielle de Rochechouart (1645–1704), Mme. de Montespan's sister, who ruled with strict and gentle autocracy over the great Royal Abbey of Fontevrault. As beautiful as her notorious sister, and the wittiest of a family whose wit was proverbial, she had been ordered into the Benedictines as a young girl, and had become an abbess at the age of twenty-two; had made a virtue of necessity, become a good nun, and an excellent superior. She had also become learned in theology, preached admirably to her community, and in her leisure hours, when not at Court, read Plato and corresponded with Boileau and Racine. Her nuns, we are told, adored her. For Mme. de Fontevrault the difficulty was not to get to Court, but to get away from it, for Louis was so attracted by her that he found it tedious to be without her company; she consented to pay him and her sister frequent visits, but firmly declined to be drawn into the amusement of the Court, preserving, we are told, a high degree of decency and dignity in a place so unsuited to a religious. It is a curious vignette of the morals of a vanished age: the King, the woman the King had seduced, and her sister the abbess, in a free and unembarrassed intimacy in the inner penetralia of the house inhabited by the King's wife. Gabrielle remained Louis' friend even after the retirement of Mme. de Montespan and the King's marriage to Mme. de Maintenon.

They were deplorable, no doubt, these worldly convents, too often religious houses in name only; but let us not overlook the many others which lived to rule, and in which vocations abounded: not to be touched upon here, for such houses have, properly speaking, no history. And surely even the worldly ones are not to be compared with their present day successors, but rather to be contrasted with the ones which they superseded.

Angélique Arnauld, whom we have already met, took the veil at the age of eight in 1599, and became Abbess of Port-Royal—on a false birth certificate by the way—in 1602: in 1608 she developed a vocation, and set about the reform of her convent with such zeal, skill, and tact, that ten years later Port-Royal, whatever may have been its doctrinal deviationism, was in all other respects a model and an inspiration to the enclosed orders of France. It was a hard struggle for the young abbess, beginning with the enforcement of enclosure. So far had the very ideas behind enclosure been lost sight of, that Angélique's mother petitioned against it on the ground that if she was excluded from the convent, she would no longer be able to search her daughter's cell for love letters and contraband literature. And her father, on being refused admission to the interior of the convent, vowed that never again would he speak to so perverted and so ungrateful a daughter. Even the convent servants reproached the abbess for her undutiful behaviour.

But this family storm was nothing to that which arose when the Cistercian Order as a whole awoke to what was going on in this obscure country convent. Abbots and monks who did not hesitate to classify idleness, luxury, and good cheer under the general heading of "the good old customs of the Order": prioresses and nuns who danced in masks at carnival time: the very assistant-general himself, a great hunting man, who had not enough Latin to translate the Lord's Prayer—all rounded upon the unfortunate girl abbess, calling her and her daughters fools, innovators, schismatics worthy of excommunication. But Angélique, supported by the general, proved too much for them, and within a few years Port-Royal, so far from being excommunicated, was sending out nuns to assist in the reform of other houses. The same Mother Angélique's memoir in justification of her action in getting her abbey removed from the control of the monks of the Order and submitting it to that of the bishop, gives an interesting idea of monastic life in the first-half of the century. If, she says, an abbess submits herself to monks, they become tyrants: if she plays the great lady, they become valets. And, she continues, I have actually seen a convent confessor employed in planting out the abbess' flower beds in her coat of arms, and carrying her train when she goes abroad. And then again, she goes on, what an intolerable expense it is to have monks about the place; true, they claim that they give their services for food and clothing alone, whilst the secular demands a fee. But this really means that an abbess has to maintain a *table d'hôte*, and a good one too, for any idle monk who cares to drop in, and often they come a dozen at a time; and, worse still, they invite their relations and entertain them at the convent's expense.

But if we would see to what lengths the scandal of a really bad convent of the old sort could go, we must turn to the Royal Abbey of Maubuisson under the reign of Angélique d'Estrées. This lady had been appointed abbess by Henri IV about the turn of the century, in order that he might use the convent as a *petite maison* for Angélique's sister Gabrielle, his famous mistress. And nothing throws a better light on the abbess's manner of life than the fact that her notorious sister used frequently to remonstrate with her on her scandalous conduct. Amongst the inhabitants of Maubuisson in 1600 we notice twelve of the abbess' illegitimate children, each being educated and boarded strictly in accordance with the rank of its father. Louis XIII succeeded Henri IV in 1610, and by 1616 the scandal of Maubuisson had reached proportions which he would no longer tolerate; a commission of monks was sent to warn Angélique to set her house in order, and found itself imprisoned in the convent cellars for its pains. A special commissioner was then sent to report upon the conduct of the abbey, and he thought himself very lucky to escape by an unguarded window after undergoing a course of floggings on bread and water. It was not until 1618 that the General of the Cistercians at last determined to put an end to this intolerable state of affairs; in that year Angélique d'Estrées was forcibly removed from her abbey and imprisoned in the *Filles Repenties* at Paris, though, as cynics did not fail to point out, she was neither *Fille* nor *Repentie*. Here one would think is the end of the story, but there is a further chapter; in September 1619 the exiled abbess escaped from her prison, and with the help of a bodyguard of gentlemen, carried Maubuisson by a *coup de main* at six in the morning, during the course of which the convent porter was wounded. The new abbess, and those nuns who favoured her régime, were expelled from the building, and it was not until the next day that Maubuisson saw the last of Angélique d'Estrées, who surrendered to a force of one hundred archers hurriedly sent to the field of battle by the Provost of Paris. One more glimpse of this odd abbess and we have done with her; years later a monk visited her in the prison of Le Châtelet in Paris, and discovered her *à la* Becky Sharp, sitting up in bed consuming wine and sausages.

It is pleasant to find that in spite of the disastrous example of their superior, the nuns of Maubuisson do not seem to have led lives much more irregular than those of many of their contemporaries. They even attended Mass daily, where the worst that could be reported of them was that their singing was of such a quality that it was difficult to know whether they were singing or quarrelling. Their ignorance was, however, dreadful; the same reporter tells us that they did not know how to confess, and at last, tired out with the reproaches of their confessor, they evolved this scheme for silencing his importunity. With much labour they produced three confessions, one for great feasts, one for Sundays, and one for weekdays; these were then written out in a book, and passed from nun to nun as each entered the confessional, and, adds our informant dryly, much time would have been saved if they had confessed in unison. For the rest, they lived in what we should call the flats into which they had divided their convent, entertaining guests both communally and in private, acting amateur theatricals, loafing in their gazebos, or strolling on a fine evening on the Paris road under the care of the prioress to meet the monks of Pontoise, with whom they would dance in the meadows.

Many of these early monasteries bore even less resemblance to religious houses, than did Maubuisson under Angélique d'Estrées. As late as 1661, when Rancé arrived at La Trappe as abbot, he found a ruined building containing six monks, or rather six brigands, armed with muskets, who, on hearing the word reform, threatened to cut the new superior's throat and fling his carcass into the fishponds. The complacency with which the Church viewed the tate of its enclosed orders by the end of the century seems less ill-founded when we realize the immense cleansing process to which conventual life had been subjected in the previous fifty years.

But if the grosser abuses were gradually eliminated or modified, one continued to flourish unchecked, that of the tenancy of Church preferment *in commendam*, which, whatever its original justification, had become in process of time merely another crutch for the support of a crippled nobility. Under this system the King had the right to appoint anyone he pleased commendatory superior of a vacant religious house; the superior *in commendam* drew the income of the abbey on condition that he kept the buildings in repair, and undertook the maintenance of the prior and the monks. Bitter experience gradually taught the monks the wisdom of having a legal contract regulating the division of revenue between themselves and their commendatory superior, but even where a contract existed, the nominal abbot usually devoted much time and ingenuity to the evasion of its provisions, especially if, as was often the case, he had never set eyes upon the abbey from which he drew his income. If, however, he was in the habit of using the abbey as a country house, the monks usually fared rather better. To be an abbot *in commendam* it was not even necessary to be a churchman under simple vows, much less a priest. The abuse had expanded, as abuses do, until an abbey *in commendam* had come to be considered a suitable award for a retired diplomatist or a distinguished soldier; Lieutenant-General de Forbin, for instance, who commanded the Grey Musqueteers, was for many years an abbot *in commendam*. What the King's private views of the system were, we do not know, but it probably caused him no uneasiness; he disapproved of religious, firstly because he regarded them as drones, mouths useless to the state, and secondly because he distrusted all divided allegiances, and the subjection of the monastic orders to the Vatican struck him as an infringement of his sovereignty. There is indeed a certain amount of evidence that he had at one time considered the suppression of all religious houses in France, but his common sense had early convinced him of the danger, or rather impossibility, of taking such a step; he had realized that the best use he could make of the monastic revenues

was to compel the religious orders to shoulder a part of that financial burden for which his own resources were inadequate. It is,
therefore, hardly to be wondered at that Louis himself was the
chief defender of Gallicanism; it was certainly a theory congenial
to his temperament, but it was also a financial necessity. Even had
his inclinations tended to Ultramontanism, it was a luxury in
which he could not have afforded to indulge. Nor could he have
afforded the luxury of reforming the monastic system, even if he
had had any wish to do so; for if an abbey *in commendam* was allowed to elect an abbot on the death of the commendatory, it was
said to have reverted to rule, that is, the King's right to nominate
on the old terms lapsed, and a valuable piece of Crown patronage
was extinguished; whereas every abbey which could be bestowed
in commendam was so much of Louis' money saved from the
throng of greedy sycophants by whom he was surrounded. It is
this aspect of the matter which explains the otherwise baffling
fact that abbots *in commendam,* such as Rancé of La Trappe, who
became converted, had every possible obstacle thrown in the way
of their desire to signalize their conversion by assuming the duties
of their titular offices. We should bear this point in mind when we
come across, as we occasionally do, a certain Pharisaic smugness
in those French writers who criticize our Henry VIII's suppression
of the monasteries; for the difference between the policies of Henry
VIII and Louis XIV is not perhaps so great as at first sight appears.
Does it in fact amount to much more than that Louis was a cleverer man than Henry? That Henry killed the goose and carved it
up amongst his nobility, whilst Louis cherished the bird and kept
his nobles in subjection with seasonable distribution of its golden
eggs?

V

The Army

Louvois is not only one of the most important figures in French military history, but also in that of Western Europe; in addition to forging the weapon which enabled Louis XIV to carry out his policy of calculated aggression, he created the type of army whose tactical and administrative methods remained virtually unchanged until the coming of the mechanical age. He found himself confronted with a feudal army and transformed it into a modern one.

When Louis XIV took over the reins of government in 1661, it was merely a polite fiction to speak of the land forces as "the King's army"; they were nothing of the sort. It was an army in which the King was, at best, one of the principal shareholders, and in the control of which the traditional status of the Crown gave him a casting vote. But as the majority of the regiments were not his property, his control was by no means absolute, and that of his War Secretary was practically non-existent. The armies which under Louis XIII and Mazarin had fought Spain, were a hard-bitten, hard-fighting, undisciplined, ill-fed, badly paid rabble, held together by the prestige of famous generals and colonels, living by loot and extortion, things of horror and terror to the civilian population, friend and foe alike. Such discipline as existed was maintained by sudden wholesale hangings, alternating with long periods of absolute licence in which even officers' persons and property were not secure against the attacks of their own men. The officers, generally speaking, were as insubordinate as the troops, and once an army had been got together and sent to the front, the control of the central government often practically ceased to operate; indeed the government's most obvious and urgent care was to get the army out of the metropolitan provinces with all possible speed, before their presence raised a revolt.

Hand in hand with indiscipline went corruption; it was the golden age for the military peculator, and there were few officers who did not see in a campaign a heaven-sent opportunity to reimburse themselves for their considerable capital outlay. Nor was there any efficient method of checking and punishing the officer's dishonesty, for he was not in our sense of the word a King's officer at all; he was an investor, who had bought a regiment or company as another man might buy a farm or a block of Paris municipal bonds; and ratification of purchase, and the subsequent grant of a commission lay not in the hands of the King but in those of two military viziers, the Colonel-General of Cavalry and the Colonel-General of Infantry, both of whom, by the way, had as likely as not bought their posts, and were now recouping themselves by collecting a brokerage on the purchase and sale of commissions. Like stock exchange values, the prices of commissions fluctuated considerably; only a very few *corps d'élite* were maintained in peacetime; so when peace was in the air, the price of all commissions fell heavily, while the market value of those in the new regiments fell to nothing. For the state admitted no obligation to recompense the holders of commissions in disbanded regiments; as on the stock exchange, the rule was *caveat emptor*. It would have been odd in the circumstances if every officer had not joined his unit determined to make hay whilst the sun shone; for his expenses were high, and the legitimate return on his investment low. For instance, in 1689 companies in the French guards were selling at rather over 3,000 louis d'or: it is true that a guards captain held the honorary rank of colonel in the army, and his pay seems to have been 12 louis d'or odd a month, as against some 4 louis d'or in the line infantry. And there was the further advantage that when army funds ran out, as they had a habit of doing in that unorganized age, it was the guards who got any money that was going, while the line were left to live as best it could; or in other words at the expense of the district in which they were quartered. But even when we take into consideration the relative security of tenure of the guards officer, a return of under five per cent on a highly speculative investment is a poor one.

Still, it was not pay but peculation that formed the bulk of an officer's income, and his opportunities for making a little on the side, as the Americans say, were many. To begin with, it must be understood that the state did no recruiting; that was the business of the captain. The state paid the soldier's pay, more or less irregularly, into the hands of the captain, who, in return for a recognized percentage of the sum received, and his recruiting grant, undertook to enlist, equip, clothe and feed say a hundred men. But though he received a fixed rate of pay per man, he in fact made the most advantageous bargain he could with his recruits, and when he had enlisted a hundred of them, marched his company to the assembly quarter to be inspected by the commissioner of war. For each recruit on parade he received about 2 louis d'or in the infantry, and nearly 10 louis d'or in the cavalry; and there appears to have been no check that the company which joined the regiment was of the same strength as that which had appeared on the muster parade. An arrangement better calculated to promote fraud could hardly be devised, and most officers took full advantage of it; as late as 1668 Luxembourg reports that if swindles were perpetrated by a few officers, he could take disciplinary action against them, but that he has in fact hardly one honest officer serving under him. And Rochefort, in the same year, ends a report on the same subject with the airy consolation that it is an evil which time alone can cure.

An obvious fraud was that the company commander could and did retain more than his legal percentage of the pay, and, in extreme cases, pocketed the lot. But this rather elementary swindle had the inconvenient result that the company usually deserted *en masse*, and even a seventeenth-century colonel was apt to object to a company whose captain was its only member. So the more intelligent contented themselves with the profit to be made out of *passe volants*. Under this system, the captain who was receiving pay for a hundred men, would in fact pay and maintain perhaps sixty, annexing the money of the imaginary forty. Inspections were few and far between, commissioners of war were conveniently blind, and their visits well advertised beforehand; on the day of the muster a collection of valets, grooms, and beggars would be issued with musket and bandolier, and would shuffle along behind the real soldiers. The commissioner would sign the muster roll, the stage soldiers would be dismissed with a *pourboire*, and the captain could put the whole matter out of his mind for another twelve months. If word came down that the commissioner was of a tiresomely observant and inquisitive disposition, it was merely necessary to give what Pooh-Bah calls a touch of artistic verisimilitude to an otherwise bald and unconvincing narrative by borrowing forty real soldiers from the nearest regiment; for as there were no uniforms, there was nothing to expose the deception which was being practised, especially as all the men on parade were obviously soldiers. The fraud was not, one must admit, peculiar to the French service; Montecuculi, the Austrian commander, in his memoirs, complains bitterly of it, and advises that the captain who employs *passe volants* be "chastiz'd with the utmost rigour": but he is silent as to the means to be employed.

There is some excuse for the juniors in that the examples set in the most exalted circles were not calculated to promote professional integrity; in 1641 that curious ruling prince, Charles IV de Lorraine, found himself short of cavalry horses, and without means of buying any. Nothing daunted, he raised the cry of the Church in danger, convened his clergy, and made them an eloquent address in the principal church of his capital. While he was so doing, his troopers stole all the horses of the assembled ecclesiastics. Again, the raising of contributions in enemy territory was a legal and normal method of subsisting an army in wartime; but it was notorious that many generals remitted to the War Office much smaller sums than they had extorted from the occupied area. And, of course, where the general was known to be feathering his nest, naturally each collecting officer did likewise.

The military aspect of the *passe volant* abuse was an even more serious matter than the financial, for it meant that a commander took the field in complete ignorance of the effective strength of his army. To be sure, he had the daily strength returns; but what percentage of the men inscribed thereon really existed? Was his army ten, twenty, or even forty per cent below its nominal strength? It follows from this state of affairs that we must be very cautious in accepting battle casualty figures in the earlier part of the century; for the captain whose company had a nominal strength of a hundred and an effective strength of seventy would undoubtedly, if he could manage to get his men under fire at all, report that he had lost thirty men in action when perhaps he had had no losses at all.

Sometimes the ingenious company commander would turn his attention from his men to their equipment; two company commanders would decide that in peacetime, with a little management, one set of muskets and bandoliers would suffice for both companies. They would then sell one set for their common profit, lending each other what was necessary for muster days. Then too, some little assistance could be got from the use of the soldier's rations in garrisons where these were provided by the King and not the company commander; a pack of hounds, for instance, was found to thrive on soldier's biscuit. And, of course, the immediate consequences of such a theft was a further outbreak of the chronic evils of desertion and looting. In the cavalry, the wide-awake officer found that there were pickings to be made out of the forage ration; it was a simple matter to loot corn for the horses from the countryside, and sell the King's corn to the commissary, who in turn sold it to the army bread contractor. Well may a contemporary complain that the ill-conduct of the officers "frequently produces very fatal inconveniences."

This glimpse of the old-style army will give us some idea of the colossal problem which confronted Louvois in 1665, when at the age of twenty-four he threw himself into the work of reforming the service. To the task he brought an energy, a clear-sightedness, and a brutality which was to make him the most feared and hated man in France, but, on the whole, the greatest administrator of the reign, not even excepting Colbert. For he had behind him the enthusiastic backing of Louis XIV, upon which his rival could never absolutely depend.

Louvois was not the man to batter his head against a brick wall: he had a clear perception of the possible and the impossible, and he wasted no time in attempting to abolish the sale of commissions. But he determined that the King should in future have some say in the conditions of purchase and the qualifications of the purchaser.

At the very outset he was cheered by an unexpected piece of good fortune: the Duc d'Epernon, Colonel-General of the Infantry, died in 1661, and Louis himself assumed the vacant post of colonel-general. Henceforth, every infantry officer thus held his commission direct from the King, and that document was countersigned by the Secretary of War. To be sure, the Colonel-General of Cavalry and the Grand Master of the Artillery still remained in office, but their positions had been fatally weakened by the disappearance of their colleague, and Louvois, sapping and mining with unwearied patience, lived to see their functions become purely decorative. Though, this being the *ancien régime,* they of course never lost the salaries paid them for the duties they had ceased to perform. Louis XIV took his colonel-general's functions seriously, and indeed, as was his wont, rather lost sight of the wood for the trees. The officer's confidential report may be said to have come into existence with his assurance to Coligny in 1664 that no one shall be informed of the tenor of Coligny's remarks on the officers under his command: and by 1673 such reports are common, and have about them a very modern ring. "D'Espagne," writes Luxembourg in that year, "is a brave man, and admirably fitted for a subordinate position; but he has not the qualifications to fit him for an independent command." This is very well, but we must feel that the King is usurping the functions of his subordinate commanders when in 1676 he not only selects the town major of Aire, but winds up by saying, "for the minor appointments I wish to have men from the Guards: but I have not yet chosen them."

Having, through the King, secured control of the infantry officers, Louvois' next care was to attack the *passe volant* evil, and simultaneously with it, the general financial laxity which pervaded the whole army. Purchase of commissions in the *Gardes du Corps* he did succeed in suppressing, but that very minor reform of a fundamentally vicious system was all that he attempted directly. Indirectly, he tried to combat the evil by ensuring that, all other things being equal, the purchase of regiments and companies should be reserved for wealthy men who would have little temptation to indulge in petty larceny, while at the same time opening a new ladder of promotion to the keen but needy officer. The army, as he found it, knew no other ranks than ensign or cornet, lieutenant, captain, colonel, and general, all of which, up to and including a colonel, were venal posts. In modern language Louvois did not introduce any new *ranks*, but instituted two important and unpurchasable *appointments*, those of lieutenant-colonel and major, filled by merit alone, and qualifying the holder for promotion to the rank of general officer. It was, and was intended to be, a severe blow to the members of the old regimental hierarchy; the lieutenant-colonel, technically the colonel's deputy, tended more and more as time went on to exclude the colonel from any detailed control of the regiment, and to place him in something like the position now occupied by the colonel of a regiment in our present-day army. The major held no command, but was responsible for the supervision of the officers, discipline, training, and administration; he was, as we should say, adjutant and quartermaster combined, and was assisted by one or more subalterns called *aide-majors*. In 1667 and 1668 came a further innovation, the introduction of brigadiers, whose functions then were the same as today; but to become a brigadier it was not necessary to have been a colonel, and a colonel who became a brigadier did not relinquish the command of his regiment.

With the introduction of brigadiers, the two ladders to the top of the tree are now complete: ensign, lieutenant, captain, colonel, brigadier, for the wealthy man; ensign or the ranks, *aide-major*, major, lieutenant-colonel, brigadier, for the needy. For it is a great mistake to imagine that the officer of the second half of the seventeenth century was invariably a noble who had entered direct by purchase; Maréchal de Catinat was not noble, and Maréchal Fabert was a ranker, to name only two exceptions.

In 1674 one Sergeant Lafleur of the Regiment de Dampierre, is mentioned for distinguished service in Holland; whereupon Louis XIV writes to his general, "His Majesty desires that Lafleur be promoted lieutenant in the Regiment de Dampierre when there is a vacancy, and that in the meantime he be given a gratuity of five hundred livres." When St. Simon is serving in the Royal

Roussillon Regiment in 1693, he mentions Boissieux, cornet of his troop, who "had started life as a swineherd, and had raised himself by sheer merit; though old, he had never learned to read or write. He was one of the best scouts in the army. . . . We all liked and respected him, as did our Generals." I quote the case, not as being in any way exceptional, but because St. Simon is the speaker; had the case been exceptional, the waspish little duke would have spoken very differently about the obligation to treat such a man as a brother officer. As a matter of fact, the number of rankers one meets with in Louis XIV's armies is remarkable, and it would not surprise me to hear that the class was commoner in the French service in 1690 than the British in 1890. And promotion by the poor man's road was very far from being a War Office dead letter, one of the King's pious hopes; when in 1684 Louis created twenty-seven new infantry regiments, there was not one of the new colonels who had not been either a major or a lieutenant-colonel.

But it is time to turn to Louvois' struggles with the *passe volant*, a struggle in which he was ultimately successful, because, unlike so many of his fellow bureaucrats, he did not content himself with issuing orders, but proceeded to enforce them. His first step was to cut off the supply of soldier impersonators; in 1663 a detected *passe volant* was flogged: in 1665 flogged and branded: and in 1667 the crime was made a capital one. Next it was the turn of the officer. Any soldier denouncing his captain for using *passe volants* is to be given his discharge and a gratuity of three hundred livres, provided by the stopping of that sum from the captain's pay: and in addition, the offending officer is to undergo at least a month's imprisonment. Next the heavy hand descends on the dishonest commissioner of war; in 1671 Louvois catches Commissioner Aubert at Dunkirk drawing a salary from the garrison for giving officers notice of his muster days—and Dunkirk knew Commissioner Aubert no longer. Belleisle was a distant garrison where a man might reasonably have hoped to live out his days as in the good old pre-Louvois times: but the rage for innovation does not spare even Belleisle. There the governor, instead of discharging a sergeant who has denounced a *passe volant*, has put him in arrest, and the news reaches the War Office. A month's forfeiture of pay for the governor, three months' for the town major, and cashiering for the captain says Louvois; adding that this is only an instalment of what the three may expect if the delator has any complaints to make about his treatment. And let them beware of showing any resentment against the commissioner who has reported the case. Here, by the way, we may correct a common impression that Louvois put the French army into uniform with the double object of checking desertion and destroying the *passe volant*. Actually, Louvois rather disapproved of the idea, and so far from uniforms being "introduced," they came into use at the whim of individual colonels, except in the case of the *Maison du Roi*, which had been clothed uniformly since 1664. It was not until 1682 that uniform was made compulsory, and even then, it was for officers only.

Whilst still keeping a vigilant eye on the administrative side of the service, Louvois now turned his attention to the hitherto almost totally neglected matter of training, particularly officers' training. The officer, not only undisciplined but ignorant, did not take kindly to Louvois' effort to improve the standard of his professional competence, but the young War Minister was both swift and merciless in his dealings with those who opposed him. Incompetents learned to their horror that their continued employment was conditional on the efficiency of their units; useless colonels and captains were tormented into selling out, and rebellious Marshals of France were sent to their estates to meditate on the unwisdom of trying to stem the tide of reform. Martinet and Fourilles, two of Louvois' discoveries, were made, the one Inspector of Infantry, the other of Cavalry, and we may guess at the nature of their performance from the name which Martinet has bequeathed to our own military vocabulary; we have no difficulty in believing that he was "a man of rare merit and firmness."

The inefficiency and insouciance of the officer of the earlier part of the century was largely due to the precarious tenure of his employment, and it seems to have been Louis XIV himself who, in seeking for a palliative to the situation, hit upon an elementary version of the modern army's reserve system. Speaking of the demobilization of 1659, he says of the disbanded officers:

Some of them had no means of subsistence but their profession, and I pitied their case . . . I put a number of them into the Musketeers, and formed the Dauphin's Light Horse to absorb others, giving them in addition to their pay, pensions calculated on their past service . . .

thereby having the means available to mobilize new units in next to no time.

It was the existence of this reserve of ex-officers which enabled France to mobilize so swiftly in 1666, and when peace came in 1668, the officers alleged to have been demobilized were in fact secretly absorbed into the permanent formations.

But it was on the young entry into the officers' corps that Louvois pinned his faith, and with them he spared no pains. In 1682 the old casual system of attaching a youngster to a regiment to pick up what he could (usually bad habits) whilst the family lawyer haggled over a company for him, was abolished and its place taken by a modern system of military education. Nine cadet companies were formed in frontier towns, commanded by the governors of the places, each with an instructional staff for the benefit of the cadets. The idea being a complete novelty, the companies naturally suffered from teething troubles, but within a very short time they were already proving their worth. By June 1683 Louis admits that not even his Musketeers make a better show on parade than the Besançon company, and a year later the Cambrai company had already passed out some four hundred satisfactory young officers. The instruction given seems to have been good, and the syllabus extensive; drill, the manual, and musketry were the most important subjects, but in addition the cadets were taught dancing, fencing, riding, geography, and the principles of mathematics. But instruction in the latter subject seems to have left much to be desired, for Louvois complains in 1685 that he has examined four Longwy cadets and found them ignorant of the first rules of the subject.

Having set on foot a training scheme for the officers, Louvois turned his attention to the problem of the men: and here too he found an ample field for the exercise of his abilities. The first thing to be done was to improve the quality of the recruit, and it is interesting to notice that Louvois at Versailles and Montecuculi at Vienna hold the same view. Both insist that the time is gone by when a satisfactory army can be manufactured out of the dregs of the people, and both are anxious to secure a better stamp of recruit. Louvois tackled the problem by tightening up the recruiting regulations, giving increased powers to the army Intendants, and improving the private soldier's opportunities and status.

Recruits were enlisted on a written attestation, and for a fixed period of four years' service: they must be physically fit, either bachelors or widowers, and under forty years of age: if intended for the *Maison du Roi*, the man must be a Roman Catholic, over twenty-eight, and if possible, a gentleman. If he is a gentleman he must have a minimum of two years' service in some other corps, and if not a gentleman, a minimum of four years.

But in spite of Louvois' exertions in this field, the quality of the recruits yielded by the overstrained economy of the country remained a constant preoccupation. As early as 1673 Louis XIV remarks that whilst he had plenty of men, they "were not of the quality needed for the capture of fortresses." In 1676 Luxembourg complains that his recruits are "deplorable; a good half of them mere children, whom I shall have to send back to France."

In 1683 the War Minister has to issue orders that soldiers must not be discharged because they are an inch or two under the average height of their comrades; the line infantry must not be measured with a tape as is done in the guards, he says. In 1689 Vauban urges a defensive campaign on the ground that the infantry is very different in quality from what it was in the last war, and almost at the same moment Duras writes from another front to complain about the quality of the cavalry. By 1690 the kidnapping of recruits in Paris had reached such proportions that the Lieutenant of Police is instructed to proceed against kidnappers with the utmost rigour. By 1703 Louis has found it necessary to offer five years' total exemption from direct taxation to any man who will enlist on a three years' engagement. The plain fact was that France, as then organized, simply had not got the manpower available to carry out the grandiose policy of Louis XIV.

Louvois was more successful in dealing with the abuse of direct peculation than he was in solving the recruiting problem. Under his reformed system the captain still received and issued the men's pay as heretofore, but his pay roll was audited by the army Intendant: and if his accounts did not balance, he could think himself lucky if he escaped with a sentence to make good the deficiency by stoppages from his pay. At about the same time Louvois made a real effort to improve the status of the common man; the infantry sergeant and his cavalry equivalent, the *maréchal de logis* were given the rank of under-officers, thus exempting them from all punishment other than that inflicted by court martial, and a system of awards for gallantry and good service was instituted. The day of decorations, even for officers, is still far distant, but Louvois provided the perhaps more powerful incentive of financial easement; exemption from the most galling direct tax, the *Taille*, was awarded for periods ranging from six months to total exemption for life to those soldiers who had distinguished themselves.

In 1670 a uniform scale of pay was laid down for each arm of the service: and not only laid down, but actually paid, which did something to reduce the enormous amount of desertion which was ordinary in the armies of the period. And even Louvois did not succeed in stamping it out; in 1677 there were forty-two cavalry deserters in one day from Luxembourg's army, and in a fortnight of the same year the Regiment Dauphin lost fifty men. In the following year the crack Regiment de Champagne had sixty-five deserters in ten days. As late as 1694 the evil was still widespread, and Louis XIV, in writing to one of his generals, says that the first step towards curing desertion is to see that the behaviour of the captains gives the men no excuse for deserting. But though desertion continued, and indiscipline was scotched rather than killed, Louvois undoubtedly raised the status of the rank and file, with beneficial effects on the efficiency of the army.

Nor were the King and his ministers without some sense of responsibility for the welfare of the men who paid so heavily for the advancement of Louis' glory and Louvois' reputation. In 1666 we find the King writing with his usual good sense on the subject of soldier's allowances when in billets, and in the same year he orders extra pay for troops serving in plague areas. In 1664 Beaufort, commanding in Algeria, is instructed to "take the greatest care of the sick and wounded. Tell them how I feel for them in their sufferings, and assure them that their wounds will always be a powerful recommendation to my favour."

And again to Beaufort in the same year: "I want to know if Captain Laurier leaves a wife and children, so that I may do something for them, being anxious that people shall see that those who die in my service continue to live in my memory."

Nor did he overlook the then generally ignored problem of those discharged as unfit for further service; in 1672 the Order of St. Lazarus and Mount Carmel was re-endowed and revivified for the benefit of indigent ex-officers, while in 1674 the *Hôtel des Invalides* was opened for ex-soldiers. Not that this was the first provision made for this class; the wounded soldier, called a *donné*, had, up to this, been billeted on a monastery, a system which was not without its inconveniences. The conversation and habits of the retired warrior had not tended to the edification of the younger brethren, and we may suspect that the cellarer found himself forced to write off a good deal of his stock to leakage. The religious orders gladly purchased exemption from the requirement to lodge destitute soldiers with an annual subscription to the new foundation of the *Invalides*. A beginning was also made in giving preferential treatment to the fit ex-service man by allowing this class a monopoly of the sedan-chair traffic in the royal palaces.

At the same time a vigorous and much needed effort was made to reform the field hospital services; and for the moment at any rate, with such success that in 1673 a wounded officer writes from Holland, "I could not be better off (than in this hospital) if I was in my mother's house . . . and the same is true of the men." A very different state of affairs from that existing in the 1667 campaign when the men preferred to die in billets rather than be admitted to the hospital. But the radical unsoundness of the hospital organization engendered constant abuses, which could be checked, but not eradicated; for the hospitals were let out to contractors at a fixed rate per patient, and a dishonest contractor had therefore every inducement to spend as little as possible on the unfortunates in his charge. But with Louvois as Secretary of War, he did so at considerable risk; in 1683 the Secretary detects frauds being perpetrated by the hospital contractor of Alsace, and gives judgment in a letter to the Intendant. The offending contractor is to be led by the common hangman through every hospital ward in the province, wearing sandwich boards with the legend *fripon public*, after which he is to be banished for life.

If Louvois did not entirely succeed in his struggle to stamp out indiscipline, he at any rate never relaxed his efforts to do so; but circumstances, the whole tone of society, were against him. And, oddly enough, it was Louvois who was responsible for much of the indiscipline against which he himself strove. With a *naïveté* remarkable in so able a man, he imagined that it was feasible to incite French armies to commit murder, rape, robbery, and arson for so long as it suited his strategical objective, and that then, on the word "halt," the troops would once more become models of soldierly discipline. It is some little consolation for the atrocities committed by Louvois' orders in Holland in 1672 and in Germany in 1689 to know that the damage thereby done to French morale was a major factor in bringing about the ultimate ruin of his master's plans.

When Louvois began to look into the question of regimental training, he found that it was not so much a reform that he had to make as a beginning. The first shock came when the commander of the Hungarian Expeditionary Force reported in 1664 that one of his chief difficulties was that many of his so-called trained soldiers had never fired a musket, and did not even know the theory of that cumbersome weapon. Musketry drill, and even musketry camps, made their appearance soon after this startling disclosure, and a rigorous inquisition into the state of the muskets of all regiments was made; those which did not conform to standard weight and measurement being withdrawn and replaced at the captain's expense. Here, for once, Louvois shows himself a reactionary; the *fusil*, a more modern weapon, had already made its appearance when the French army was being rearmed with the musket. But Louvois would have nothing to do with the *fusil*; the musket was the traditional weapon of the French infantry, and to change, said Louvois, was to disarm: an argument with which we are not unfamiliar, even today. It was not until 1670 that he consented to the experimental introduction of four fusiliers into each infantry company. He was equally conservative over the pike, with which about a third of each company was armed until 1703, in spite of frequent reports that whenever the enemy infantry was routed in battle, the first thing the Frenchman did was to throw away his pike or musket and pick up an abandoned *fusil*. The obstinate retention of the pike is the more inexplicable, seeing that in 1687 Vauban had invented the bayonet, which gave the infantryman a musket and pike in one. Apropos of muskets, let us note a point arising out of the correspondence, which shows Louvois' amazing capacity for entering into detail without, like Louis XIV, losing sight of major issues. In 1683 he circularizes inspectors of infantry on the advantage of having a leather pad sewn on to the left shoulder of the tunic to take the friction of the musket when on the march.

As late as 1688 the relative weakness of French fire power was still causing Louvois anxiety; in that year officers are ordered to provide themselves with muskets, to practise on the range, and to introduce company pool shooting-competitions. And in 1692 Louis is enquiring into the report that at Steenkirke the whole of the French fire power was produced by the fusiliers alone.

Cavalry was still, and for many years to come, considered to be the arm which won battles; the rôle of the infantry being to soften up the enemy line in preparation for the cavalry charge. Consequently, cavalry training was better understood and better carried out than that of the infantry. Cavalry camps were held annually, where new tactics and weapons were tried out, and one result was that in 1679 the sabre replaced the sword as the standard cavalry weapon. In the same year cavalry fire power had its modest beginnings in the addition of two carbineers to each squadron.

In dealing with problems of administration Louvois was as indefatigable and as fertile in expedients as in those of discipline and training: and if the administrative side of Louis XIV's armies strikes us as amateurish, it is largely because we contrast it with the administration of today, instead of with that of Louis' opponents. Louvois' major contribution to the problem of field maintenance was the introduction of the magazine: one of those ideas which is so obvious, once someone else has thought of it. The magazine conferred a strategic power on Louis XIV's armies which took Europe off its guard; hitherto it had been accepted as a law of nature that cavalry could not take the field until the spring herbage was sufficiently grown to supply it with forage. Now, thanks to magazines, French cavalry could both march and manoeuvre in any month of the year; and further, the existence of magazines helped to offset the French cavalry's notorious extravagance in the matter of forage consumption. Certainly from 1693 onwards there were authorized scales of forage issue, but an attention to such details was a clerkly activity unbecoming an officer and a gentleman.

And the same attitude was taken towards the feeding of the troops. The staple ration of the French soldier was bread, and on the march, biscuit, the latter baked hard, with a hole in the middle, so that the ration could be strung on the bandolier. Of these biscuits, a soldier could carry enough for six days. But it never seems to have occurred to the officers to check consumption; at the first night's halt the men would barter their biscuit for wine, with the result that a formation badly wanted at the front would be found immobile and three days' march from its destination, having run out of rations. One French general suggests as a remedy that the men should be given an allowance in cash instead of the biscuit ration; but it would seem unlikely that the French, or any other soldier of the period, would have wasted the money on bread. The Austrian Montecuculi is a strong advocate of the system of supply by contract; which suggests that either Montecuculi was very lucky in his contractors, or else took very little interest in his supply problems. If the regimental officer was careless about the conservation of rations, he could point to an equal and more criminal carelessness on the part of his superiors. When Boufflers defended Lille in 1708, he had to surrender for lack of provisions; but the shortage was caused by the issue of rations throughout the siege for the same number of men as on its opening day, no regard being paid to the very heavy casualties sustained by the defence. Indiscipline as well as negligence played its part in complicating the work of the French supply service; in 1673 the whole of Luxembourg's army was put under stoppages of pay as a punishment for looting their own magazines. And where the troops did not loot, there was the ever present difficulty of the dishonest contractor; Berwick, commanding on the Spanish front in 1704, complains that his bread comes up bad, by reason of the contractor only half-baking it so as to make it weigh more.

Ration scales varied considerably according to the troop's tasks and the resources of the *terrain;* the army in Lorraine in 1670 had an issue of fresh meat daily, Fridays excepted, but the general is told to make it clear to the men that meat is an extra to which they have no right, and which is given them by the King, and not by their captain. Again, in 1677, on the Rhine, the order is that each infantryman is to have one-third of a pound of meat daily, and each cavalryman a quarter: but while the infantry get a free issue, the value of the cavalryman's ration is to be stopped from his pay. And the issue of meat is to cease as soon as there is an abundance of peas and beans. In 1690 the authorized meat issue is three pounds a week, free to the infantry, and at a reduced rate to the cavalry, while the *Maison du Roi* pay full contract price.

Louis XIV is himself credited with one contribution towards solving the problem of rations in the field, that of introducing the portable oven, which in one day's halt could bake enough bread for the next six days. I am inclined to suspect that this is truly his own idea; it is just the sort of administrative detail at which the King, nothing of a general, but an excellent junior staff officer, excelled.

Wherever we turn, we find the generals hampered by having to rely on the contract system for the performance of duties which are now regarded as an integral part of the functions of an army; even the artillery was, until 1672, a civilian commercial enterprise, in which the contractor hired soldiers to mount his batteries, and was paid so much for each gun brought into action, a system only one degree less bad than that obtaining in the contemporary Spanish army, where the contractor was paid for every time he moved a gun. The result naturally being that Spanish artillery was constantly on the move, and hardly ever in action. The supply and transportation of rations was organized also on a contractual basis, with results which were sometimes disastrous. In 1675 Maréchal de Créqui was beaten at Consaarbruck without having succeeded in bringing a single gun into action; the post mortem revealed the fact that the artillery contractor, expecting a quiet day, had lent his horses to the commissariat to bring in a convoy. And where were the commissariat contractor's own horses? We are not told, but I have a strong suspicion that they were out on hire to the neighbouring farmers. The whole system cried out, not for more detailed supervision from Versailles, but for the appointment of a general officer charged solely with the duties of administration in the field: and this solution seems to have occurred to no one. Each army had indeed its military Intendant, but that official was as overworked as his Home Office *confrère*, and was operating in a milieu unsuited to the technique of the civilian administrator. And the general, so far from regarding him as a member of his staff, usually was at daggers drawn with him, regarding the Intendant, not without reason, as a spy. In 1678 the War Minister writes to the Intendant of the army in Roussillon, "Your first duty is to let me know everything that is said, projected, and done in the army."

At best, the general saw in the Intendant a superior sort of clerk, detailed to act as his man of business, whilst to Louvois and his successors, the Intendant was the channel through which they exercised control over the general; the situation was rich in opportunities for friction, and friction there was. Nor were the soldiers entirely to blame. In 1665 Louvois has to write to an Intendant thus: "A War Commissioner has no right to pretend to any command over troops, nor over the inhabitants of the district in which the army is operating . . . and if you do so, I shall be unable to uphold you."

In 1669 the boot is on the other foot, and it is the Intendant who is energetically supported in his complaint that he has received nothing but *paroles assez fâcheuses* from an officer whose men's weapons are in a bad state. Dozens of other examples could be quoted to show the difficulties of the precarious equilibrium which Louvois managed to impose on those uneasy bedfellows, the general and the Intendant.

In the sphere of higher tactics there was a latent weakness in the new model French army, which does not reveal its full danger until the second half of the personal reign. Remote and overcentralized control was the evil, and it had its birth not only in Louvois' love of power, but in the history and character of the King himself. Two factors combined to imbue Louis XIV with the fatal notion that he could control battles and manoeuvres from his room at Versailles; firstly, his boyhood and youth had taught him the national danger, and what he felt even more deeply, the personal humiliation, which could be inflicted by semi-independent and potentially rebellious generals. If he could not reduce his commanders-in-chief to impotence as he had done his nobles, he could at least make sure that they should be ever conscious of the hand of the master. Secondly, Louis, like so many men, fancied his skill in the one sphere in which he was palpably at his worst, namely, that of a military commander; and, having a fine natural vanity, his easy successes when in command had convinced him that nothing was so easy as to be a successful soldier. Moreover, his generals, one of whose chief preoccupations was to keep the King away from the front, were constant in their flattering assurances to His Majesty that he could exercise the supreme command as easily from the palace as from his tent in the field. The soldiers thus kept the King at home in many campaigns, but at a heavy price; Louis took their flattery seriously; control from Versailles became ever stricter and more detailed until in Louis XIV's last war, it was practically unknown for a general in the field to threaten an enemy place or even strike camp without sending off a courier to the King for his instructions. And by the time orders arrived, a change in the situation had rendered their execution impracticable. The performances of the French higher command in the 1701–12 war is a sufficient comment on the working of the theory of remote control.

But when all has been said, the reform, or rather the re-creation, of the French army remains one of the most remarkable achievements of seventeenth-century France; the work of the pioneer is by its very nature imperfect, and those who look back on it tend to criticize what was left undone rather than to appreciate what was accomplished. And the accomplishment of the army created by Louvois was that it kept Louis XIV's crown on his head in his last disastrous war, and quite possibly prevented the fall of the monarchy.

VI

The Country Gentleman

In law the *noblesse* formed one of the three estates of the realm, its members enjoying the same privileges and performing the same duties, distinguished from each other only by the adventitious demarcations of wealth and title. But by the middle of the reign, the nobility had in fact become split into two classes, between which there was little sympathy and little contact—the *noblesse de la cour* and the *noblesse campagnard*. A sixteenth-century noble would not have understood the distinction, which indeed barely existed in his day; there were, to be sure, the King's favourites and his high officers, who naturally spent more time at the Louvre than in their own *châteaux*; but except for such people, a noble pleased himself whether he lived in the country or at Court. Any gentleman probably paid his respects to the King once in two or three years, or at least once in his lifetime, but no one, not even the King, thought any the worse of him if he lived from one year's end to another on his estates. Indeed, many of the nobles of highest rank were never seen at Court, and rather looked down upon the courtier; when one of the breed, in his ribbons and fashionable clothes, sought the hospitality of his manor, he would say aside, like Hamlet, "Dost know this water-fly?"

But Louis XIV had deliberately enforced a policy which turned the tables in favour of the courtier; not to be seen constantly at Court was in his reign to condemn yourself to obscurity and your children to poverty. Not even a loyal friend at Versailles could win you the smallest favour if you insisted on living in the country—"He is a man I never see," would be the royal answer, and that answer was final and irrevocable. It was now the turn of the courtier to jeer at his country cousin, his poverty, his antiquated good breeding, and his out-of-date clothes; to live in the country, he would explain condescendingly, was not only to become a vegetable with powers of locomotion, but was to inflict upon yourself the most dreadful penalty which the King could inflict: namely, banishment from his royal presence.

Molière made the country gentleman the joke of polite society, poets ridiculed him, the courtiers mimicked him. The *campagnard* on a visit to Paris, his poverty, his boastings, how he is swindled out of his money and tricked into a discreditable marriage, becomes the stock in trade of the writer of ephemeral farces. If the courtier condescends to spend a night with his country cousin, he does so as a matter of pure convenience, and hardly troubles to conceal the depth of his contempt for his host and hostess; indifferent to the trouble and expense to which he puts them, he regards their hospitality as material from which to fashion a good story which will raise a laugh when he retails it on his return to Court. Let us take a typical example of the attitude of the man of fashion towards the country squire. Bussy-Rabutin, travelling with his mistress and a friend, arrives without warning late at night in midwinter, at the house of his lady's relations:

We stopped the night with one of her relations, whom we didn't see, as he had a quartern ague, and luckily the fit took him just as we arrived. Our happiness would have been complete if his wife had had the fever too, for we could not have had worse cheer than we did, and we would at least have been at our ease. We were received in a hall lower than the courtyard, where I am certain the walls would be damp in the dog-days: in many places it was unpaved, so that one could cross it only in jumps. While the servants went to cut a tree for us to warm ourselves at, we were given hard-bottomed chairs in front of an empty fireplace. There was a cold and dismal silence, for after the usual commonplaces which one makes use of in arriving, we didn't know what to say to the woman, or she to us. She was not so stupid as to be unashamed of the absurd reception she had offered us, and we were too miserable to have any pity for her. I was dying to go and warm myself at the kitchen fire, which I could hear crackling. . . but it wouldn't do to leave my mistress. Beauvoir, who was just as cold as I was, and hadn't the same reasons for scrupling, went out, he said, to hurry on those who were getting the wood, and settled down to give assistance in front of the kitchen fire. A quarter of an hour afterwards two peasants came in with a veritable wagon-load of wood, covered with snow, which they put on the fire-dogs; then came a girl with a bundle of straw which was so wet that she couldn't get it to light properly and we were nearly suffocated. In the end she had to take a paillasse off a bed, and all that it succeeded in doing was to melt the snow on the wood, making a sort of lake, which, as often as it crept up to our toes, drove us out farther into the middle of the room. . . . . The supper was on a par with the fire; the soups were hot water; the meat had been alive when we arrived; the bread wasn't baked, the wine was sour and muddy; the linen wasn't damp, it was wet, and the heat of the soup made the napkins smoke. This fog helped to extinguish what light two small candles afforded. That nothing might be lacking to this detestable meal, it was very long, and, if one could have eaten anything, one would have digested the first course whilst waiting for the second.

The whole account is too long to quote, but the bedroom and its appointments surpassed in discomfort "even that accursed hall where we had suffered so." It is doubtless all very witty and amusing, but we do not wish to become better acquainted with M. le Comte de Bussy-Rabutin, Colonel-General of the Light Horse of France; in fact it is with considerable satisfaction that we learn that he was subsequently exiled, and forced to spend seventeen years in the country with no other society than that of the *campagnards* whom he so despised.

Mme. de Sévigné was much more of a countrywoman than the majority of her contemporaries; but even that gracious lady is not guiltless of a touch of patronage when she comes to talk to us of her country adventures. On a fine May evening in 1680, she breaks the axle of her carriage, miles from anywhere in the Orléans district, and a country gentleman comes to her rescue—"he was

M. de Sottenville to the life," she writes, "a man who would write the Georgics himself, if they were not already written . . . we were two hours in his company without boredom, owing to the novelty of a conversation and a language entirely new to us. We afterwards made several reflections on the gentleman's perfect contentment." June of the same year finds her in Brittany, where she suffers acutely from the sociable habits of the local *noblesse*; there is a Mme. de La Hamelinière, in a carriage, with

six beautiful grey horses, the property of M. le Marquis: the carriage is also the property of M. le Marquis: she speaks unceasingly and unendingly of M. le Marquis . . . she has nothing to do but pay visits; she has come from twenty leagues away, and dropped here like a bomb, when I least expected her. I hid in the woods to put off my martyrdom, but of course I had to return in the end . . . we have supper, and to stop my continuous yawns, I keep myself awake by talking to her daughter. . . . this woman has been here three days . . . no doubt she will go when it pleases God.

A few days later there arrives "a *garçon*, young, blond . . . with an air which took me. I was delighted . . . but, alas, every time he opened his mouth he laughed, until I nearly cried."

And so the country gentleman, unpitied even by Mme. de Sévigné, was left to struggle with his difficulties unaided, the butt of courtier and comedian alike, and ignored by the King; yet he should have been the natural complement of the peasant, an asset to the state, whereas we can faithfully apply to his cadging, servile Court cousin a contemptuous epithet known to every schoolboy, with the possible exception of Macaulay's.

How did he live, this much despised countryman whose Court gossip was a year out of date, and who, dressed in the same homespun as his own farmers, carried his produce to market with a sword by his side? Many of us today will have a vivid appreciation of one aspect of his life which would have struck home less forcibly to our fathers: for he was before all, a man with a fixed income in a world in which the value of money was continuously falling. Not only the etiquette of his caste but the law prevented him from engaging in trade, the civil service was a *bourgeois* preserve, the legal world was to the noble a closed shop; he had in fact a choice of three ways of life: he could live in ever growing penury on his estate, he could enter the army, or he could try the desper-

Louis XIV

From the portrait by Mignard engraved by Nanteuil

Louis XIV
From the portrait by Charles Lebrun in the Louvre

Louis XIV receiving the homage of the peers at his Coronation in
Rheims Cathedral

From a contemporary engraving

The "Lever du Roi"

The Grand Master of the Order of St. Lazarus taking the oath before
the King in the chapel of Versailles on 18 December, 1695

From an engraving by Sebastien Le Clerc

La Taxe Par Teste

D'vne taxe legere la douceur on impose
A vn peuple tout prest d'en accepter la loy
Heureux sy l'on pouuoit pour si modique chose
Achepter vne Paix aux vœux de notre Roy.

The Poll Tax
From an anonymous print of the period

Distribution du Pain du Roy au Louvre

Distribution of the King's bread at the Louvre
From an anonymous contemporary print

LE PRINTEMPS

On plante le May

Enfans des beaux jours
ture passagère;

Nous apprend qu'une loy Severe,
En doit bientost finir le cours.

Putting up a Maypole

From Mariette's "Scenes de la Vie Rurale"

Wrestling at a country fair: "whoever falls, pays"
From a contemporary print

Raising the militia in a country parish
From an anonymous print of 1705

Prison visiting
From an engraving by Abraham Bosse

The Schoolmaster

From an engraving by Abraham Bosse

The Galleys: loading and unloading

From a drawing by Rigaud

The Lying-in

From an engraving by Abraham Bosse

The Bleeding

From an engraving by Abraham Bosse

Lady of Quality dressing for a ball
From an engraving after Mariette

Gallery of the Royal Palace
From an engraving by Abraham Bosse

ate gamble of joining in the hunt for crumbs under the rich man's table at Versailles. Here I propose to deal mainly with the man who elected to remain on his estates.

The whole deliberate trend of Louis XIV's policy was to turn the *seigneur* into a courtier, to make him an anachronism in the countryside: to deprive him of all duties, whilst letting him retain his privileges and emoluments. This state of affairs is at the bottom of the smouldering exasperation with which the *seigneur* and peasant regarded each other. Neither was an economist, nor even a clear thinker; but the peasant understood very well that it was to the Intendant that he must now look for protection, and not to the *seigneur*, though he must continue to pay the *seigneur* for the duties which he no longer performed, whilst the Intendant's services were gratuitous, or at least they seemed so to the peasant. In actual fact, of course, he was paying the Intendant's salary, though he did not realize it. The *seigneur*, on the other hand, regarded the situation with a bewildered resentment; he was caught up in an economic change which he did not understand; the income which had been nearly sufficient (no income is ever sufficient) for his father's wants was utterly inadequate for his. And then there was a nasty spirit abroad in the village; the people were getting impudent, slacker about paying their feudal dues, and sulking about the performance of manorial *Corvées*. In some districts peasants have begun "to stare proudly and insolently" at their lord, and are "putting their hands in their pockets instead of saluting him." In Auvergne things are even worse, owing to the King's disastrous attack on the status of the *noblesse* of that province in 1665; peasants are reported to be buying gloves, and to be offering their protection to persons of quality who are in fear of the King's justice. A noble has been executed for squeezing his peasants a little too hard; it is becoming quite common for peasants to go to law with their *seigneur*. Things have come to a pretty pass in France.

But it would be wrong to think of *château* and village as two permanently hostile camps; the frictions and annoyances produced by the working of a force which was beyond the comprehension or control of either, were often in abeyance, and in many cases there was normally a real sympathy and friendliness between the two parties. After all, the *seigneur* had grown up amongst the village children, and his own children had played with the sons and daughters of his old companions; his daughter, as likely as not, had a village couple for her Godparents, and the squire himself was not above taking a social glass with his old playmates in the village inn. It was not to the peasantry but to the *bourgeois* and the *nouveau riche* that the noble displayed his arrogance and insolence, to the moneyed man of obscure origin who was trying to buy him out of his dilapidated *château* and set up for a country gentleman.

Much has been made of the severity with which the *seigneur* extorted from the villager the uttermost farthing of his feudal dues; but what was the unfortunate man to do? His elder son in the county regiment was bombarding him with appeals for help; the younger, being intended for the Church, must have a college education; and his daughter, whether he intended to marry her or put her into religion, must have a dowry. For to make a religious of a girl was not the cheap way out of a financial difficulty which it is often assumed to have been; all convents insisted on a dowry as a *sine qua non*, and many of them demanded a sum for which the girl could have had a country squire for her husband. Three thousand livres is not a high figure for the country convent to ask. But it would be an exceptional *seigneur* who found himself with only three children to provide for; many, perhaps most, had a dozen or more, to say nothing of those born on the wrong side of the blanket for whom some sort of modest provision must be made. The philoprogenitive habits of the French *seigneur* of the seventeenth century are not without a certain significance in underlining the inherent monotony of his existence; rather than ponder upon the financial implications of the Chinese proverb that "he who goes to bed to save candles, begets twins," he preferred to concentrate his energies on qualifying at the earliest moment for the gratuity of 2,000 livres which the King paid to those of his nobles who had more than ten children.

How did he live, this rustic nobleman, what was his income, from what sources was it drawn? In general, he lived a hand-to-mouth existence, and his income was made up of an odd collection of miscellaneous receipts. Firstly, there was his land, and that might be managed in a variety of ways: rarely by the ordinary landlord and tenant method of modern times, which in the seventeenth century was virtually confined to the big estates of the wealthy nobility. One of the chief causes of the small estate's poverty was the type of cultivation known as *baux à cens*, a system dating back to the thirteenth century. At that time there had been an acute shortage of agricultural labour, and many landowners, as the only alternative to letting their fields go out of cultivation, had been compelled to let the land to peasants in perpetuity, at a fixed rent; it is perhaps hardly worth pointing out that what had been a fair rent in 1460 had become an absurd one in 1660, and that the in‹ heritors of such unprofitable contracts started out heavily handicapped in their struggle to wrest a living from the family estate. The *seigneur* would perhaps farm some of his land himself, but much the most usual arrangement was a *métayerie*; under this system the *seigneur* entered into partnership with a peasant farmer, called a *métayer*. The *seigneur* advanced the capital for stocking the land, whilst the peasant worked it and paid him a percentage of the fruits. From the *seigneur's* point of view the system had two serious drawbacks; firstly, considerable capital had to be laid out, and the dividend on it was precarious, depending as it did on the weather and the prices of food-stuffs: secondly, he was at the mercy of the dishonest *métayer* who, if the bargain looked like turning out badly for him, could and did do what the Irish call "a moonlight flit," often burning down a barn or so before he went as an indication of his dissatisfaction. The *seigneur* could, of course, pursue him criminally, but this would benefit no one but the local attorney. It was merely throwing good money after bad. But, unsatisfactory as the system was, four-sevenths of the land in France was being cultivated *en métayerie*.

For the rest of his income, the *seigneur* depended upon his feudal dues, which were of such diversity, of such different values, and of such disputable legality that the subject gave employment to a special class of lawyer who engaged in no other practice. Here we must limit ourselves to a cursory glance at a subject on which many learned volumes have been written.

The *baux à cens* we have already dealt with, and, as we have seen, its yield had dropped to a mere trifle, next in antiquity came the *Lods et ventes*, a payment of approximately one-sixth of the sale value of any land farmed under the *baux à cens* and sold by the perpetual tenant. But this, it will be noted, was not income but a windfall of capital. *Terrage*, one of the *seigneur's* more important sources of income, was a percentage tax on a crop raised on seigneurial land. As we glance through the interminable catalogue, *Bordelage, Marciage, Dîme, Parcière, Carpot* and the rest, we find what we expected to find, namely, that in conformity with the whole pattern of the age, there is neither uniformity nor standardization of yield in the feudal dues. This one is payable only in Burgundy, that in the Nivernais; here a due is unknown, there a due is half as much again as in a neighbouring province. What is a *Banalité*? How did the *droit de Banvin* operate? Whose is the *droit de Blairie*? Let us not enquire, but content ourselves with saying that each brought in a driblet of produce or cash to make up the *seigneur's* income.

Amongst this mass of rights, we look in vain for the only seigneurial due known to the modern reader, the notorious *droit du Seigneur*; it is a fiction, or had at any rate become one by the reign of Louis XIV. But if it had not at some time been enforced, it is difficult to understand the custom of the *seigneur* putting a leg into the bride's bed after the wedding feast. Some historians would persuade us that this ceremony is the origin of the popular legend about the *droit du Seigneur*; to me it seems much more probable that it was the *seigneur's* formal assertion of the continued legality of a right whose exercise he had ceased to demand.

One more seigneurial due may perhaps be mentioned before we leave the subject: the lord of the manor had a right to all rain-water that fell on the manorial roads. One regrets that no cartoonist has given us a drawing of the *seigneur* engaged in the collection of this portion of his rent. The peasant showed a certain resignation towards most of the dues which we have so far mentioned; some fell upon him infrequently, the others he met in the same spirit with which he regarded an inundation in spring or a thunderstorm before harvest. It was the daily nuisance of the remaining dues which exasperated him into enquiring "Why?" That "why" which is the first faint rumble of the storm which was to break over the country in 1789. The peasant's corn could be ground only at the *seigneur's* mill: his bread must be baked in the *seigneur's* oven, and every sixteenth loaf was for the *seigneur*: he paid an eighth of his grape harvest to the seigneurial wine vat, and was forbidden to use any other. Even more than the tax, the farmer resented the waste of time and labour which this antiquated method of payment involved; for it would often happen that a tenant living on the outskirts of a *seigneurie* would have a ten or twelve mile journey with his crops, whilst within a mile of him there would be a wine press and a mill which he dare not use. An even greater hardship was the law which forbade him to kill the *seigneur's* game, whatever damage it might do to his crops, or to supplement his Lenten fare by fishing the seigneurial waters.

Indeed, the more we read of seigneurial rights, the more surprised we are to discover that relations between *seigneur* and peasant were, generally speaking, amicable. Perhaps it was an instance of the working of the seventeenth-century practice of making severe laws, and then giving nearly everyone an exemption from their provisions; I have little doubt that in the better *seigneuries* permission to trap a rabbit or fish a stream was not difficult to obtain. It would be odd if it had been, seeing that the *seigneur* had played on the same dung hill with the men who would ask such a favour. We at least know for a fact that in some provinces, Brittany, for example, when the *seigneur* was going hunting, the village bell was rung, and *curé* and peasants, with their guns, hurried to the *château* to join in the sport. Brittany, in fact, seems to have been the earthly paradise of old France; there are few contemporary writers who do not comment on the good fellowship that existed between a Breton squire and his people, the feastings, hunts, dances, and festivities of all kinds in which they shared. But then Brittany was a *Pays d'Etat*.

It is characteristic of the age that the *seigneur* should have been more tenacious of his honorific rights than of those which were of some practical importance, and nowhere did he show himself more determined to fight for his privileges than in the village church. The word "fight" is here used not only in its metaphorical but in its literal sense, for it was by no means uncommon for two gentlemen to come to blows and even pistol shots in the church, and that during the service itself, on a point of precedence; and if the *curé* interfered, he was apt to get his ears boxed. Where a parish church was used by two or more noble families, the occasions for quarrelling were endless, and the probability of a brawl on Sunday morning was very strong; *seigneur* A's ancestors have endowed the living, but B's have built the choir. Which of them is entitled to the coveted distinctions of a closed pew, of being received processionally at the porch, of being prayed for by name, and of being given holy water, not by aspersion, but by having the brush presented to him? Only one member of the congregation could be so indulged, and in the case of a dispute, it was impossible to discover which *seigneur* was the happy man without taking the case to the highest court at a cost which was utterly beyond the means of either disputant. Sometimes the *curé* would join battle with his *seigneur*; he might have strong views on the matter of aspersion, and would rule that even the *seigneur* was not entitled to the use of the *goupillon* or holy-water brush; one *curé* emphasized his point of view by providing himself with a brush of such dimensions that under pretext of aspersing the *seigneur's* lady, he drove her out of church with her best finery soaking wet. We would sympathize more with the lady did we not know that her husband on an earlier Sunday had protested against the *curé's* attitude towards aspersion by knocking him down after service.

It is singularly difficult to generalize about the life of a country gentleman in the seventeenth century, but as we turn from one source book to another, we get a gradually strengthening impression of narrow means, dilapidated homesteads, frustration. Men of strong character fight with adverse circumstances, even to the extent of themselves labouring in the fields, while the weak live from day to day in drunkenness and debauchery. For all, it is a life without a future. The *campagnard* is reproached for living in the country: but how many of this class did so from choice? His critics overlook the fact that a large, perhaps the largest, section of the country *noblesse* were retired army officers, crippled with wounds and debt, who had come back to the village to discover that their return was hotly resented by the peasants; in the twenty or thirty years of his absence, a generation had grown up which pulled down manorial walls for building material, made free with the fishponds, and had become squatters on some of the best land in the estate. Already poor, the ex-officer was soon poorer still, owing to the litigation into which he was plunged in order to recover his property and to resume his seigneurial rights. What could he do but remain in the country to defend the remnant of his ruined estate?

A still less fortunate section had perhaps been too poor ever to serve at all, and found itself doomed to live out its days on much the same footing as the peasant. It was all very fine for the pension-fed Court noble to reproach his country relation with his indifference to the call of honour and the welfare of the state; but he overlooked the fact that in Louis XIV's, as in all armies officered by an aristocracy, the pay was quite insufficient for the necessities of existence, even in the cheapest regiments. A striking instance of the poverty of the country noble is afforded by the calling out of the *Arrière-ban* in 1674. This was a feudal cavalry force, a levy of landowners, in which each man was required to equip and mount himself for one campaign; but on this occasion so ludicrous and pitiable were the efforts of the gentry to fulfil their obligations, that Louis had to step in and provide the equipment himself. Incidentally, it was the last time the *Arrière-ban* was mobilized, and the report on its performances in 1674 is the epitaph of the old feudal chivalry of France—touchy paupers, good at looting, but no use for fighting. Soldiering had become a profession, and there was no longer a place for the occasional campaigner of the sixteenth-century type. Professional officer or farmer, there was now no other choice open to the *campagnard*, though in isolated instances a younger son would enlist in the ranks, or go to sea before the mast. The best of the country gentlemen, by dint of sheer hard work, managed to maintain themselves in modest comfort, or, at worst, in a precarious solvency, buttressed by occasional cash grants from the Intendant or the controller-general; but in only too many cases, the grandsons of the men who had kept open house and a pack of hounds, sunk into peasants who wore a sword and paid no *Taille*. Those who were both destitute and unprincipled "ran the roads," or in other words became highwaymen; or collected around them a group of broken gentry and adopted a life of organized brigandage and extortion; but sooner or later the heavy arm of the central government made short work of those who tried this profession. The *Grands Jours*[1] held in Auvergne, a particularly disorderly province, in 1665, afford striking evidence of just how bad things could be in a bad district in the earlier years of the reign; the facts brought to light by this tribunal, in the teeth of passive obstruction from a venal magistracy and a terrified countryside, go far to justify Louis' policy of replacing the *seigneur* by the Intendant and reducing the former to administrative impotence. For a system which facilitates the abuse of privilege cannot be defended on the ground that most of the privileged do not in fact abuse it.

As a sample of what was going on in Auvergne let us glance at the following cases.

There was M. le Baron de Sénéges, who had imposed his own

[1] The name given to a specially constituted court of assize, sent to a province which had got out of hand, and which was armed with special powers to revise sentences imposed by the local magistracy, institute criminal proceedings, give judgment in civil matters, and in fact to override the normal judicial machinery of the province for the duration of the court's commission.

taxes on his district, and collected them with the aid of a small private army of foot and horse: had established his own table of weights and measures: had taken by force the Church's *Dîme*, the property of the local priory: and had used his peasantry as slave labour. The third head of his indictment adds rather perfunctorily that he had "also committed two or three murders and several ransomings . . . conducted with an extraordinary violence." We notice with regret that he escaped beheading by seven votes to six, but he was sentenced to the confiscation of all his property, the destruction of his *château*, and banishment for life. Another gentleman of much the same kidney, one La Mothe, was sent to the galleys for three years, to the horror and indignation of all Auvergne—*noble* Auvergne I assume this means—and those with guilty consciences set out hurriedly on foreign travel.

Others, who had no means of flight, were reduced to soliciting their peasants for testimonials of good character, armed with which they retired to their manors and lived behind bolted doors for the duration of the assize. In the meantime the *Grands Jours* were hot on the trail of the Marquis de Canillac, described as "the oldest sinner in the province," a man whose exploits seem to belong rather to the realm of Spenser's *Faerie Queene* than that of France. Dotted about his estates were the towers of a dozen scoundrels whom he called his twelve apostles, men who had fallen so low that they had become nameless; one was called *Brise-tout*, another *Sans-Fiancé*, and so on. At their head the Marquis would ravage the countryside, "catechizing with sword and stick" as he called it; for he was a merry gentleman was M. le Marquis, always with a laugh and a joke on his lips, whether he was burning down a peasant's cottage, or persuading an imprisoned traveller to pay him a large ransom. I am sorry to say that he was too cunning for the *Grands Jours*, whose officers found that their bird had flown; and the court had to be content with hanging him in effigy and confiscating his property.

But we must beware of taking the Auvergnat *noblesse* as in any way typical of the whole of France: indeed the very fact that Louis found it necessary to hold *Grands Jours* there and nowhere else, is in itself proof that the province was exceptional.

Nor must we assume that all country gentlemen were poverty-stricken money-grabbers; the Duc de Luynes' *Devoirs des Seigneurs*, published in 1668, a copy of which was to be found in many a manorial kitchen, plainly presupposes a sufficiency, and indeed a degree of wealth, amongst this class. The *seigneur,* says Luynes, is to live economically in order that he may have money available for charity to hospitals, and when visiting the poor; he is to make frequent visits to the outlying parts of his estates, especially on Sundays, when he can meet all his people; and he is at all times to behave himself modestly and piously. Under the latter heading is included the duty of not keeping the *curé* waiting for him at Mass. And there seem to have been many *seigneurs* who profited by Luynes' advice. Some built cottage hospitals and maintained them at their own expense: many were in the habit of giving *fêtes* to the village: others would pay a doctor to set up in practice on their estates. The majority acted well by their people according to their perhaps rather dim lights, but however the *seigneur* acted, there could be no permanent removal of the underlying irritation which his privileged and irresponsible position aroused in the taxpayer; and when in 1693 his right of appointing the village judge virtually passed to the Intendant, the last vestige of the *seigneur's* claim to be the paternal ruler of his people vanished. Gradually the criticism of his position begins to assume a sharper edge, or rather a new shape, as the war years militarize his peasantry; hitherto, criticism of the seigneurial system had been concentrated on the anomaly of taxes exacted without any return in service, now his position as the only wearer of a sword in the community was challenged. The *seigneur* is still nominally the *homme d'épée,* the man whom the village subsidized to go to the wars on its behalf; but perhaps he has never held a commission at all, and the hard-bitten discharged soldiers in the village tavern suspend their talk over old battles to grin at the *seigneur* as, sword on hip, he passes down the street. "M. le Baron," they remark sarcastically, "prefers shooting pheasants to shooting Germans: yet we have to pay him for his military services." That ominous "Why?" is heard again, and this time a little louder.

When we enquire into the life of the country gentleman in his own home, we find little to satisfy our curiosity; days of hard field work, varied by an occasional journey to the market town with produce, or to see the lawyer about his latest lawsuit, make dull reading, even where the records survive. And they rarely do. If the squire was in moderately easy circumstances, he spent his time as such men have probably spent it from the beginning of things:

hunting, shooting, fishing, quarrelling, dicing and drabbing, all day in the saddle, retailing his day's adventures before the kitchen fire of an evening, or towsing Liselotte in the barn; riding out on a non-hunting morning to look at his fields, or to call on a neighbour with whom he happened to be on speaking terms, and killing the day with a dinner lasting three or four hours. Here and there we may find a French Jonathan Oldbuck who rides some hobby horse, usually of the genealogical order; more rarely still, one with a taste for *belles lettres* of the old sixteenth-century school; possibly one with a smack of theology, coupled with a pious hatred of all foreigners and heretics. But generally speaking, the literary occupation of the country gentleman was to compose petitions to the long-suffering Intendant, in which were set out what he liked to call his "rights" to financial assistance out of the public funds.

Marrying and giving in marriage afforded unlimited opportunities for wasting time with the neighbours, for the *campagnard* was not bashful about volunteering his advice to any neighbour with a son or a daughter in need of a partner. In some provinces marriage customs were still primitive rather than medieval; in one, we learn with astonishment that the simulated abduction is still the *vraie galanterie*. The marriage contract would be drawn up in the usual hard-headed manner, but then the girl's parents would arrange with the prospective groom that his bride should be sent on a journey in the family coach, and would be at such and such a place on an arranged day; there the coach would be ambushed by the groom and a party of friends, and the girl, screaming and protesting, would be thrown on horseback at the pistol's point. After which the cavalcade galloped off to the groom's *château*, where a priest was in readiness to celebrate the marriage. One young gentleman of a romantic turn improved upon the conventional arrangement by knocking a hole in the wall of the convent in which his destined bride was lodging, and carrying her off under the nose of the infuriated mother superior. That lady, apparently ignorant of the customs of the province, appealed to the King, with cries of sacrilege, and Louis XIV ordered the offender to be tried on a capital charge. Oddly enough, the Law failed to lay hands on the wanted man, and the judge had to sentence him to be hanged in effigy; on the very day on which the sentence was carried out, the newly wed couple entertained the judge who had sentenced the husband, at an uproarious supper.

In such a state of society any evidence of an aesthetic enjoyment of the country is hardly to be looked for, though there are a few rhapsodic passages on the subject of well-tilled fields and heavy crops which can hardly be called purely utilitarian. The first person to enjoy the country in the modern sense of the term was Mme. de Sévigné; but then she was an exceptional woman, and hardly a countrywoman proper. She has a foot in both camps, spending her winters in Paris, and her summers in her beloved Brittany, visiting Court occasionally, on speaking terms with the King, but more at home amongst her Bretons than at Versailles. There is a curiously modern ring about some of her letters from Brittany: "Here I have found May triumphant; the nightingale, the cuckoo, and the warbler have brought spring to my forest . . . I am writing to you this evening in the garden, where I am deafened by three or four nightingales, just above my head." In the same month "we have been to Issy, where the whitethorn, the lilac, and the fountains, gave us all the innocent pleasure we could desire." Later in the year she is planting at Rochers: "Pilois, my gardener, is still my favourite, and I much prefer his conversation to that of MM. les Chevaliers of the Parlement of Rennes." In July she is strolling alone in the woods until eight o'clock at night, "in a silence, a tranquillity, a solitude which it is not easy to discover elsewhere." If the weather be wet, she solaces herself indoors with Pascal's *Provinciales, Don Quixote*, and Lucian; or entertains a peasant who comes in to pay his rent, loaded with sacks, and producing canvas bags from every pocket. She has visions of unexpected wealth, but finds that his whole load amounts to thirty francs in sous. Her days slip by with a soothing monotony of pleasant routine; she gets up at eight, strolls in the woods until the bell rings for Mass at nine, then dresses for the day. Until dinnertime she gathers wild flowers, then reads or works until five, when she takes her second walk, with two books, one gay and one serious, for the second walk. And so, "thinking a little of God and His providence," she strolls until supper is served at eight: and bed follows after a little idle chat with her guests, or her women if there are no guests.

But one fears that few country *châteaux* bore much resemblance to Rochers, and that still fewer *campagnards* had either the means or the good sense to live such a life in the country as did Mme. de Sévigné.

VII

The Town

The latent hostility, or at least divergence of interests, between town and country, probably as old as civilization itself, is rooted in the basic fact that the countryman produces while the townsman consumes. No nation has yet evolved a policy that satisfies both classes, and the France of Louis XIV was less fitted to solve the problem than most. For the encumbering vestiges of feudalism which hampered seventeenth-century France at every turn, engendered a friction between the country noble and the town *bourgeois*, which appears scarcely to have existed in the contemporary England. To the English squire the neighbouring town was the social and commercial headquarters of the countryside, whilst to the French noble, it was a portion of his *seigneurie* which had enfranchised itself from his yoke, obtained many financial privileges, and was growing steadily richer while he grew poorer and more insignificant. He hated and despised a *bourgeois*, whilst the *bourgeois*, increasing in wealth and importance, asked himself why he should put up with the intolerable insolence of the beggarly squireen. A time came quite early on, when a noble who attempted to cane a *bourgeois* in the street would find himself rabbled and hooted out of the town; the noble's only possible retort was to wash his hands of the town and seek the company of his own caste in the fields. In inflicting on himself this voluntary banishment from the town and exclusion from municipal office, the noble made a grave strategic error; had he, like his ancestors, solicited election as mayor or alderman, had the noble and the *bourgeois* realized that they had common interests, the centralizing policy of Richelieu and the later Bourbons would have encountered an obstacle which might very possibly have modified the whole course of seventeenth-century history. Here and there a noble may have had a glimmering of such an idea, or at least had an instinct which prompted him to keep a finger in the town pie; Maréchal d'Estrades, for instance, was perpetual Mayor of Bordeaux; the Duc de Grammont, hereditary Mayor of Bayonne; and the Duc de Villeroi had a preponderant influence in the affairs of the City of Lyons. But, broadly speaking, the nobles withdrew from the towns, creating a vacuum which was promptly filled by the Crown. Henceforward, the towns were the King's protégés, his chief counterpoise against the nobility, and within the towns grew up a municipal aristocracy to replace the self-exiled nobles. And the towns, though they were far from being democracies, and were under the royal protection, tended to become centres of resistance to arbitrary power, and indeed retained a remarkable degree of independence, even under Louis XIV; the town of Provins, for instance, in 1682 rejected an edict of the Council of State on the ground that it was contrary to the liberties of the province: and the edict was withdrawn.

On the whole, we may say that a well-to-do *bourgeois* of one of Louis XIV's *bonnes villes* was the most comfortably situated man of any estate in the realm, but the fact that the constitutions and problems of no two towns are the same, makes generalization very difficult. And indeed conditions of life were often different in different quarters of the same town. Surrounding the town was the *banlieue*, often a considerable area of country; if you lived in one of the thirty-five villages of the *banlieue* of Rouen, you enjoyed the privileges of that city. But not one of the villages of the *banlieue* of Bordeaux enjoyed any municipal privileges at all. Inside the towns themselves the *faubourgs* would often pay the *Taille*, whilst the old municipal area in the centre of the town would be exempt; sometimes one *faubourg* would pay *Taille* while another would not. But even the least-favoured *faubourg* of the most oppressive town offered a better way of life to the ambitious commoner than did the countryside, and the drift to the towns was as serious a problem to Louis XIV's government as it is to many modern ones.

To become a townsman was by no means easy, for not only did the Crown seek to stay this drift to the city, but the cities themselves kept a sharp eye on intruders who seemed likely, in our language, to "come on the bread line"; as early as 1646 the central government had decreed that any peasant settling in a town must pay *Taille* in his last place of residence for the next ten years, while most of the towns demanded a financial guarantee from the intending settler. For instance, the municipality of Rethel in 1682 refused to allow anyone to take up residence in the town who could not pay a five-franc *Taille*. At Boulogne there was a domiciliary fee of twelve francs, and at Gray in 1698 there was a scale of domiciliary fees ranging from eight to seventeen francs according to the trade of the applicant. On the other hand, a man whose services would be valuable to the town was usually given free domiciliary rights, and was sometimes even offered a salary to settle.

The attitude of the *corps de ville* towards the admission of religious orders within the walls was a cautious one, for the establishment of a new religious house raised all sorts of municipal problems. Would the parish priest's income fall off? Would the revenue of the other houses of religious decline? If the order was a mendicant one, what would be the effect on the town charities? Teaching orders were, however, welcome, and so too were the popular Capuchins, for a curious reason. Fire brigades did not exist before 1699, and, somehow or other, the Capuchins had become expert firefighters; in emergencies, in which the modern Londoner dials "fire," the seventeenth-century householder sent for the Capuchins. Finally, all towns fought hard, but generally unsuccessfully, to prevent the Jesuits settling in their midst.

Domiciliary rights, be it noted, did not make the settler a *bourgeois*. For at this time the word "*bourgeois*" did not mean inhabitant of a *bourg*, and still less was it a derogatory adjective applicable to a political theory distasteful to the speaker. Qualifications were required to become a *bourgeois*, and we may perhaps think of him as a man on whom has been conferred the Freedom of the City. The domiciled man had civil rights, the *bourgeois* had both civil and municipal rights; to become a *bourgeois*, a qualifying period of residence was always required, varying from between ten and five years. At Paris, a *bourgeois* forfeited his rank if he failed to spend seven months each year in the city. In nearly all towns an oath of allegiance to the city was demanded from the new *bourgeois*, and everywhere a sharp look-out was kept for the bogus *bourgeois*; it was much easier in old France to become a sham nobleman than a sham *bourgeois*.

The *bourgeois* no doubt valued his municipal rights, which generally included that of trial by a special tribunal, but the privilege which was naturally treasured above all others was that the rank gave exemption from the hated and oppressive *Taille*. Amongst many other privileges we notice that the *bourgeoisie* often had collective hunting rights in the *banlieue*, and that at Paris, every *bourgeois* had a right to own a tax-free farm, providing that it employed two carts.

The only man not noticeably less well off in the town than in the country was the parish priest, and that for a variety of reasons. Firstly, many towns took the view that as he owed allegiance to an external authority, he was not eligible to become a *bourgeois*; the nature of town life rendered the bond between priest and flock weaker than in the country; and he had of course no agricultural *Dîme*, while only the oldest of the town parishes were endowed. Consequently, he had to look either to the civic authorities or to his parishioners for his stipend, generally to the latter; and whoever paid him insensibly acquired a right of interfering in parish matters which was unknown in the country, and whose extent can be clearly seen in an edict of 1675, which lays it down that the churchwardens, ex-churchwardens, and the incumbent, form the committee charged with the conduct of the parish. At Gray in 1697 it is the magistrates, one notices, and not the parish priest, who draw up the tariff of fees for burials and marriages. But if there is an almost congregational air about a city parish of the period, the parish priest seems generally to have been popular, unlike the monks and the higher clergy. For if the town was a bishopric, the bishop, too, had his troubles; frequently he or the Chapter would hold the *seigneurie* of the town, which involved him in endless quarrels with the municipality, to say nothing of the clash between seigneurial and municipal justice. But the bishop, on the other hand, held a trump card, in that he could usually appeal to the King via the royal confessor and Mme. de Maintenon, whilst the municipality could only invoke the dangerous aid of the Intendant. Dangerous because, whilst he was always ready to support his town against the local aristocracy, the Parlement, and the provincial estates, he was an adept at fishing in troubled waters. By playing off the military against the municipality, the *seigneur* against the magistrates, he sooner or later produced a situation in which all concerned awoke to find that whilst they had been quarrelling, the Intendant had become the town dictator.

Municipal government under Louis XIV shows the same lack of uniformity which characterizes every aspect of life, and which makes it difficult to arrive at a picture which shall be even approximately true for the whole country. Office by election, purchase, and royal nomination, government by assemblies of the *bourgeoisie*, government by elective assembly, wide differences in the composition of elective and elected bodies meet us at every turn; and all that emerges clearly from the confusion is an over-all picture of the Crown struggling for *de facto* control of the towns, with the towns fighting, on the whole successfully, for local self-government. In no case is there a formal absolute control of a town by the central government, and in every case there is a clear recognition of the elective principle within the town.

Let us look into the typical pattern in outline.

The townspeople fell into three broad divisions: an aristocracy consisting of the officers of justice, financiers, holders of Crown offices, and members of the Parlement if there was one: the merchants, with whom this aristocracy was often at loggerheads: and the artisans, who, by and large, sided with the merchants. The two latter classes were subdivided into trade groups, each forming as it were little republics, self-governing within the city state; thus at Paris the merchants formed seven *corps*, drapers, grocers, silk-merchants, furriers, hatmakers, and wine merchants, all under the general control of the provost of the merchants, who was the senior city magistrate.

The artisan class was split into *corporations*, very roughly corresponding to trade unions, and the member, called a *compagnon*, held a recognized legal status. He was forbidden to form any combination outside his *corporation*, though in fact he was often a member of some secret trade guild as well. It should be noted that while the artisan, the member of a *corporation*, was the social inferior of the tradesman, it not infrequently happened that the artisan was the richer man of the two. In addition to the normal advantages of trades guilds, both *corps* and *corporations* had the benefit of a recognized business court, that of the *Juges-Consuls*, elected by themselves, and empowered to judge all trades disputes. The *corporations* were, of course, more numerous than the *corps*, and in Paris, by 1673, there were sixty of the former to seven of the latter. Organization was a mania in Louis XIV's France, and to live in a town made membership of a *corps* or a *corporation* inevitable. One would have thought that at least the unemployed *rentier* would have been exempt; but not a bit of it. If you were in that happy position, you were automatically a member of the *corps of bourgeois* "living nobly," and liable to be elected to office, under the usual penalties in case of non-compliance. Even prison did not enfranchise you from guild membership; at Troyes in 1643 we find the prisoners, with the approval and indeed encouragement of their keepers, forming themselves into a *corporation*, with a formally elected provost, sub-provost, and lieutenant to undertake the proper conduct of their affairs. For each *corps* and *corporation* had, of course, its elected officers, as sumptuously robed as its finances would permit, its patron saint, its annual feast, and its communal Mass. Office-bearing in either, and indeed membership, put the individual to considerable expense. But the system was cherished as clothing the common man in a little brief authority and dignity; "you would have enjoyed," writes Racine from Uzès in 1661, "seeing the carpenter, Gaillard, in his red robe." We need hardly add that, this being old France, the various *corps* and *corporations* spent a great deal of their time in quarrelling with each other over matters of precedence, and that some *corps* and *corporations* had been at law with each other for over two hundred years; and naturally, where trades overlapped, as in the case of the bakers and the pastry cooks, there was endless friction and litigation. The aristocracy of the town quarrelled as energetically as did their inferiors, generally in defence of their beloved precedence, and frequently in public.

A ceremony which had begun with a pompous procession and a distribution of largesse to the *canaille*, might easily end, as did one in Lyons in 1679, when the provost of the merchants was knocked down with a halbert in the cathedral whilst trying to pass in front of the senior magistrate.

Entry to a *corporation* was by apprenticeship, followed by a practical examination, and the payment of certain dues to the guild chest. The members of the *corps* and *corporations* normally formed the municipal roll of voters, and by their votes the municipal government was elected. The sovereignty of the city had formerly resided in the general assembly, but as towns grew in size and business became more complex, an elective assembly took its place. Furthermore, the old general assembly, being a source of tumult and disorder, was looked upon unfavourably by the central government, which did all in its power to abolish it, and usually succeeded in doing so. By the middle of the century the usual, but by no means invariable, government of a French town, was by mayor, aldermen, and city councillors, the latter being partly *ex officio* and partly elected; thus at Abbeville in 1714 all ex-mayors were councillors, and in some towns so were all the law officers of the city. The authority of these officers, whether elected or *ex officio*, was collective only, and no authority rested in the hands of individual members.

These town governments, curious islands of democracy in the sea of French absolutism, had the defects of their qualities, the chief one being that the *corporations* or working-classes had the weight of numbers on their side, and thus generally secured a majority on the council. Not only were the artisan councillors accused of accepting bribes from their fellow-citizens, but their ignorance and stubbornness often gave rise to situations which gave the central government a plausible excuse for interfering in the affairs of the town. Colbert, for instance, complains to the King in 1670 that of the twenty-four Aldermen of Niort, not one is a merchant, and reinforces his case against the elective system by pointing out that at Condom in 1664, criminals condemned to death had been elected to the town council.

The number and functions of the municipal body, the *corps de ville*, varied as widely as did the manner of its election; but it is impossible to go into the matter in any detail, as may be realized when we discover that Paris, for instance, had more than three thousand officials, ranging from the provost of the merchants down to the controller of oranges. Even the mayorial system was not made compulsory until 1692. But the broad general pattern throughout is a mayor and aldermen, supported by a city council, and including under various names, a certain number of indispensable officers. Firstly, the *Procureur du Roi*, officially described as "the counterpoise to the Mayor," the guardian of tradition and precedent, whose duty it was to oppose the council in the interests of the populace, and who acts as officer of the Crown when the council sits in a judicial capacity. Next in seniority comes the *Greffier* or town clerk, a permanent official whose functions tended to become hereditary, and whose permanence made him the most important of municipal statesmen; he was the man who knew all the ins and outs of the *Hôtel de Ville*, and without consulting whom, no one dare act, not even the all-powerful Intendant. The duties of the *Treasurer* and the *Overseer of Public Works* require no explanation, and with the innumerable juniors we need not concern ourselves.

Louis XIV, by temperament and policy, disliked the whole idea of municipal government, and would gladly have substituted for it control of all urban business by the Intendant. But this would have been too ticklish a matter, especially in the *Midi*, the most municipally minded portion of his kingdom, and the part in which royal infiltration was most strenuously resisted. He found himself reduced to a policy of nibbling, coupled with bluff in the case of weak municipalities; he could and did use his immense prestige to influence the municipal elections, and sometimes went so far as to advise troublesome voters to try a change of air during election week. But on the whole, the municipalities struggled successfully against both his threats and his blandishments; we notice, for instance, that in the Dijon elections of 1659, the King's candidate for the mayoralty polled 318 votes out of a total of 1,420.

It was not until the 'nineties that Louis, taking advantage of sundry municipal scandals, appeared to open a direct frontal attack on the liberties of the towns. His edict, after a fatherly preamble on his desire to secure for his good towns that enlightened government which can only be ensured by having substantial citizens for municipal officers, goes on to make the leading posts permanent, and purchasable. But Louis was in fact not seeking to destroy the elective system in the towns, he was trying to raise money: and the towns reacted to the edict in the way he had guessed they would. In almost every case the towns repurchased the right of election from the Crown, thus retaining municipal independence; things went on just as before, and the hard-pressed controller-general in Paris was the richer by a handsome windfall. Henceforward, the intervention of the Crown in municipal matters is limited to the blackmailing of the city fathers by the creation of new officers which they had to buy up to retain their liberty; and as disaster thickened around the King, more and more offices were created for the express purpose of being bought. This, of course, rendered municipal taxes, or rates, as we should call them, more and more burdensome as the reign drew to its close, but there was a certain rough justice in this; for it helped to level out the glaring inequalities of urban and rural taxation. Where posts had to be purchased there was a salary attached, which was generally fixed at the current rate of interest on the purchase money; and the salary rarely comprised the total emolument. Most mayors and aldermen, for instance, got an allowance for the upkeep of their robes, certain traditional presents, and a number of valuable privileges; for instance, exemption from militia service and from the lodging of troops. Some of the traditional presents are curious; at Dijon we notice that the mayor's wife is entitled to a new three-crown hat every year at the expense of the ratepayers.

One infliction, common to town and country, was the billeting of troops, the greatest scourge of the period; it of course fell with particular severity on the frontier and lines of communication towns. The charges were heavy, sometimes as high as five francs a day per man, plus free bed and board, and these were aggravated by that social injustice which permeated the whole structure of society; generally speaking, the wealthier citizens were exempted from lodging troops on one pretext or another, and the burden fell entirely on those least able to support it. Its severity may be imagined from the fact that at Rambervilliers in 1675 most of the people fled the town, leaving their property at the mercy of the soldiers, rather than endure the presence of their unwelcome guests; and this was a case of normal routine billeting. It throws a sinister light on the state of the Huguenot towns under the punitive billeting system designed to bring the inhabitants back into the bosom of the Church, when the soldiers were given a strong hint to behave as badly as possible. In the country in general, however, things improved greatly after 1692, in which year the construction of barracks began, not as a method of easing the townsfolk's burdens, but as a means of tightening up military discipline; though as late as 1712 at Verdun, the town council is complaining of the ill-treatment of *bourgeois* by the soldiers.

What with billeting and local defence, care of hospitals, education, town finance, regulation and inspection of town manufactures, sanitation, roads, and a host of other matters which are now largely the responsibility of the central government, membership of the *corps de ville* was no sinecure. There was a full and active municipal life which was controlled with remarkable success, considering the inherent limitations of the social system. Nearly every town had its hospital, supported by local taxation, street collections, annual lotteries, and the sale of articles manufactured by orphans, who seem usually to have been boarded in the hospital.

Education was taken seriously and showed good results; as early as 1647 every town had its parish schools under the direction of the incumbents, but staffed with lay masters, where reading, writing, and arithmetic were taught, as well as religion, and, somewhat surprisingly, manners. It is by the way amusing to notice that the national love of office penetrates even into the classroom of the parish school, where there were twelve pupil officers, amongst whom we find a *receiver of ink and powder*. School hours were generally from eight to eleven, and from two to five, and in some towns primary education was both free and compulsory. But as usual there is no uniformity in any aspect of education, and there is, of course, constant friction between the rival guilds of schoolmasters; the *corporation* of writing masters fought the parish schoolmasters, and both fought the Salesians, who gradually acquired a virtual monopoly in primary education, boys' education, that is, for female education largely remained in the hands of the nuns and the lay schoolmistresses, the former being more esteemed by prudent parents; but it was not so much the quality of the education as the advantages of enclosure which dictated the choice.

Many towns had their universities, mostly of what we should call the "red brick" type, in which the *corps de ville* appointed the regent and the professors, paid their salaries, and attended prize givings and "literary exercises" in state; but the subjection of the university to the *corps de ville* was tempered by the fact that the regent and the professors were *ex officio* members of the town council, and that they had the sole control of the funds accruing from undergraduates' fees. But tuition fees seem to have been very low; at Troyes University, for example, in 1710 they were about seven francs a year. The most pleasing feature of these provincial universities was that they seem to have been genuine democracies of learning; at the College of Mans in 1668, for instance, we find that out of the forty-one undergraduates in the senior division, eleven were the sons of working-class fathers.

In most towns efficient policing was rendered impossible by the lethargy of the people and the welter of competing jurisdictions—royal, seigneurial, ecclesiastical, and municipal. When a criminal was brought to trial, it must have been a very stupid defending lawyer who could not enter a successful plea in bar of trial on the ground that the court was incompetent to deal with the case.

The modern reader discovers with some surprise that one of the most important police duties was the enforcement of fasting in Lent, and that these duties were efficiently performed; by an ordinance of 1648, hotels and restaurants are forbidden to serve meat in Lent or on fast days. In 1659 the Paris police raid a monastery during Lent and there surprise twelve monks dining off partridges, pies, hams, and many bottles of wine; and the monks go to jail. In the same year a butcher is put in the pillory with a leg of veal hung around his neck for selling meat on a fast day; and in 1671 the police are given the right to search all houses in Lent, even those of ambassadors, for forbidden articles of diet, and any found are confiscated and given to the hospitals. In the whole of Paris only five shops were licensed to sell meat in Lent, and during that period the licensed shops were operated, not by their proprietors, but by the hospital authorities.

Even the amenities were not neglected by the seventeenth-century *corps de ville*; if the Louis cult filled squares and public places with indifferent statues of the King, their presence at least awoke an interest in sculpture which had hitherto been lacking; but more valuable work was done in laying out malls and public gardens in the spaces liberated by the demolition of old fortifications. Most towns, however, drew the line at the introduction of street lighting, which the King had made compulsory in 1697; like most of the central government's legislation on municipal matters, the edict was simply ignored.

Intellectual activities too were not neglected. Where there was a college, its library was open to the public twice a week, and few towns were without their academies or at least their learned societies, which were the spoilt children of the *corps de ville*. These bodies were under an obligation to give free public lectures, which were usually well attended; poetry, rhetoric, and philosophy were the usual subjects, but historical and scientific lectures were also given. Parisians seem greatly to have exaggerated the stagnation of intellectual life in the provinces, for, if there was no important work being done outside the capital, the provinces can at any rate show a considerable degree of intellectual energy. Brossette, a Lyons lawyer who had the ambition but not the genius to become Boileau's Boswell, gives us some attractive glimpses of the life of the *bourgeoisie* in a large city in the second half of the reign. In 1700 he writes to give his hero the news that he is one of an informal society which meets weekly to read papers on Science and Belles Lettres, and that the first two meetings have been devoted to a discussion on the adequacy of Descartes' demonstration of the existence of God. But the group languished, and the manner of its resuscitation in 1709 is characteristic of the age. The Intendant steps in, gives them *un établissement plus solide et mieux réglé*, and announces that in future the society will meet every Monday under his chairmanship; and at the first of the new meetings, Brossette reads a paper on the burial customs of the ancients. At another, science comes into its own with a discussion on magnetism. But the monthly letter to Boileau at Paris is by no means entirely devoted to the affairs of the debating society; in 1706 Brossette announces with pride that he has been commissioned by the *corps de ville* to write the history of Lyons, and that his first volume will deal with the glories of his native city in Roman times. In the previous year—very Boswellian this—we find him worrying Boileau for a Latin inscription, to be placed in the Hôtel de Ville, and warning him that their municipal buildings are "beyond any question the most beautiful in France." From a previous letter we learn that the main square of Lyons, in which the council is putting up an equestrian statue of Louis XIV, "passes for the most beautiful in Europe"; in 1702 he describes in great detail the splendours of the observatory which the Lyons Jesuits are building; and more than once he reminds Boileau that Lyons is a far older and more famous city than Paris, and that all its doctors and advocates are *noble*. There is here little trace of that self-depreciation and sighing after Paris which was supposed to characterize the provincial.

Municipal government was least successful in that department of its duty whose efficiency we now take for granted, namely, public hygiene and sanitation. And Paris was perhaps the dirtiest city in France. Paris mud left an indelible stain on all it touched, and from whatever direction you approached the capital, Paris mud could be smelt two miles outside the gates. Only those who have travelled on foot through a Chinese town can form any accurate idea of a Paris street, and the resemblance between the two must have been remarkable. In Paris, the stroller would find the same narrow thoroughfare, carpeted in filth, with the central gutter, or rather succession of stagnant pools, choked with dung, entrails, litter of all kinds: the droves of foraging pigs and poultry, the dark open-fronted cavernous shops, each with its trade sign suspended on a gallows and almost touching that of the shop on the other side of the street: the mounds of human excrement and kitchen rubbish outside the doors, awaiting the arrival of the municipal cart to transport it out of the city, where it will be seized upon for manure by the suburban market gardener: the well-to-do in sedan chairs, whose bearers may at any moment deposit the chair in a midden for greater ease whilst expostulating with a clumsy carter. It was not until I first entered a Chinese city that I suddenly understood why Louis XIV's Parisians always wore scented gloves in the streets.

For this state of affairs the municipality was not entirely to blame. Paris contained several large *seigneuries*, each with full seigneurial rights, and within whose bounds the city was powerless to interfere; worse still, the Parisian *seigneurs* were not as a rule individuals, but religious orders, chapters, *commanderies* and the like, and such bodies are notoriously hard to move. Furthermore, all Parisians offered a stubborn passive resistance to all sanitary regulations, and as the middle of the street invariably formed the boundary between competing jurisdictions, any uniform policy of street cleansing was an impossibility, even had the inhabitants desired it, which they didn't. As early as 1644 it had been enacted that all latrines in the city must be emptied by the municipal scavengers before six in summer and before seven in winter, but with the usual result; the edict was reluctantly obeyed for a few days, then tacitly ignored, and as late as 1697 all household filth was still being disposed of by being flung out of the windows. In 1666 a further law was passed making the provision of sanitary accommodation compulsory in every Paris house; but several years later the city was found to have many tenements housing twenty to twenty-five families, with no sanitary arrangements whatever. In fact, generally speaking, no notice was taken of police regulations in Paris, or in any other city in the kingdom. Some little improvement is however noticeable after La Reynie became lieutenant of police in 1667, and especially after he persuaded Louis to clip the wings of the *seigneuries* in 1674. If La Reynie did not succeed in cleansing the streets, he at least made them cleanable by paving them, with the result that heavy rain swept away the worst of the dirt instead of turning an evil smelling mud lane into an impassable bog. An attempt too was made to get builders to conform to a municipal specification for new constructions. But right up to the end of the reign and beyond it, complaints from a not oversensitive generation about the filth and stench of Paris are frequent and vigorous.

That such a street loving age could have tolerated this state of affairs speaks volumes for its insensibility; for to see the stir, to reap the harvest of a quiet eye, to stroll and gossip, was the chief amusement of the *canaille* and the lesser *bourgeoisie*. The true Parisian loved his dirty streets, and was never happier than when showing them off to a stranger. Let us play country cousin to Berthaud, and under his guidance explore this vanished Paris, going with him first to the Pont Neuf, which offers the appearance of a demented fairground, with more than its noise; the bridge is the rendezvous of *charlatans, passe volants*, quack ointment sellers, toothdrawers, street singers, pimps, cutpurses, cloak-snatchers, conjurors, booksellers, and all, with the exception of the pimps, cutpurses and cloak-snatchers, yelling, "Come, buy, buy, buy," at the full pitch of their lungs. Equally vociferous are the proprietors of the shooting galleries which line the bridge, who offer you three shots a penny, with the certainty of your winning a magnificent prize. The prize is your choice from an old box filled with battered books, dirty rosettes, nutcrackers, tobacco boxes, flutes, broken masks, seedy hats, and a quantity of other miscellaneous rubbish. A very little of the Pont Neuf goes a long way, and we cross the river, which here serves the triple purpose of open sewer, town drinking-water supply, and the washerwomen's place of business; though by the way, the washing of clothes in the Seine at Paris has been strictly prohibited since 1667. But nobody takes any notice of the edict. Here we are at the palace; not the King's palace of the Louvre, for the word "palace" has not yet acquired its modern meaning; the King's residences are *châteaux*, whilst palaces are law courts. The palace is a favourite strolling place, dirty and ill-smelling, even by Parisian standards, but probably no more disgusting than the Louvre, where visitors relieve themselves not only in the courtyards, but on the balconies, and staircases, and behind the doors.

Complaints of its condition were common as late as 1670, and when in the 'eighties the Court moved out to Versailles, one of the things that most surprised visitors about the new residence was that the King there insisted on the same degree of decency and cleanliness which was to be found in a private house. We find the gallery of the law courts full of little shops, and here is the place where the bookbuyer hunts for bargains, undaunted by the fact that the bookseller, like all other tradesmen, sells her wares by personal canvass, and issues a deafening catalogue of the less salable works while we turn over her stock—*Cassandra*, Arnauld's works, Bellerose, Molière, Montaigne, Rabelais, "come buy, come buy!" Next door to her a girl is shouting her handkerchiefs and lace, pin boxes, and scissors, and from farther down the gallery come lusty praises of the next stall-keeper's Polish knives, English leather jerkins, and felt hats for wet weather, "as worn in Turkey"; while a rival tries to shout him down with his chant of collars and shirts.

Inside the hall of the palace the turmoil is nearly as great; here a lackey is caning a gingerbread seller, there we are shocked to see a man performing an operation which is not usually conducted in such publicity; not that the publicity shocks us, it is the fact that the man is in full view of a statue of the King. The room is full of attorneys of the lowest standing, and their ragtag and bobtail clientele brief them with a noisy repetitiveness and a wealth of gesticulation against which they are apparently hardened by long practice. The combined bar and restaurant of the palace is open to the public, and here we should have enjoyed our pint of wine, had we been able to shake off our hostess, who is infected with the general mania of shouting her wares, and plagues us unceasingly to order various singularly unattractive dishes; so gulping off our drink we emerge into the street to find ourselves in the middle of a fracas. Traffic, foot, horse, and wheeled, has stopped to take sides in the quarrel between that great lady's coachman and a carter, who has locked his wheel in that of the coach. Both drivers have dismounted to do themselves more justice, and the cloak-snatchers are turning the diversion to account, when a squad of archers puts an end to the entanglement with an impartial distribution of *coups de bâton*, during which we take refuge in a shop. We emerge when the storm is over, and a minute later find ourselves passing the police headquarters, the *Châtelet*; here it behoves us to be both swift and unobtrusive, for the place swarms with archers and attorney's clerks, who have a playful habit of identifying the passer-by as some badly wanted criminal and holding him to ransom. We omit the Place de La Grève from our sight-seeing trip, for we have unfortunately hit upon a day when there is nothing to be seen there; had it been yesterday or tomorrow, we could have had the pleasure of watching a batch of women being flogged and branded, or a selection of rascals turned off on the gallows—dancing on air as we call it. For this, too, is one of the sights of Paris. Dr. Patin, writing to the father of his pupil, Noel Falconnet, tells him that the boy has been working so well that tomorrow he is taking him as a treat to see a man broken on the wheel. Forcing our way through a mob of itinerant image sellers, picture sellers, piemen, begging friars, led captains, and loafers, we arrive at the Cemetery of the Innocents where the professional letter-writers sit on the flat tomb stones awaiting custom. That young footman has been snared by a pretty face at a window, and is commissioning a declaration of love in as high-flown a style as the writer thinks consistent with a fee of ten sous; the cookmaid in earnest colloquy with that other writer wants to *shoe the mule* as it is called, or in other words seeks his assistance in the preparation of a set of fraudulent housekeeping books; while the squint-eyed fellow in the shabby black suit wants help in drawing up a really taking circular advertising his infallible cure for syphilis.

From the cemetery we make our way to the thieves' market, a dirty, neglected street where the cloak-snatchers take their plunder to be dyed, altered, and sold, and where sometimes one can pick up a bargain. Here, as elsewhere, sales are made by patter, but the fences have a technique of their own. Commonly the dealer in stolen clothes poses as a retired soldier who has had some wonderful strokes of luck in looting; finger over lips he takes us into the darkest recess of the shop and produces a tarnished cloak, which he took off the Grandee of Spain he shot at Rocroi, wishes he had never brought it home, for its extreme richness makes it difficult to dispose of, even at a sacrificial figure. Or, gentlemen, here is something very special; this pistol I had from a man who had it from the lackey who stole it from M. de Turenne; the actual pistol of the immortal Turenne, just think of that! But we don't think of it, and leaving the shop amidst a shower of curses, we set out for the fish market, the *Halles*.

It would be interesting to discover the connection between fish selling and bad language, which is evidently not peculiar to England; for it is clear from contemporary accounts that "the language of the *Halles*" can be best translated by the single word "billingsgate." Berthaud gives us a sample of a quarrel between two rival fishwives, conducted with a creditable pungency on both sides, but with a freedom of personal criticism and simile which unfits it for reproduction, even in a footnote. A formidable body, these ladies of the *Halles*, and, rather surprisingly, much addicted to hero-worship.

When the Duc de Beaufort was thought to have been taken prisoner by the Turks in 1669, they guaranteed a sum for his ransom that worked out at about seven louis d'or per head for the whole of their guild.

Their present favourite is Monseigneur, who sneaks into Paris as often as he thinks it safe to do so, and is in consequence very popular in the city; last time he was ill, a deputation of the corporation of fishwives went out to Versailles in cabs, were admitted to his sickroom, kissed him, promised to have Masses said for him, and after dining at Monseigneur's expense, was sent back to Paris at his charge. A periodical saunter round the *Halles* is essential to the Parisian man about town who wants to keep up-to-date, for in addition to displaying that animation which is so dear to his heart, the *Halles* is the grand manufactory of the type of story which in modern London is supposed to emanate from the Stock Exchange.

We have now exhausted the free entertainment afforded by the capital, unless you are adventurous enough to go home through the Rue de La Huchette, but most prudent visitors decline this item on hearing that its only interest lies in the fact that it is the residential quarter for the cutpurses and cloak-snatchers.

Court, country, town, which of them would we have disliked least? On the whole one is inclined to think the town.

VIII

The Medical World

Throughout the seventeenth century the French medical profession had what we should call a thoroughly bad press; Molière has conferred upon its members an inglorious immortality, the satirists have done their worst with them, and in private correspondence the physician is almost always presented as a cross between a murderer and a buffoon.

Two facts go far to explain this climate of opinion; firstly, the physicians, particularly those of the Paris faculty, had not yet learnt the unwisdom of washing their dirty linen in public; that first rule of all professions, that dog does not eat dog, was broken by a constant war of scurrilous and venomous pamphlets which was an intellectual treat to the cynical layman. And the war of pamphlets was supported by an endless stream of appeals to the law courts and petitions to the Crown, nearly all of them damaging to public confidence in the medical profession. Secondly, one must remember that all writing, or at least all critical France, was Parisian by birth or by choice, and to the Parisian a doctor meant a graduate of the medical school of Paris University; for there was no privilege which the Paris physicians guarded more jealously than that which forbade graduates of other schools to practice in the capital. And unfortunately for the doctor's reputation, the medical faculty of the university was a target which the veriest recruit to the army of letters could not fail to hit with his first shot. For the Paris faculty, now in the fifth century of its existence, had sunk into a state of mind which rather resembled that of old China than anything to be looked for in Western Europe. Its unpublished, but none the less firmly held, creed was that medicine was invented by Apollo, improved by Aesculapius, and brought to perfection by Hippocrates; though if you were of modernist leanings, it was permissible to maintain that Galen had perfected the perfection of Hippocrates, and carried the science as far as human reason could reach. Granted this creed, the logical sequel followed: let the aspiring student learn the masters by heart and have their defence at his finger-tips; let him shun like the poison it was, all so-called "discovery" in medicine. For how, granting the premiss, could there be any "discoveries" in a science which had reached perfection more than twelve centuries earlier? The acquisition of clinical knowledge was discouraged for the same reason; it could only result in observing what had already been observed by countless forerunners, or else in committing the absurdity of claiming to have observed the non-existent. So, having written "finis" on the last page of the book of medical science, the faculty fell into a complacent slumber, only awakening from time to time to fall savagely on innovators, or those who encroached upon its privileges. Having chosen stagnation, its members now sat round the council table in their red gowns and square caps, disputing mediaeval syllogisms and complimenting each other in flowing Ciceronian periods on the profundity of their own erudition. The only strong emotion which now ever rippled those calm waters was hate; and it would not be easy to say who or what the Paris faculty hated most—chemistry, and chemical medicine, alleged discoveries, surgeons, royal physicians, apothecaries, each in turn had been fiercely attacked; but perhaps its permanent mental attitudes may be described as a deep loathing of other physicians and a profound contempt for surgeons.

Dr. Gui Patin (1601–72), who became Doyen of the Faculty

in 1652, is the fine flower of this school of physicians, and, luckily for us, he was a voluminous letter writer. A singularly unlikable man this Dr. Patin, who stands self-revealed as a spiteful liar, a dishonest controversialist, and a hater of all mankind; Paris, in 1653, he tells us, was "full of thieves, impostors, purse cutters, and men who prescribed antimony." Nor has the position improved four years later, when life in the capital is rendered intolerable by hordes of "charlatans, chemists, monks ('mutton souls,' he calls them), Jesuits, courtiers, and financiers." But particularly did he detest women, fellow-practitioners, and surgeons. Prefixed to the 1710 edition of his *Table Talk* we have an engraving of the author as a young man, perhaps executed when he had just qualified in 1624, which we feel at once is Patin to the life—the smooth, maddeningly complacent face with its wisp of black moustache, the faint smile of complete satisfaction with which he peruses a fat octavo entitled *The Wit of Gui Patin*, the two busts in the background—doubtless Aesculapius and Hippocrates—the scarlet and ermine robe and the square bonnet—yes, this is undoubtedly Gui Patin.

Amongst the surging multitude of hates which filled that malevolent head, perhaps hatred of the defenders of inorganic medicine was most frequently uppermost, and on the subject of antimony in particular, he can hardly contain himself; when his son, who had evidently taken the measure of his father's foot, chooses for his Doctorate Thesis the proposition that "the principles of the chemists are ridiculous and chimerical," his delight knows no bounds. And on his own appointment as King's Professor of Medicine he vows to himself "to protect his students from the impostures of the chemists." He hears that Vallot, the Royal Physician, is favourably inclined to the new drugs; whereupon Vallot becomes "a doctor, or at least a man who attempts to carry out the duties of a doctor"; d'Avaux, the diplomat, a patient of Vautier's, dies, and this time Patin brings down two birds with one stone—"Mazarin," we are told, "bribed Vautier to kill him with antimony"; the Princesse de Condé is "killed by the chemical poisoner Guènaud." But Patin did not discharge all his bile on inorganic medicines or on his fellow-practitioners; Dutch physicians, we are told, are "hangmen rather than doctors"; and he is almost as indignant at the quinine treatment for fever as he is about the use of antimony—"fools run after it," he says, "because it is expensive: but everyone derides it . . . quinine never cured anyone, and is now completely discredited." Sometimes, but very rarely, he even has a word of praise, or at least of exoneration, for another doctor; when Mme. de Mercoeur dies in 1657, he thinks her death was due to her disease as much as to her physician. But the balance of the verdict is neatly restored when he comes to discuss Louis XIV's serious illness in 1658— "He is in grave danger, both from the nature of his illness and of his physician." And let it be remembered that so far we have not heard Patin criticize any of the men he really dislikes: none of these doctors has graduated from that abominable den of quackery, the medical faculty of the University of Montpellier. In the conduct of his own extensive practice, Patin, we need hardly say, showed himself a physician of the most orthodox Paris school, convinced like his forerunners that bleeding and purging were the twin pillars of the temple; modern medicine he leaves to "charlatans, unfrocked monks, chemists, apothecaries and suchlike . . . as long as we have cassia, senna, and syrup of roses, it does not matter how dear drugs may be."

As we have seen, Patin is very free with charges of murder against fellow-doctors, but what we should like to have is a glimpse of Dr. Patin's own case-book. How many of his victims responded to his theory that constant bleeding was the only safe treatment for fevers, pains in the side, blood-spitting, pleurisy, and inflammation of the lungs? What was the subsequent history of the three-months-old child whom he bled twice for a cold in the head? Or of the man of eighty who was let seventy-two ounces of blood in a month, followed by "four good purgings," as a cure for a lung complaint? Incidentally, whatever the merits or demerits of Patin's treatment, one feels that his bedside manner would have been anything but cheering; for he lays it down that when seeing a patient, nothing becomes a physician like "a gravity, natural or affected, and a melancholy air." But it is perhaps unfair to single out Patin for condemnation, seeing that a heroic use of the lancet was common to the whole Paris school. Some doctors indeed went further than Patin did; for instance, one bled a baby of three days old for erysipelas; the King's own doctor had himself bled sixty-four times in eight months as a cure for rheumatism; and in 1659 one Dr. Boralis, at the age of eighty-one, was let blood eleven times in six days. Bleeding is the sovereign specific, and the universal precaution, even in pregnancy, when a woman must, whatever her state of health, be bled at four and a half, seven, and nine months. Bleeding is also the infallible cure for a toothache, though it is apparent that the public disbelieved this. I have spoken somewhat carelessly of a physician "bleeding" his patients, but it must of course be understood that he did not in fact so degrade himself; he brought a surgeon with him for the vulgar labour of handling the lancet, whilst he supervised, doubtless "with a melancholy air."

Ferocious purgatives were used as frequently and with as little mercy as the knife; the Dauphine was once bled twenty-two times in a couple of months; Louis XIII, in one year, received 215 doses of purgative and 212 enemas, to say nothing of forty-seven bleedings: and Vallot, Louis XIV's physician, pinned his faith on a "purgative soup" which, when tried on the King in 1688, acted eleven times in eight hours; after which even Louis felt himself "somewhat fatigued" and retired early to rest. We begin to understand the justness of the cynic's remark that Louis XIV resisted the care of his physicians for over seventy-seven years.

Even as late as the second half of the seventeenth century, medicine in the Paris faculty had not thrown off the trammels of astrology: and indeed in order to qualify, a knowledge of that subject was needed. Vallot, whom we have just mentioned, was a keen astrologer, a drawer of horoscopes, and before administering treatment, often enquired into the patient's lucky and unlucky numbers. In 1658 Louis' surgeon-in-ordinary advised that the King should be bled in the first and last quarters of the moon, "because at this time the humours have retired to the centre of the body." In 1699, in the final *viva voce* examination at Paris, one of the questions posed was "Does a comet presage disease?" and, more remarkable still, in 1707, finalists were asked, "Has the moon any power over the human body?" But in the latter case at least, it would appear that a negative answer was desired. We are in a superstitious world, lit here and there by a false dawn of common sense; for instance, in 1607, just one hundred years earlier than the examination question concerning the influence of the moon, a physician, and a Paris physician at that, had asserted that one way to reduce plague epidemic in Paris would be to keep the streets and gutters clean. But he at once vanishes into obscurity, overwhelmed with a ridicule as universal as that which would now assail a practitioner who should assert the then orthodox theory that plague was caused by "a malign conjunction of the planets."

Throughout the century the physician's best allies were the saints, who between them shared the care of every ailment to which the human frame was liable; no fewer than a hundred and twenty-three could be invoked in cases of fever, but the number dwindles to ten for those who suffer from convulsions. No doubt in the vast majority of cases, both physician and patient sought such aid with reverence and devotion, but sometimes faith seems to have degenerated into a superstition which was, to say the least of it, unseemly. To the modern reader it cannot but be nauseating to learn that the prudent man about town, anxious to avoid the results of incautious sexual promiscuity, should invoke the protection of St. Job. It is pleasant after this to turn the page and find that some saints, if one may so express it, had veterinary practices; St. Gertrude cared for sick cats, whilst St. Ambrose watched over the bees.

The first attack on the slumbering medical faculty of Paris was delivered by a very remarkable man, one Dr. Théophraste Renaudot (1586–1653), who had graduated from the University of Montpellier in 1606, and proceeded to build up a good country town practice at Loudun. There, in 1611, he caught the eye of Richelieu, always on the look-out for talent, who at once realized that there were possibilities in this young doctor, and took him under his protection. In 1618 he was appointed Commissioner-General of the Poor of Paris, and in 1625 he settled in the capital, where he soon built up as flourishing a practice as that which he had abandoned at the beckoning of the cardinal. At this point the reader may ask how it came about that the Paris faculty had allowed a Montpellier graduate to set up practice in its own preserves? Richelieu had foreseen that difficulty, and had in 1612 caused Renaudot to be appointed Physician to Louis XIII; no rule is without its exception under the *ancien régime*, and a physician to the King, or for that matter to any member of the royal family, could practice where he pleased, not only without a Paris degree, but, so far as I can discover, without any degree at all.

Renaudot is one of the most striking examples of that amazing energy which was so characteristic of the century; he seems to be not one man, but half-a-dozen, and a long essay might be written on any one of his multifarious activities. Setting aside Renaudot the doctor, let us glance briefly at his other occupations, always remembering that these were the side lines of a busy medical man.

As Commissioner of the Poor he was, of course, immediately struck with the problem of unemployment, for which no better solutions had hitherto been found than those of casual charity and sporadic forced labour. This was not good enough for Renaudot, who in 1630 opened at his own expense what he called the *bureau d'adresse et de rencontre*, where masters could seek workpeople, and the unemployed, employers; he had in fact created the first labour exchange. But what of the sick? Renaudot soon found a partial solution in expanding his labour bureau into what was in some sense the germ of the modern health service; within a short time there were exposed at the bureau the names and addresses of pious persons who were prepared to aid the sick poor, together with a list of Paris doctors and surgeons who had undertaken to give free consultations and treatment to any person sent to them from Renaudot's bureau. The ordinary man might here have drawn in his horns, but not Renaudot; soon the bureau is dealing with masters seeking servants, apprentices seeking masters, the sale of house property, a registry office business for nurses, and an information service on marriage problems and on foreign travel. All the services of the bureau were free to the poor and available at a small fee to the general public, and how varied were the services rendered can be seen from an advertisement issued in 1633, which begins with a list of houses to let, and closes with the offer for sale of a young dromedary "at a reasonable price." Our indefatigable doctor is already half-way towards the discovery of the pawn shop; and by the end of the 'thirties he is, in addition to everything else, a pawn-broker and a furniture warehouse proprietor. Early in the enterprise, the expense and difficulty of publicity by leaflet had become irksome to Renaudot, and in 1631 he had dealt with the problem characteristically by founding the first French newspaper, the *Gazette de France*, with, of course, himself as editor. This had needed the permission of Richelieu, and in seeking his patronage Renaudot had got rather more support from the formidable cardinal than he had either wished or bargained for. Richelieu had not only given his consent, but had informed the doctor that he would himself write the political leading articles, which he proceeded to do, except when he compelled the unfortunate Louis XIII to write them for him. The *Gazette* thus became virtually an official journal in which Renaudot had an advertising monopoly, and it was perhaps a wish to have a freer hand which led him to acquire the *Mercure François* in 1638; this he edited until 1644, whilst still retaining the editorship of the *Gazette*.

Here was, indeed, a pretty colleague for the dignified pedants of the Paris faculty of medicine, a fellow with a pen behind his ear, giving free consultations to the poor, with his pockets stuffed with advertisement proofs! But bad though all this was, it was for Renaudot the doctor that the faculty reserved the deepest of its hatred; and indeed Renaudot combined in his own person almost every single quality calculated to rouse the fury of the Paris school. To begin with, he was a graduate of Montpellier, and the Paris men affected to believe that at Montpellier medical degrees were sold for hard cash after a farcical examination. Nor was this the only or even the heaviest count in the indictment against the southern university; Montpellier had a long tradition of contact with the Middle East, and was known to have spoken favourably of the Arabian pharmacopoeia; the Montpellier men were known to set much value by clinical experience, to believe in the circulation of the blood, to have denied that blood making was the function of the liver; they were the foremost defenders of the use of antimony, and, worst of all, they openly derided the scholastic learning of Paris. Of each and everyone of these heresies Renaudot was a leading defender. A collision was inevitable, and it was not long in coming. On 23rd October 1640 the Paris faculty appealed to the courts to forbid the "empiric," as they now called Renaudot, to practise in the capital, or to prepare and sell drugs; a long and complicated legal battle ensued, from which Renaudot emerged triumphant. But his victory was shortlived; Richelieu, his protector, died in December 1642, and the death of Louis XIII in the following May deprived him of the post of Physician to the King. In 1644 the Parlement declared that all his non-literary activities were illegal, and forbade him to practise in Paris. But even the faculty could not eradicate the effect of his twenty years of work and propaganda; it could not prevent his *Treatise on Diagnosis*, published in 1642, from becoming the standard work on the subject; and it could not prevent the acceptance of much of Renaudot's theory and practice by the younger graduates of the university. Perhaps the most significant proof of his influence on contemporary medicine is that nine years after his death 92 of the 102 physicians of the Paris school were prescribing antimony; and, more remarkable still, Gui Patin's egregious son Charles was forced in 1685 to admit the fact of the circulation of the blood, in a letter which is a masterpiece of the Paris school. The ancients, he says, touched so slightly on this fact that their knowledge of it has been overlooked, and Harvey and his contemporaries may therefore justly claim the credit of having been *restituteurs*.

But the struggles of the old guard could not conceal the fact that Renaudot had burst open the door of the Paris faculty, and that a faint current of fresh air was circulating in that stagnant atmosphere; Gui Patin, before his retirement from practice, had begun to tell his patients that there was nothing injurious to health in the frequent washing of the hands, and though the up-to-date treatment for abscess of the liver was still a draught of pearls dissolved in potable gold, and Mazarin was being given tea for gout, Ranchin was allowed to express publicly his doubts about castration being an infallible cure for leprosy.

But if the new ideas were tolerated in debate, the course and syllabus of the Paris faculty were unaffected by them, and the long, stately and expensive process of degree-getting remained what it had been for centuries past. To enter the faculty as a student, the applicant had to be a Master of Arts, and a practising Roman Catholic with a certificate of good conduct from his parish priest. At the end of his second year he presented himself for his preliminary examination, which lasted for three days, and is described as being "on things natural, unnatural, and contrary to nature"; after which he had to deliver an impromptu dissertation on an axiom of Hippocrates. During the next two years the successful aspirant witnessed dissections, and once a week "sustained a thesis." Which sounds a more severe infliction than it perhaps actually was; for we must remember that in every examination conducted by the Paris faculty, what was required was not a show of knowledge but a display of rhetoric, not a knowledge of fact but an elegant Latin style. A *viva voce* examination of medical students resembled rather a meeting of a tumultuous debating society than an examination, and the room rang with shouts of "Distinguo" and "I dispute your major." We can perhaps best get the feel of a Paris *viva voce* from glancing at some of the questions asked in the second half of the century:

Whether the cure of Tobias by a fish's gall was natural?

From what part proceeded the water which flowed from the side of the dead Christ when pierced by the spear?

Whether the ninth day be critical?

Is woman an imperfect work of nature? [A question, by the way, calling for an affirmative answer.]

Are pretty women more fertile than others?

Is woman more lascivious than man?

Should a decoction of onions be administered to a drunken man?

The *viva voce* must have been a fearsome ordeal, even for a strong young man with a natural turn for classical rhetoric, for it began at six in the morning and continued until midday. In the cold dawn the senior examiner gave out an axiom, which the candidate was apparently allowed to study until eight o'clock; from eight to eleven he had to refute the objections to it which were put forward by the board of nine examiners, and the final hour was devoted to an interrogation of the victim on some subject outside the set thesis. Perhaps the crowning hardship of a gruelling day was the candidate's obligation to provide in an adjoining room a cold buffet, with wine and beer, to which the examiners, but not the candidate himself, could from time to time repair for refreshment.

Having taken his qualifying examination, the *de praxi medica*, the newly fledged bachelor paid a ceremonial call on the Parlement, the sovereign Courts, and the Provost of Paris, after which came his formal reception by the faculty. Finally, he paid a state visit to the archbishopric to receive the Church's licence to set up in practice. But before beginning to do so, most bachelors took their *Vesperie* or Doctorate examination, which consisted in the inevitable "sustaining of a thesis," followed by a medical debate, after or during the course of which, the initiate would be given a few hints on professional conduct. He must never visit a sick person without being summoned to do so: he must observe the strictest secrecy about what he sees, hears, or deduces in a sickroom: he must be invariably polite to his juniors, and always get up when a senior doctor enters the room: he must not visit a sick person more than twice without demanding to see his certificate of confession and absolution, signed by the *curé* of the parish: and finally, he must always make a pretence of refusing a fee until he has been repeatedly pressed to accept it.

The profession into which the new doctor found himself launched was on the whole a lucrative one. Fees were high and doctors few; one notices that in 1657 the population of Paris was 600,000 and that in the following year the number of qualified doctors in the capital was 110. But the possibilities before the doctor were by no means as good as these figures would lead one to believe, for the seventeenth century was the golden age of the quack, and Paris in particular was infested with the species; on the Pont Neuf could be bought a cure for any disease under the sun, sworn to contain the same ingredients as the doctor's potion, and at a fraction of the cost: *eau thériacale*, the sovereign remedy for syphilis, and *orviétan*, the universal specific, with its twenty-seven ingredients.

But on the whole, the medical profession seems to have been prosperous, and there were prizes to be gathered at the top of the tree; Fagon, First Physician to Louis XIV, had 2,000 louis d'or a year, a patent of nobility, the title of count, and the governorship of all the Spas in France. Great men paid their physicians proportionately, and in a wealthy private practice, a hundred francs a visit seems to have been the usual fee. But we must beware of imagining that the physician of the seventeenth century, even the fashionable physician, enjoyed the social status of his modern counterpart; an anonymous eulogist tells us that Patin's company was so eagerly relished at the best tables that he could rely on finding a louis d'or under his side plate for the entertainment which he had afforded the company: and let us remember that Patin was then at the head of his profession.

But if the status of the physician upsets the modern reader's preconceptions, how much more surprised he is by that of the surgeon, who in law, as well as in the estimation of the physician, was until well on into the century nothing more nor less than a manual labourer. The physician, who would not degrade himself by the practice of a manual art, called in the aid of a surgeon in much the same spirit as an architect might summon a plumber to repair a leaking gas pipe. The reason for the gulf dividing the two branches of the art of healing is not far to seek; for the surgeon is the professional child of the barber, and indeed was in this century still graduating from the barber's shop. Though here an explanation is necessary, for the organization of the surgical profession under Louis XIV is a somewhat complicated one.

The story goes back to the year 1371 when the existence of two separate classes of surgeons was recognized, and that of yet a third tolerated; all three classes still existed in the reign of Louis XIV, though the first two joined forces during the reign. By 1507 the medical faculty of Paris had succeeded in making two of the three classes its vassals, or rather serfs, and it was not until 1577 that the physicians renounced their right of examining candidates for a licence to practice surgery, whilst retaining their suzerainty over the surgical profession.

The first class, the surgeon-barbers, sworn surgeons, or surgeons of the long robe, was recruited by each master of surgery taking one premium-paying apprentice, who was educated at the surgical headquarters, St. Côme, which had been recognized as a college since 1533, but was not a portion of Paris University. The St. Côme men, however, aped the Paris faculty of medicine in every possible way; Latin only was talked, robes and bonnets were worn, and degrees awarded, in spite of the unconcealed anger of the physicians, who were anything but gratified at the obsequious flattery of the surgeons. Let us hear our old friend Patin on the subject—"Hair-oil sellers, miserable rascals, toothdrawers . . . they talk of giving licentiates, which is positively indecent in the case of these lackeys . . . conceited trash." And when he hears that they have installed an arm-chair in their hall for the use of their doyen, his fury boils over again—"the insolence of these lackeys," he cries. But St. Côme continued to imitate the faculty, some of the St. Côme surgeons carrying their imitation to the absurd length of refusing to perform operations at all, as being manual work derogatory to their dignity; the dyed-in-the-wool St. Côme man took with him to a bedside an assistant to do the actual work under his direction. So that, as a surgeon was forbidden to operate except under the instructions of a physician, the public was treated to the farcical spectacle of a physician pretending to direct a surgeon who was pretending to direct the man who was actually performing the operation. But we need waste little more time on St. Côme; it paid the penalty of its folly by sinking into an ineptitude in which it equalled if it did not surpass its model, the medical faculty of Paris. Throughout its existence St. Côme did not produce a single surgeon who stood high, even in the second flight of the profession, and ultimately its members reaped the harvest of their own stupidity. In 1655 they were forced to pocket their pride and solicit a union with their rivals, the barber-surgeons or surgeons of the short robe.

By the term of the treaty, the St..Côme surgeon was now entitled to set up a shop, while the barber-surgeon was given the freedom of St. Côme. But the union was more apparent than real, and it was the barber-surgeon who continued to secure the most lucrative of the available practice. This latter class had originally consisted of barbers pure and simple, but so far back as 1371 the barber-surgeon had been given permission to operate. In 1505 his community had fallen under the control of the Paris faculty of medicine, and thenceforward a physician, assisted by two St. Côme surgeons, had issued barber-surgeon's certificates of competence. The medical faculty viewed the union of the two classes with grave disapproval, apparently for no better reason than that it was an innovation, and in 1660, by dint of lobbying, lying, and intrigue, scored what was, on the face of it, a great triumph; the Parlement was persuaded to decree that, whilst the fusion of the two bodies was legal, the reformed St. Côme should be subordinated to the faculty of medicine, its members forbidden to style themselves doctors or bachelors, to wear the bonnet and long robe, or to call St. Côme a college: "the whipped dogs have come to heel," writes Patin joyously. But the whipped dogs were by no means so beaten as Patin had imagined. They riposted by resurrecting a decree of 1371, which placed all barbers in France under the control of the King's Barber, and carried their point.

Now by 1660 the office of King's Barber had been absorbed into that of King's Surgeon, a very important personage indeed, and utterly outside the control of the faculty of medicine or any other body; so that when the medical mandarins called a halt in their rejoicings to consolidate their victory, they awoke to the fact that their position had been not bettered but worsened. What had in fact happened was that the surgeon-barber had been put in the way of acquiring a better professional technique from his new associate, and the barber-surgeon had acquired a more assured social status from his inclusion within the ranks of St. Côme: and further, the physicians were no longer able to play one class off against the other by trading on their common jealousies, whilst any collision with the surgeons now meant a collision with the King's Barber, who was far too influential a person to be offended. The great victory turned out to be a Pyrrhic one.

The fusion does not seem to have affected the methods of entry into the surgical profession, which continued to be by the old two different methods. The surgeon-barber still took his paying pupil whilst the barber-surgeon's was the long and steep road to the upper ranks; but it was also the inexpensive one, and the one which provided the best training. Its chief drawback was the length of the apprenticeship: six years for the barber-surgeon's *garçon-chirurgien* as against two years for the ignorant surgeon-barber's ignorant pupil. On the other hand, the *garçon* not only paid no premium, but was lodged and boarded by his master, and, from the start, made a little pocket money from tips in the shop; for every barber-surgeon kept a shop where the *garçons* gave shaves and haircuts, and did simple dressings while the master went on his surgical rounds. The six-years' apprenticeship decided whether the youth would become a surgeon proper or remain a mere barber for life; if he was smart, and showed some manual dexterity, he would soon be more or less quit of the shop and accompanying the master on his rounds, acting as his assistant and dresser, and watching the performance of operations. Soon he would be carrying out simple operations himself in the shop, under the eye of the senior *garçon*. When his apprenticeship ended, the *garçon* became a *compagnon*, virtually a junior partner in his master's business, and as a *compagnon* he spent a further seven years. Then, and only then, was he at last in a position to take his examinations. Like those of the medical school, they were long and formidable; first came an elementary *viva voce* examination, conducted by the four Provosts of the Community, followed by the *tentative* and the *First Examination*. The candidate who satisfied the examiners in all three could proceed to take his final examination, called *The Four Weeks*. The subjects dealt with were osteology, demonstrated upon skeletons; anatomy, in which the candidate performed various operations on a human corpse; phlebotomy, demonstrated upon the poor of the town, who joyfully seized the opportunity to get a free bleeding; and finally a paper on medicine. Such was the ordinary *garçon's* road to a Mastership of Surgery, but the brilliant or lucky youth could reduce the period considerably by getting himself attached to a hospital; in that case, six years sufficed to qualify him for his master's examination, and the examination was of a formal and perfunctory nature.

In the matter of dissections, the surgeons of the day were faced with a formidable difficulty. That pampered child, the faculty of medicine, had in 1634 taken the whim to establish a Chair of Surgery, and had at the same time acquired a monopoly on the bodies of all executed felons, the only corpses available for their purpose. The faculty dissections, though open to surgeons and their pupils, were valuable rather to the budding orator than the embryo surgical man, and the problem of finding means of carrying out modern dissection at St. Côme was a chronic one. Let it be said to the credit of St. Côme that the surgeons there do not seem ever to have attempted to get out of the difficulty by the aid of the resurrection man; the normal solution was to bribe the hangman to allow corpses to be stolen from him by the *garçons*. The bodies so obtained were conveyed by night to St. Côme, and there dissected behind locked doors. And the courts came to tolerate the practice; in 1657 the penalty for a surgeon found in possession of a corpse was to be struck off the register; by 1683 the penalty had become "an admonition." The faculty of medicine, needless to say, neither acquiesced in or approved of this tolerance, and there were some spirited protests. In 1672 physicians and medical students stormed the dissection room at St. Côme and caught a surgeon and his pupils *in flagrante delicto*; but the surgicals proved themselves the better men. Headed by their teacher, the dissectors defeated the long robes of the university with heavy loss, and thrashed their auxiliaries, the Paris police, doubtless subsequently finding on the stricken field an ample number of subjects for the practice of surgical first aid.

If the path of the *garçon-chirurgien* was a steep and toilsome one, the rewards at the top of the professional hill were such as would make a present day surgeon blink; in 1686 Felix, the King's Surgeon, operated on Louis XIV for an anal fistula, with complete success. For so doing he received about 15,000 louis d'or, a country estate, and a patent of nobility, which included a special clause that he was not to be held to have degraded his rank by continuing in practice. And all this in spite of the fact that he was in receipt of a salary of about 1,200 louis d'or a year.

We may note in passing that the operation took place at seven o'clock in the morning, and that Louis insisted on holding his *lever* as usual at the accustomed hour of eight. Perhaps even more remarkable was the result of the operation on the courtiers; were it not so well attested, we should find it difficult to believe that above thirty of these sycophants entreated that Felix should perform the same operation upon them, and were annoyed when they were told that there was not the faintest reason for his doing so; while those who were really suffering from anal fistulas "could not contain their pride and joy."

Felix's success brought about a social revolution in the status of the surgeon; his ennoblement put an end to the taunt that surgeons were mere day labourers; and when in 1699 surgery was decreed to be a liberal art, its exponents began to assume the rank in society which they have held ever since.

Yet a third class of surgeon remains to be noticed, the *inciseur*, whose knowledge was empirical and often hereditary, and who was at once perhaps the worst and best qualified operator in the profession. The *inciseur* had had no theoretical training whatsoever, but far more practical experience than his more distinguished brethren of the knife. His practice lay mainly among the poor, and in his earlier years he must have been indistinguishable from an assassin; but when he had acquired a sufficiency of surgical knowledge by vivisecting his unfortunate fellow-citizens, a patient was probably as safe in his hands as in those of the barber-surgeon, and a deal safer than if he had entrusted himself to a surgeon-barber. The *inciseur* had no degree, but enjoyed legal protection in virtue of an edict forbidding him to operate except in the presence of a surgeon-barber: a restriction on his practice which was usually ignored by patient and *inciseur* alike, and which was indeed unenforceable. For the *inciseur* was largely an itinerant tradesman, working in the town in the winter and tramping the country districts in the summer with his bag of instruments over his shoulder, not disdaining to bleed a horse or a pig if no better client offered. He had a surprising number of successful operations to his credit and does not seem to have killed many more of his patients than did the other two classes. For it was a tough age, and patients took a lot of killing; in 1669 Hauterive, at the age of 85, had himself cut for the stone and survived it. A Paris monk, having undergone the same operation, set off on horseback five days later for Rome, and rode back again without suffering any ill effects; Fagon, Louis XIV's best-known physician—a Montpellier man by the way—chatted with his surgeon whilst being operated upon for the stone. Truly they were men in those days, and it detracts but little from our admiration of their fortitude to find how short was the time taken to perform this dreaded operation; Mareschal, the best surgeon of his day, could cut eight patients for the stone in half an hour.

What were then the camp followers of the medical world, osteopaths, oculists, midwives and dentists, were all under some form of professional control by the middle of the century. Osteopaths had to possess a St. Côme diploma, as had oculists, who were really surgeons specializing in the operation for cataract. By the decree of 1699, midwives had to be Roman Catholics of good morals, with either three months' hospital experience, or three years' apprenticeship to a qualified midwife; the midwife, too, had to hold a St. Côme diploma. It is interesting to note that in the case of a midwife, some elementary hygienic precautions are exacted: she must always remove her rings and wash her hands before touching a patient. But the most extravagant superstitions still were to be found in orthodox midwifery practice; if a woman had a fall during pregnancy, all ill consequences could be obviated by giving her a morsel of crimson silk, cut up small, and served in an egg; pain at childbirth could be minimized by placing the husband's hat on the woman's belly; and as soon as a woman was delivered, her loins must be wrapped in the fleece of a newly killed black sheep, still warm from the carcass. Among the upper classes the midwife was gradually replaced by the *accoucheur*, though not without protests both from the Church and the more conservative laity, who held that the employment of a man at such a time was grossly indecent; but when Clement not only became *accoucheur* to the royal family, but was ennobled for his services, society rid itself of its lingering hesitations.

Whether deserved or not, the dentist's reputation was an unfortunate one; "to lie like a toothdrawer" was a proverbial expression, and when St. Simon indulges in one of his celebrated tirades against a fellow-peer, he can think of nothing more crushingly contemptuous to say than that "he looked just like a country toothdrawer." Probably, however, he had in mind the vast army of dental quacks which swarmed everywhere in his day, rather than the qualified members of the profession; for the quack dentist was even commoner than the quack doctor, and considerably noisier. His technique was the time-honoured one of the glib tongue, the big drum, and what actors call the "feed"—the assistant who gets the worst of the crosstalk and is hooted by the audience. In the seventeenth century, professions were not so specialized as they are today, and many street dentists carried on auxiliary trades; one, for instance, sold a powder which was guaranteed to turn water into wine. But in spite of their reputation the dentists had made considerable progress in mastering their subject before the turn of the century, a stimulus being given to their researches by the fact that Louis XIV had a very poor head of teeth.

By the middle of the reign false teeth could be obtained, either singly, or in sets, bound together with fine gold wire; but they were for appearance only, *dents de parade*. Mlle. de Gournay is praised for the nice conduct of hers; at dinner she kept them by her plate, and inserted them *assez adroitement* whenever she was going to speak—removing them again of course before continuing her meal. Bleeding is, we need hardly say, the sovereign remedy for a toothache, but there were many others, of which spirit of nicotine seems to have been the most popular; and it is surprising to find that it was used by courtiers, although they knew that the King swore by essence of cloves. Cotton wool, saturated in oil of sage, poppy, henbane, or mandragora is also recommended, and here is a recipe for non-operational tooth extraction which the reader may care to try, though I give no guarantee of its efficacy: first boil, then reduce to ashes, some earthworms; fill the hollow tooth with this powder, seal it in with wax, and the tooth will soon fall out.

There is much, very much to be said against the misfortune of having to live in the twentieth century; but who would put the clock back to the seventeenth on condition of spending half an hour tomorrow morning with the village *inciseur* or the travelling dentist?

IX

The Art of Living

The growing austerity of Louis XIV's Court after his marriage with Mme. de Maintenon in 1684, widened a rift in French society which had first become perceptible when the King abandoned Paris fot Versailles in the late 'seventies. Not all Louis' nobility shared his distaste for the capital, and so long as the Louvre remained the chief royal residence, it had been possible for a man to spend much of his time in town society without any obvious neglect of his duties as a courtier. But the move to Versailles confronted the town lover with a choice: that of abandoning Paris for Versailles, or of abandoning the Court for the town; it was, of course, still possible to have a foot in both camps, but it was a precarious and fatiguing existence, adopted only by those who, whilst their fortunes depended on the King, found the lure of Paris irresistible. The clique which chose to cut Versailles and live in Paris was naturally a small one, for to join it involved giving unpardonable offence to Louis, which in turn presupposed an unassailable financial status and a total lack of ambition. It was a witty, eccentric, pleasure-seeking little world, which had revolted against regimentation, and whose followers were recruited, not for birth or even for wealth, but for the contribution which they could make to the common stock of enjoyment. In it lived, for instance, the *bourgeoise* Mme. Cornuel, whose *mots* had earned her a place in the best houses; she who had christened the batch of Marshals promoted after Turenne's death in 1675, "the small change for M. de Turenne": who, being asked why the notorious and ageing Mme. de Lyonne continued to paint and load herself with jewellery, replied "It's the cheese in the mousetrap"; who, when the eccentric Comtesse de Fiesque denied that she was in any way peculiar, retorted, "My dear, you are in the position of a person who has been eating garlic": and on her deathbed said to Soubise, who was boasting of the birth and wealth of his new daughter-in-law, the deplorable Duchesse de Ventadour, "what a splendid marriage this will be in seventy or eighty years' time!" Then there was the Duc de Nevers, one of the wealthiest men in Europe, who did his own marketing on foot and kept his larder in his bedroom: and his sister, the Duchesse de Bouillon, at whose hôtel the company was entirely masculine, for no woman with any reputation to lose dare enter it: the two Vendômes, and a host of poets, fast men of the gown, freethinking abbés, wits, and men who were as we should say, "something in the City." In short, the underground movement which in 1716 was to emerge as Regency France.

Occasionally overlapping with this world, but in the main sharply distinct from it, was the close corporation of the famous old legal families, the *noblesse of the gown*, learned, inbred, a little pedantic, living with sober and unostentatious splendour a life which combined something of the dignity of Versailles with the liberty of the fast set; and below this class came the wealthy *bourgeoisie*, the *rentiers*, merchants, civil servants, and men of affairs, if Mme. de Maintenon is to be believed, the worst educated class in France, but possibly the most comfortable.

Through the seeming variety of designs of urban life, Court, fast set, magistracy, and *bourgeois*, runs, however, the unvarying pattern of comfort sacrificed to ostentation. "Costly thy habit as thy purse can buy" is the general rule of life, and an unflinching acceptance of it strained even the handsomest incomes; the Parisian *seigneur* strove to model his household on that of the King, the *bourgeois* aped, indeed often outdid, the *seigneur*, and the shop-keeper imitated the *bourgeois*. In the higher ranks, establishments were extravagant and expenses enormous. Dress in particular formed a very heavy item in the domestic budget; St. Simon, who was no fop, tells us that his own and his wife's clothes for the wedding of the Duke of Burgundy in 1697 cost him 800 louis d'or. Let us glance into Audiger's *La Maison Réglée*, published in 1692, and see how things should be done by a *seigneur*. And, parenthetically, we should like to know more of our author; a man who was successively butler to the Comtesse de Soissons, lieutenant in the Regiment de Lorraine, and proprietor of the best-known lemonade and liqueur shop in Paris, might have given us interesting memoirs, but unluckily his book is entirely professional. Here, according to Audiger, who had always lived in the best houses, is the indispensable apparatus of existence for a bachelor *seigneur*: thirty-seven servants, of whom five are the personal attendants of the five senior servants, fourteen carriage horses, sixteen riding horses; each horse, we are glad to notice, must have straw, "as much for his amusement as for bedding"; and we also observe that the chaplain gets a third less wages than the cook. Each servant gets a free pint of wine every day, and the butler, who keeps the key of the cellar, has certain perquisites in addition; he, for instance, receives the wine in barrels of 280 pints, but is expected to account for 265 pints only out of every barrel; the lees of the wine are his property, and the baker has to supply him with thirteen loaves for every dozen ordered. On the whole, Audiger concludes, with a proper and reasonable economy, the total of a bachelor's household expenses should not exceed 1,600 louis d'or a year. Marriage, however, adds sixteen servants to the establishment, and if there are children, another seven, of whom one is the nurse's personal maid. Madame's arrival adds to the cares of the butler, for Madame will often eat separately, and for her dinner nothing can be arranged in advance—*tout s'y gouverne à sa fantaisie*. The provision of a *valet de chambre* for Madame is another preoccupation for the butler: for not only must he be *sage et fidèle*, but a man of much discretion. If the couple have a country house, this involves keeping yet another twelve servants.

The Intendant of a Minister of State, writing about the same time, has even larger ideas than has Audiger on the fitting way of life for a *seigneur*; for a childless couple he considers sixty-seven servants to be the minimum, and, like Audiger, he adds another seven if there are children. The Intendant considers that in such a household, the wages bill alone will come to some 2,500 louis d'or a year.

It is a relief to turn from the estimates of these great men's great men to Mme. de Maintenon's letters to her spendthrift brother, where we find ourselves in a domestic economy in which most of us breathe more easily. Mme. de Maintenon, who knew only too well how many francs make a crown, is an unsparing critic of Mme. d'Aubigné, her stupid, extravagant little sister-in-law, and generally replies to d'Aubigné's begging letters with an essay on housekeeping with modest means. Forty louis d'or a year is, she says, an ample dress allowance for Madame, which certainly does not err on the side of generosity when we consider the price of clothes as drawn from Mme. de Maintenon's own letters—a *robe de chambre* of flame-coloured plush, 12 louis d'or odd: a violet satin skirt, the same: a velvet sack, the same again: a habit, 4 louis d'or odd: a pair of corsets, six crowns. D'Aubigné had apparently brought some of his army bluster with him to Paris, for about this time we find his sister giving him the unexpected warning that Paris tradespeople cannot be intimidated by threats, but insist upon payment, even from the courtiers. In 1697 the d'Aubigné household consisted of twelve people, Monsieur and Madame, three women servants, four lackeys, two coachmen, and a *valet de chambre*; an establishment into which Mme. de Maintenon goes in great detail and satisfies herself that it should be run at a cost of about 450 louis d'or a year, inclusive of an ambiguous item described as "the magnificences of Monsieur." She even enters into the discreet management of candles at eight to the pound, of which not more than half a pound should be consumed each day: one for the ante-room, one for the kitchen, one for the women and one for the stable. And we note that she is writing at the end of September. Wood, fruit, sugar, meat—fifteen louis d'or a day of the last for the twelve of them—nothing is forgotten; well may she conclude, "you will agree that I know the ins and outs of a *ménage*." But circumstances had made Mme. de Maintenon a model of thrift, and I fear her domestic budget is one to which few housewives could have restricted themselves, and least of all Mme. d'Aubigné. And it is difficult to reconcile it with a contemporary estimate that a bachelor with four servants, who so demeans himself as to employ a woman cook, can make do on 200 louis d'or a year for all household expenses.

The ostentation of the seventeenth-century householder created for him his own servant problem, which was acute, however little we may sympathize with him in these servantless days. The demand for good servants was always in excess of the supply, and most great houses were in consequence filled with swarms of underpaid lackeys, who considered their master's liveries gave them a right to "hang loose upon the town" with all the arrogance of soldiers in a conquered city, with, of course, the consequence that lackey's broils became master's feuds. Often the lackey was not paid at all, was not *à gages*, but *à la fantaisie du maître*: that is to say that he received such intermittent gratuities as his master saw fit to give him. The knavish lackeys of contemporary comedy, the Scapins and the Leporellos, belong to this latter class.

To those of us who can remember the glacial contact between employer and employed in too many English households of yesterday, it is difficult to visualize the situation of a domestic servant in seventeenth-century France. Scolded, kicked, beaten, but with a liberty of speech which would not have been tolerated two hundred years later, the domestic's was then a rougher but a more human life, in which it was never forgotten on either side that the servant was one of the family. To our ideas, startlingly so at times. There were fewer haughtier men in France than the Duc de La Rochefoucauld, but he thought nothing of sitting down to a game of chess with one of his footmen; and, more extraordinary still, his sister was married to one of the Rochefoucauld footmen, the celebrated Gourville; and the marriage, though never acknowledged, was an open secret both in the family and in society.

St. Simon, rather unexpectedly, speaks with approval of the Duchesse d'Orléans' chambermaid, who was "familiar, like all good old servants," and did not mince her words in reproving the duke himself when she thought he deserved it. Nor need we waste much indignation on the habit of beating servants, for it was a pleasure which it was safer to discuss than to practise; the Princesse d'Harcourt was much given to it until she engaged a new maid, a strong country girl unaccustomed to beatings, and not caring much for the novelty: without more ado the maid knocked her mistress down and gave her such a thrashing as had not come her way since she left the schoolroom. And society was so amused that the princess did not dare to seek her revenge.

It is interesting to note that the first qualification for a servant is that he or she should not be a drunkard; but perhaps not surprising in a world in which drunkenness seems to have been common in the highest ranks, in spite of the King's example. For, until he was twenty, Louis drank only water, and thereafter, watered wine; and he never in his life tasted spirits. But fashionable society, especially that of Paris, did not follow his lead, and the women were as notorious as the men; the Duchesse de Berri, the Duchesse de Bourbon, Mme. de Montespan, and Mme. de Richelieu were all notorious hard drinkers, and we find even the charming Mme. de Caylus, after a quarrel with her lover, "drowning her grief in wine and burnt brandy."

The servant problem was sufficiently serious to engage the attention of an Academician, the Abbé de Fleury (1640–1723), who in 1688 published his *Devoirs des Maîtres et des Domestiques*, which seems to have had a considerable success. He had himself been tutor to the children of one of the Princes of the Blood, and knew intimately the interior working of a great house, and had evidently arrived at the conclusion that everyone employs far too many servants. Don't, he says, imagine that by employing a multitude of servants, you are showing charity, and don't make the excuse that you are helping to reduce unemployment. What you are doing is to save a number of idlers from the necessity of earning their bread usefully. And remember that the most numerous class of servants, the lackeys, being mainly kept for show, are the idlest. The prudent master will engage his servants very young, bringing them from his own estates if possible, and will encourage them to seek promotion within his household rather than engage trained servants who may often prove unsatisfactory; for he will remember that the *seigneur* who frequently changes his servants lowers his own character in society.

Let the master never forget that he stands responsible to God for the religious instruction and moral welfare of his domestics; he must keep a stock of good books for their use, and if he cannot afford a chaplain, must arrange for some virtuous priest to visit the servants once a week. And he will, of course, see to it that the whole household attends Mass every day, as well as evening prayers;

the stable staff will probably not be able to attend evening prayer, so the chaplain or visiting priest must provide them with written prayers to be said when their duties permit.

It is for the master to point out to his servants how comfortable is their life compared with that in the village, and how much easier it therefore is for them to fulfil their religious duties, seeing that they all have the greater part of the day to themselves. The God-fearing master never forgets that he stands in the place of a father to his servants, and prefers to beat, rather than to dismiss them; and he keeps the strictest eye on their morals. Not only are the maids' rooms as far from those of the menservants as possible, but the sexes have separate dining-rooms, or at least take their meals apart, and at different hours. But, adds Fleury, it is very wrong to hinder servants from marrying; at best, such hindrance leads to deception, and at worst, to deadly sin; and the master whose selfish rules have brought a servant to wrongdoing, will be held responsible before God. A sick servant must not be sent to hospital, for that would be to deprive a poor patient of a bed; the proper place for a servant who falls ill is what we should call a nursing home. But the ideal arrangement is that there should be a servants' sick-room in the house, furnished with dressing gowns, good books, and all things necessary, where the master or the mistress will visit the sick daily. If the doctor declares a servant to be incurable, Christian charity demands that the invalid be maintained in the house for the rest of his or her life.

If at the end of an agreed period a servant wishes to leave service, it is the master's duty to settle him in some honest trade and keep an eye on his future well-being; and old servants who have gone into business should always be invited to a meal with the domestic staff on feast days.

Fleury speaks with approval of the rules of conduct laid down for the household of his own former employer, the Prince de Conti; duelling, cards, dice, the theatre, blasphemy, and impiety were strictly forbidden, and every servant had to be indoors by six in the winter and by eight in summer, when the doors were locked for the night. Incidentally, we notice that, as in all houses great and small, the doors were kept shut during family prayers and whilst meals were in progress; at those hours it was not even permitted to pay the formal call which consisted in writing your name in the visitor's book.

The daily time-table of the pages gives us a glimpse into what was really the public school of a boy of noble birth in the first half of the century. These boys rise at six and proceed to the chapel for religious instruction before Mass; after Mass comes breakfast, followed by fencing, reading, and study, until dinner. After dinner there are two hours for recreation. On fête days, but apparently on no others, the boys attend Vespers; then follows supper and recreation until household prayer time. At ten the pages go to bed.

Fleury agrees with all contemporaries in insisting on the duty of showing politeness to servants. But it was hardly necessary to emphasize this point. Probably no fact about the *Grand Monarque* is better known than that he never passed a charwoman at Versailles without taking off his hat to her, and society was quick to catch his tone; to Mme. de Maintenon, for instance, the most glaring evidence of her sister-in-law's vulgarity is that she will accept something at table from a footman without thanking him for his service. It is a pleasant trait in the century, even if the point of good breeding is sometimes exaggerated to absurdity; St. Simon, driving back from Fontainebleau with his wife and two maids in the carriage, had the misfortune to meet the Duc de Coislin, the politest man in France, broken down on the road, and of course stopped to offer him a lift. As the exchange of preliminary compliments threatened to be interminable, St. Simon was forced to get out into the mud himself and entreat his fellow-peer to join him. Only then did Coislin discover the presence of the maids, "the young ladies," as he called them; he would not think of depriving them of their places: the war of compliment began all over again, in spite of St. Simon's insistence that the "young ladies" could follow on in Coislin's coach when it had been repaired. After a long delay Coislin was tricked into entering St. Simon's coach, where St. Simon had to hold him down to prevent him from climbing out of the window to offer a final apology to the maids.

Stories of the Duc de Coislin's excessive politeness are numerous; at his Paris hôtel he once poured out so many compliments on a German visitor that the German, in despair, bolted from the room and locked the door behind him rather than continue the argument as to whether his host should re-conduct him to his carriage or no. When the German reached the courtyard there was Coislin again, who had rejoined him by jumping out of the window, and had put his thumb out of joint in so doing. The King's Surgeon set the thumb, and there ensued a polite struggle between the duke and the medical man as to who should open the door: at the end of the contest Coislin found that his thumb was out of joint again. To his family he seems to have been a constant source of exasperation, and his brother the Chevalier once took his revenge upon him in a manner which is entirely characteristic of the century. The two had spent the night in a provincial town, and in the morning before entering the coach, the duke must needs pay a few well-turned compliments to his hostess; the rain poured down on the bareheaded brothers, and there seemed no reason why the duke's speech should ever end. So the Chevalier went indoors, re-emerged some time later, and at last got his brother to enter his carriage. After they had gone a few miles, the Chevalier remarked that he would like to know what their hostess now thought of his brother's politeness. "Why?" said the duke. "Because," said the Chevalier, "while you were making that infernal speech of yours, I slipped up to your bedroom and put the floor to a use for which it was not intended."

But Coislin's behaviour was merely an exaggeration of a code of elaborate politeness which governed intercourse between all classes and did something to cloak a fundamental grossness. The numerous books on etiquette which were published during the reign show both the demand for such works and the seriousness with which the subject was taken. One of the best of them, Courtin's *Nouveau Traité de la Civilité*, published in 1675, has much to tell us of the art of paying and receiving calls; if a lady calls upon you, you must put on your sword and mantle, go out to her carriage, lead her in, give her an arm-chair, and sit down yourself upon a stool; and when the visit is at an end, re-conduct her to her carriage and stand in the street bare-headed until the carriage is out of sight. Here the matter is comparatively simple, because with a lady there can be no contest in civility; but if you are being visited by a man, or visiting one, the matter is not so straightforward. Should, for instance, your host insist upon seeing you off, you in your turn must insist upon his reentering his house before you get into your carriage. If he refuses to do so, there is then nothing for it but for you to set off on foot, making a sign to your coachman to follow you, and you must not get into your carriage until you are out of sight of the house. And note by the way while you are plodding along, that should you meet a friend, it is the height of bad manners to ask him where he has come from, or where he is going to.

Some of Courtin's "do's" and "don'ts" for social intercourse throw a curious light on contemporary society; a woman, we learn, in mixed company, should not pull her skirts up to her thighs to warm her legs at the fire, and a man should not enter a room with any portion of his clothing unbuttoned which the tailor intended to be buttoned; a man should not fidget with his hat, gloves, and stick, nor with his hostess' fire-irons; he must not yawn, spit, take snuff, or offer his hostess the loan of his handkerchief. In telling your host a story, don't take him by a button, or underline your point by hitting him in the stomach. It is ill-bred to say "God bless you" out loud when anyone sneezes, but correct to say it silently to yourself, at the same time taking off your hat; but otherwise it is grossly uncivil to take off your hat in the interior of the house, except when you speak to a person of the very highest quality, when it becomes a mark of respect. Above all, never in any circumstances sit down to a meal without your hat on; but until the whole company is seated, you should keep your hat in your hand. At dinner, in addition to your hat, you wear your sword and your cloak. But there are exceptions to the rule of keeping your hat on indoors; for instance, civility demands that you go hatless in the ante-room. And should you happen to be an army officer, and have the honour of eating at the King's table in the field, remember that the King will be bareheaded and everyone else will have his hat on his head.

Then, as now, all Frenchmen took their meals seriously, and amongst the Parisian upper *bourgeoisie* eating held an even more important place in life than it did at Versailles. Or at any rate, there were more meals.

Louis, as we have seen, contented himself with two meals a day, but by the end of the 'sixties the wealthy Parisian was having a *desjeune* before his midday dinner, and a *gousté* between his dinner and his eight o'clock supper. More than one contemporary work survives on the elaborate ceremonial of eating and drinking, and from them we get some vivid impressions of life in a rich household of the period. Table laying already showed a high degree of sophistication; the cloth, of Dutch linen, must touch the ground on all sides, for its overhangs must be long enough to serve the diners for a common napkin. Such at least was the original object, but a separate napkin for each guest came into use about 1660, and within a few years the efficient footman had to know the twenty-seven different ways of folding it. By about 1648 the plate had replaced the old slice of bread which had formerly done duty for it, and by 1655 it had become customary to lay clean plates for each course.

In some ways life at Versailles was more primitive than at Paris; Louis XIV ate with his fingers to the end of his life, but at Paris the fork was in fairly common use by 1648. If we found ourselves the dinner guests of a wealthy Parisian in the second half of the century, we should find nothing odd about the room, for draughts and uncomfortable chairs are unfortunately not peculiar to the age of Louis XIV. The tapestry hangings of our host's father would have been replaced by wall paper, as expensive as Gobelin's tapestry, and of some light colour, probably blue; for Mme. de Rambouillet's refusal to content herself with the orthodox monotony of reds and browns for interior decoration has now become universal. Over the mantelpiece hangs perhaps a framed family tree, and elsewhere a religious painting or two. Nor would the table layout strike us as unfamiliar; in the centre would be the *surtout*, a piece of goldsmith's work something like a soup tureen, but having a base large enough to accommodate salt, pepper, spices, and toothpicks. At the right of our plate we should find a spoon, fork, and a knife with its cutting edge turned towards the plate: the knife having a white bone handle, though in most houses a set of black-handled knives was kept for use during Lent. In addition to the *surtout*, the room might be decorated with a *nef*, an elaborate ornamental piece, perhaps a gold model of a full-rigged ship; this on the sideboard not on the table. The *nef* had originally been the receptacle which held the King's knife and spoon, and had only recently become an adornment for the commoner's table.

In the earlier part of the reign soup was not served in plates but in a two-handled porringer, from which each guest drank in turn; and even when tureen and soup plates came into existence, everyone dipped into the tureen with his own soup spoon. Sixteen ninety-five seems to have been a revolutionary year in matters of table deportment; Coulanges then expresses his disgust at a lady helping him to sauce with a spoon which she has just removed from her own mouth for the purpose, and at the same time the Duc de Montausier, who was held to carry cleanliness to the point of absurdity, invented the soup ladle.

Until well on into the second half of the century, meat was served cut into convenient morsels, to which the diners helped themselves with their fingers; it is true that as early as 1658 Mademoiselle expresses her disgust at the King allowing other people to put their fingers in his dish, but her objection is obviously based on its being a sacrilegious, not an unhygienic, practice. A casual remark of Mme. de Motteville's shows how very nasty the habit would have seemed to our eyes: when the Queen of Sweden visited the French Court, Mme. de Motteville looked forward to criticizing the beauty of her hands, which was famous throughout Europe, but was unable to do so at dinner, because they were so encrusted with dirt that it was not possible to judge of their shape.

By 1681 a dinner seems to have conformed very roughly to modern ideas, if we may take the meal offered by Louvois to the Queen in that year to have been typical. It was of four "services," or as we should say, courses, but the courses were gargantuan; the first service consisted of forty plates, that is forty dishes, of entrée: the second, of forty plates of roasts and salads: the third was of hot and cold *entremets:* and the fourth was "an exquisite and rare dessert." Melon was served before, and oranges with the roasts.

Here is a supper menu of 1662:

1st Service

Centre Plate:	Oille. [A stew of spiced duck, partridges, pigeons, etc.]
Entrées:	Partridge in cabbage: fillet of duck: galantine of chicken: fillet of beef with cucumber.
Hors d'œuvre:	Chickens cooked on hot embers.

2nd Service

Centre Plate:	Quarter of veal.
Roasts:	Two hens and four rabbits.
Hors d'œuvre:	Two salads.

3rd Service

Centre Plate:	Partridge pie.
Plats Moyens:	Vegetables and fruits.
Hors d'œuvre:	Fried sheep's testicles: slices of roast beef spread with kidneys, onions, and cheese.

It is not clear whether this is what we should call an *à la carte*
menu, or whether it is in fact a choice of three distinct suppers,
or whether the guests worked their way through the whole bill of
fare: but it seems a pretty satisfying meal, whatever interpretation
we accept.

By this time the habit of sharing one or two drinking cups
amongst the whole company had disappeared, and each guest had
his own vessel; not on the table, but on the buffet behind him,
from which he had to demand it whenever he wished to drink.
A nice test of manners this for the thirsty diner, for it was bad
form to call for wine out loud: you must do so in a low voice, or
better still, by making a sign to a lackey.

Apropos of drinks, we notice that old wine seems to have been
unknown to the seventeenth century, and that most of the wine
drunk at Parisian tables came from the environs of Paris. Champagne had begun the century as a still red wine, and had somehow
changed itself into the modern beverage by 1695. Cider was well
known, but was thought by right-minded men to be God's judgment on the Normans for their rascality. Liqueurs, but apparently
not coffee, were served after dessert, the best known being *Rossolis*,
made from brandy and certain spices.

Courtin and others have ably charted the many reefs on which
the unwary diner might make shipwreck. Here are a few of them.
When the priest, or in his absence the youngest child, had said
grace, and you sit down, with the host not at the head but in the
middle of the table, bowls of scented water will circulate, in which
you are expected to wash your hands; but don't dip in the same
bowl as your host, or with anyone of a higher quality than yourself, unless you are specially invited to do so. If you must spit at
table, turn your head aside and do it dextrously; don't tear your
meat like a rustic, but cut it with your knife, and the same rule
applies to your bread. Don't put your elbows on the table; fill
your mouth so full that you can't answer a question; or eat so
much that you give yourself the hiccups. Don't help yourself to salt
with a greasy knife; eat fish with your fork or your fingers; don't
dip into a dish before your betters, and always wipe your spoon
before dipping into a fresh dish, for there are people so fastid-
iously constituted that they object to eating what you have disar-
ranged with a spoon which you have just taken out of your mouth.
Don't make a noise when eating, don't blow on your soup to cool

it, and remember that to lick your fingers is the height of impropriety, only surpassed by the *lâcheté* of picking your teeth with your knife or fork, or rinsing out your mouth in full view of persons of higher rank than yourself. If you must clean your teeth, do so with the toothpicks and silk thread provided for the purpose.

To discuss the menu, or for that matter, to talk about eating during dinner, is not considered the best of form, nor should you tell your fellow-guests that you never eat such and such a dish, or don't care for so and so. It is uncivil to offer to carve. If you are the host, don't press your guests to eat, but let them enjoy their victuals as they please. If boiled eggs appear on the menu, remember that a well-bred person cuts off the small end, not the big, and if there is no cream for the strawberries, pour some wine over them. And finally, don't at the end of dinner pocket sweets, fruit and suchlike to take home with you. If you are the host, remember that you give the signal that the meal is over by rising and bowing to the principal guest.

Failure to observe the etiquette of the dinner table could involve the delinquent in unpleasant consequences. In 1715 an adventurous lackey dubbed himself the Marquis de Ruffec, and set out on a tour of the country houses of the *Midi*; all went well until one day, whilst dining with the Commandant of Bayonne, he helped himself to olives with a fork. The commandant saw it, had him arrested as soon as dinner was over, and denounced him as an impostor.

Cookery books were as common as books on etiquette, and even better thumbed; Lavarenne's ran through eight editions between 1651 and 1726, and five editions of Bonnefons' book were called for in eighty years. In the 'seventies an increasing fastidiousness in matters of cuisine must have become apparent judging from Robert's cookery book of 1674, in which he says that "we no longer have confused heaps of different kinds of meats, mountainous roasts, and *entremets* oddly served." The "roast," by the way, is not what we should call a "joint," but something much more resembling an immense mixed grill; Boileau, for instance, mentions a "roast" which consisted of a hare, six chickens, three rabbits, and six pigeons, all served on the same dish.

Were provisions more plentiful and cheaper, one might toy with the idea of giving a seventeenth-century dinner, but I doubt if we should enjoy it; one fears the guests' reactions would be similar to those of the eighteenth-century Englishman who, confronted with a helping of peacock stuffed with asafoetida at a reconstructed Roman banquet, was betrayed into the ejaculation, "Lord, what beastly fellows these Romans were!" To begin with, everything must have been much overdone, especially all boiled meats; the *ragoûts* of which Louis XIV and his subjects were so fond, would, I fancy, have struck us as an unsuccessful attempt at mutton broth, for the recipe is to place a number of different kinds of flesh and fowl in a cauldron, add a large quantity of spice, and stew for ten or twelve hours; this sounds unpromising, and I do not think that the dish would be saved at the twelfth hour by a lavish top dressing of musk, amber, and assorted perfumes.

Amongst the recipes for *ragoûts* we look in vain for any mention of lamb, which seems to have been unpopular, though its complement, green peas, was one of the dishes most prized by *gourmets*; "we are still on the chapter of peas," writes Mme. de Maintenon from Marly in 1696: "impatience to eat them, the pleasure of having eaten them, and the anticipation of eating them again are the three subjects I have heard very thoroughly dealt with. . . . Some women having supped, and supped well, at the King's table, have peas waiting for them in their rooms to eat before going to bed." Early green peas were a luxury on which no expense was spared; in 1660 Louis XIV got a consignment from Italy, packed in herbs and roses to keep them fresh.

The consumption of fish was, generally speaking, confined to fast days, though oysters were popular, either served raw, or grilled in their shells with butter and pepper: and sardines are recommended to bring out the flavour of wine. Salmon, too, seems to have been eaten by choice, not of necessity, and is mentioned with ham and salted tongues as one of the items which at a dinner party may remain in the centre of the table throughout the meal; but the less noble fish figure in a well designed feast as a kickshaw to be served for form's sake when the demand for meat and game is slackening. The only prominent fish eater by choice whom I know of was the Duc de Vendôme, and he preferred it stale to fresh and stinking to stale, a perversity of taste which ultimately killed him.

Much as the Parisian esteemed good eating and drinking, he loved talk even more; and conversation is essentially an indoor game. Such being his tastes it followed that his outdoor amusements were few. Indeed, a contemporary doctor congratulates himself on the sedentary habits of the people of Paris, which, coupled with their *gourmandise*, made the Paris practitioner the wealthiest in the kingdom. It is therefore with considerable surprise that we find bathing to have been a popular amusement with both sexes; if indeed it was regarded as a pleasure, and not as a duty imposed upon the loyal citizen by the fact that the King was fond of the river, and gave several bathing parties every summer in his earlier years. But however that may have been, there were well patronized bathing places scattered along the Seine within easy reach of the city; the men seem to have bathed where they pleased, but women could do so only in the open air baths which were made by fencing in a portion of the river. Total or even partial immersion was, however, not popular except in the height of summer, though as early as 1675 the gentleman who aspires to cleanliness had been advised to wash his feet periodically. But the Turkish bath or *stew* was popular, even if soap and water were not, and was used by men of the highest fashion; discretion is, significantly enough, the first qualification for a Turkish bath attendant, for the baths were largely used by young gentlemen who visited Paris incognito, and were anxious to conceal their whereabouts from the King. For it was possible not only to sleep at the baths but to have meals on the premises. But the stews had their bona fide users too, and were often recommended for rheumatic patients, who, if unable to move, could have a portable Turkish bath brought to their houses.

The Paris of Louis XIV already had a long established reputation as the home of the *magasin de luxe*, and even the least energetic of Parisians must have spent an hour or so a day strolling through the shops. Many of them were already doing a considerable export trade: the ladies' tailors, for instance, who had made good their footing by 1675, in spite of the violent protests of jealous husbands and suspicious mothers: the glovemakers, who enjoyed a monopoly of the manufacture and sale of face powder: the barbers, who dealt in soaps, perfumes, toothache cures and suchlike: and the wigmakers, whose business received a considerable fillip when the King ceased to wear his own hair in 1673. With a hazy recollection of Rigaud's portraits in our minds, we are apt to think of the seventeenth-century wig as a standardized article, but it was in fact of various shapes, sizes, and materials. The cheapest variety was made of horsehair. That in which Rigaud painted his clients was the *in folio,* the full-dress Court wig.

When the men and women of the period were not engaged in the pleasures of conversation, they found their chief enjoyment in listening to the professional rhetoricians of the law courts, the stage, and the pulpit; for to hear a sermon was at that time as much a diversion of the worldly as it was a duty for the devout. Or perhaps it would be more charitable to say that a seventeenth-century congregation could derive no profit from the matter of a sermon if it was not also a finished piece of oratory. So well understood was this by the preachers, that some of the best of them were in the habit of rehearsing their gestures in front of a full-length mirror. The Paris theatres were open from Easter to Lent, and Lent being the climax of the preaching season, bridged very opportunely what would otherwise have been a tiresome gap in the year's round of pleasure. Most of the famous specimens of pulpit eloquence, other than funeral sermons, will be found to have been delivered in Lent, and to be invited to preach at Court during those forty days was virtually an official announcement that your name was on the short list for the next vacant see. The most casual inspection of the private correspondence of the *Grand Siècle* shows what a large part sermons played in the lives of the educated classes; to Mme. de Sévigné it is one of her daughter's best founded grievances against the provinces that there one hears such poor sermons; and she rarely writes to her daughter without mentioning the sermons which she herself has been hearing; and often with detailed criticism both of the matter and of its delivery. Personally, I have a suspicion that we should have found in the great preachers a ranting style and a wealth of theatrical gesture which would have offended us more from the pulpit than it would have done even in the contemporary theatre, the headquarters of rant.

What, one wonders, must have been the Duchesse du Maine's style of acting, who was blamed by her audiences for her excessive ranting?

In Paris the theatre opened at five o'clock, as did its rival, the opera. The latter was a comparative novelty, which had established itself only in 1671. The opera was what we should call a musical comedy theatre which specialized in very elaborate stage sets and effects: winged goddesses descended from Olympus upon gardens in which played real cascades and fountains, amidst the rolling of a thunderstorm, and so forth. The opera owed its success largely to the King's love of music, and ballet-opera was especially popular. The age was fortunate in finding Quinault to provide librettos for Lulli's music, a partnership which in its day was as happy and famous as that of Gilbert and Sullivan in a later era.

It was not possible to book seats at either house, but a lackey could be sent to reserve a seat as soon as the theatre opened; and it was as well for him to be early, for there was nearly always a full pit, owing to the amount of paper in the house; for the *Maison du Roi*, over three thousand strong, had a long standing right of free admission, which was not contested until comparatively late in the reign. It was also wise to tell the lackey to reserve you a place well out into the middle of the pit; for one avoided a seat under the boxes for precisely the same reason that one avoided walking close under the overhanging windows in the street.

Here, by the way, let us correct a common error about the status of the French actor of the seventeenth century. In spite of the fact that he was often refused burial in consecrated ground, he was not, like his English *confrère*, an official rogue and vagabond; Floridor, one of the best actors of the first half of the reign, had his claim to nobility confirmed by letters patent of 1668, with the usual clause that he did not derogate from his rank by performing on the stage.

We should have had many criticisms to make about a seventeenth-century production. Perhaps the first would have been of the badness of the players who filled the minor rôles, a badness which becomes understandable when we discover that they are not actors at all, but the servants of the stars, whose contracts obliged them to fill up the cast at their own expense. Then the *tirades*. Most of us, in reading even the most famous of the French classical plays, have probably felt the *longueurs* of these *tirades* put into the mouths of the leading performers; Racine, with his admirable sense of the stage, no doubt felt it too, but the practice was forced upon him by the actors. Each performer insisted on his or her *tirade*, which was an individual exhibition, deliberately holding up the action for the benefit of the star, and delivered in a sort of chant which was never used in the dialogue. Some of the conventions of costume would also have struck us as highly ridiculous; the title rôle of *Polyeucte*, for instance, had to be played in white gloves, and a hat twice the size of that of any other performer; the correct way to play Augustus in *Cinna* was in the manner of a soldier of fortune, and wearing a gigantic wig, spangled with laurel leaves and hanging down to the hips, the whole surmounted by an enormous hat covered in red plumes.

After the theatre, coach or sedan chair would be waiting to take up the playgoer to find the supper table where he might best shine in airing his views on the play; if it were a summer evening in the earlier part of the reign, he might decide to go to the Jardin Reynard, a sort of Vauxhall at the extremity of the Tuileries, where in addition to having supper he could see fireworks, listen to the band, and admire the sumptuousness of the decorations. But we hear nothing of the Jardin Reynard after the middle of the century, and the place seems to have had no successor.

And so the Parisian day ends. There was, of course, another Paris, close packed in its stinking alleys and dark lanes, but little had been heard of it since the end of the civil war; the Day of the Barricades was now ancient history, and Louis XIV will have been dead for seventy odd years before the voice of the submerged tenth is heard again. And next time it will be Napoleon and not the Monarchy who silences it.

X

The Galleys

Until the coming of the concentration camp, the galley held an undisputed pre-eminence as the darkest blot on Western civilization; a galley, said a poetic observer shudderingly, would cast a shadow in the blackest midnight. In the seventeenth century, the great age of the galleys, the particularly bad reputation of those of Louis XIV is fortuitous; all the Mediterranean powers possessed galleys, and the brutalities practised on those of other powers were often more horrible than anything that would have been tolerated in the French service. And the galleys can enter a strong plea in condonation of their existence, namely, that the convict existed for the galley, not the galley for the convict. The navies of the seventeenth century had to conform to the limited strategic and tactical plan imposed upon them by their two possible propellants, wind and oar; and in consequence the galley, with its perpetual mobility, was the important fast tactical unit of a Mediterranean navy. Until the coming of steam the galley, under many conditions of weather, was the fastest thing afloat on the inland sea; it composed to a considerable extent the scouting division of the fleet. In light airs the galleys, and only the galleys, could protect the coast against the Barbary pirate or hunt him down in the open sea; in a fleet action the galley was the only thing which could remove a damaged capital ship from its place in the line of battle; in amphibious operations its shallow draft made it the ideal landing-craft, whilst its main armament could engage closer inshore than that of the lightest vessels of the fleet proper. The galley was in fact indispensable.

The experiment of propelling galleys by free men hired for the oar had been tried and had failed; the commanders concerned had reported that with such a bank neither the speed nor the endurance essential could be obtained. Only the whip, with the threat of worse brutalities in reserve, could send the long, lean, cranky craft into action at the requisite speed. Given the necessity for the galley on the one hand, and a country swarming with criminals on the other, the *galérien* was the obvious, indeed the only, solution, the cheap fuel so callously expended in driving these fast ships.

Who was the typical *galérien*? The society of the bench fell into five distinct classes: Turks, bought by the French Government for the service, deserters, salt smugglers, genuine criminals, and, after 1685, Huguenots—the first category being definitely the least badly treated, and the last on the whole the worst. Even before the coming of the Huguenot, the *galériens* were by no means, as is often supposed, drawn exclusively from the dregs of France; at the battle of Genoa in 1638 the galley *La Cardinale* was saved by the exertions of a convict, the Chevalier de Margaillet, who was doing time for the rape of his niece; when Mlle. de Scudéry was at Marseilles in 1644 she notices that *galériens* of good social standing were allowed a considerable degree of liberty, and in their spare hours were to be met in the best *salons* of the town; in 1670 Mme. de Sévigné is assured by the General of the Galleys that her protégé Valcroissant, a *galérien*, is "living as he pleases, ashore in Marseilles, and without chains." The conductor of the orchestra of the galley *La Palme* had been a performer in the private band of Louis XIV, had thrown up his post in a fit of pique, enlisted and then deserted. And there were many other similar cases. In the earlier part of the reign the *galérien* is dumb;

we catch a glimpse of him only from the outside, or at best we look down from the poop on his crowded misery.

We went to visit the galleys [writes Evelyn in 1644]; The Captaine of the Galley Royal gave us a most courteous entertainment in his Cabine, the slaves in the interim playing both loud and soft musiq very rarely. Then he show'd us how he commanded their motions with a nod and his whistle, making them row out. The spectacle was to me new and strange, to see so many hundreds of miserably naked persons, having their heads shaven close and having only high red bonnets and payre of coarse canvas drawers, their whole backs and leggs naked and made fast to their seats about their middles and leggs in couples, and all commanded in a trice by an imperious and cruell seaman. . . . I was amaz'd to contemplate how these miserable catyfs lie in their galley crouded together, yet there is hardly one but had some occupation by which, as leisure and calms permitted, they gat some little money. Their rising and falling back at their oare is a miserable spectacle, and the noise of their chaines with the roaring of the beaten waters has something of strange and fearefull to one unaccustomed to it. They are rul'd and chastiz'd by strokes on their backs and soles of their feete on the least disorder and without the least humanity; yet they are cherefull and full of knavery.

With the Revocation of the Edict of Nantes in 1685 the bench becomes vocal, a light shines into the sinister interior of the galley. From letters of Huguenot convicts, and the memoirs of such as survived to write them after their release in 1712, we are able to piece together a tolerably accurate account of the *galérien's* life. Bad though the story is, it is not wholly bad; its sombre texture is shot through with gleams of humanity, almost of kindliness, for the officers were often less brutal than the system which they administered.

Once condemned to the galleys, the convict was consigned to the nearest jail where he might spend a considerable time in almost any variety and degree of comfort or suffering whilst awaiting the order for his transfer to the chain assembly-point—Lille for the galleys of Dunkirk, Paris for those of Marseilles. Their hands bound, and with an escort of provost's archers, the sad little groups tramped the country roads which converged on their last land prison. A Huguenot merchant, who was condemned in 1701 for trying to escape from France, has left us a description of the chain assembly-prison at Lille—a large room in St. Peter's tower, so dark that day was but darkness made visible, without fire or candle, a little broken straw, innumerable rats and mice, and the society of thirty of the most depraved scoundrels in France. . . . But for our Huguenot there was temporary deliverance in sight. The prison of Lille was under the orders of the Grand Provost of Flanders, a distant connection of a relation of the prisoner's, a tenuous lifeline enough we may think nowadays, who know nothing of the immense solidarity of seventeenth-century relationship. At any rate, the claim was instantly recognized by the provost to the extent of moving his relation and a chosen companion into a comfortable bed-sitting-room, with every alleviation of their lot which money could provide; nor did his assistance end there, for, having delayed their departure until the last draft, he then had them carried in carts behind the chain to Dunkirk. Marolles, another Huguenot, who in 1686 found himself in La Tournelle, the Paris assembly-point, has a grimmer story to tell; after complaining of the "filthiness and execrable blasphemies" to which he is subjected, he goes on: "We lie 53 of us in a place which is not above 30 feet in length and 9 in breadth. There lies on the right side of me a sick peasant, with his head to my feet and his feet to my head. There is scarce one among us who does not envy the condition of several dogs and horses"; and the conclusion of his letter to his wife is worthy to be written in letters of gold—"When I reflect on the merciful providence of God towards me, I am ravished with admiration and do evidently discover the secret steps of Providence which hath formed me from my youth after a requisite manner to bear what I suffer."

At last the almost-wished-for day came when the chain started on its long march to the Mediterranean; the weather was cold and frosty, but the convicts, weakened by ill-usage and burdened by their chains, sweated on the march. Charenton was reached in the evening, and at nine o'clock the convicts were ordered into the courtyard of an inn and made to strip naked—ostensibly to search their clothing for contraband, actually to steal from them their few poor remaining comforts. For two hours they stood naked in the frost, and when ordered to move were incapable of doing so, though "the bull's sinew whips fell like hail." As a result of the search eighteen of the convicts died during the night. And so the ghastly march continued under the lash of the archers. At night the convicts were locked in stables, where the luckiest or the strongest proceeded to bury themselves in the dung to keep warm, after dining off the "King's Bread"—literally the king's bread, 1½ lb. of it per man. By day the trail of blood left on the road would deceive travellers into thinking there was a convoy of wine carts in front of them. It may be objected that it was, at the lowest, the King's fuel which was being wasted by this brutality; why were there not regulations for getting it to Marseilles in consumable condition? There were, but petty officialdom, our old friend the white Babu, was active then as now, and the capitation grant had been cut to a figure at which it cost more to bring a prisoner alive to Marseilles in the hospital van than to let him die by the roadside: and the result was that of every five who set out, only four reached the coast, and of those four one had to be sent to the galley hospital. If he was fortunate or unfortunate enough to reach port alive, the *galérien* was sent to the depot galley where he could make himself acquainted with the layout of his future home.

The galley was in essence an open boat with makeshift accommodation and storage space. We may picture it as having about it a suggestion of the English canal barge—long for its beam, with a freeboard of only three feet, and much smaller than one would gather from the pictures; about a hundred and forty feet long. Forward was a forecastle on which was mounted the ship's main armament, and aft of the forecastle a half-deck over the rower's space, which provided accommodation for the 120 marines. One mast was stepped through the forecastle right forward, and the other amidships: each mast carried a large lateen sail. Below the forecastle were some cubbyholes and store-rooms. Fore and aft beneath the half-deck, and the complete length of the ship, ran the gangway from which the petty officers stimulated the exertions of the rowers. Aft was a poop, below which was a small cabin for the captain, and below the captain's cabin were store-rooms. The position of the other accommodations is not very clear—latrines, *cale* or hold, where the marines slept, ship's kitchen, "tavern" or wet canteen, a speculation of the chief petty officer: and I am inclined to suspect from various accounts that the interior layout of all galleys was not uniform. When these small craft were in commission there would be a complement of over 400 souls on board, and such was the overcrowding that even the captain's cabin was common to all officers except at night: for "the cabin" was in fact the only real accommodation in the ship.

Soon after their arrival at the depot galley the convicts would be assembled, stripped, sorted into gangs of five, and drawn for by lot by the *Comites* of the various galleys needing reinforcements. Each five men, arbitrarily selected for physical reasons, were now entered into the closest of life partnerships, *La Vogue*: rarely again to eat, sleep, or work apart, to be literally in close contact with each other until the end of their days. They had ceased to be men, they had become "an oar," one of fifty such oars carried by a galley.

But if they reached the port at the turn of the year, their rowing days were still three months ahead of them; the galleys, stripped to their hulls, would be emerging from their winter hibernation to face another commission. In this case the work in front of them was only one degree less arduous than that of the oar. No officers would yet have appeared on board, though a junior or two might be living ashore in the town. The seniors would be at Paris or Versailles, and the ships in the hands of the *Comites* and their *Sous-Comites*. The dictionary, I see, translates *Comite* "boatswain," which is misleading, for there never was, thank God, an English version of the word. The *Comite* was the chief slave-driver, the man with the *nerf de boeuf* or bull-sinew whip. The first, indeed the only, qualification for a *Comite* was brutality; though even *Comites* varied, and the anonymous Huguenot whom I have already quoted found in his *Comite* a protector and almost a friend. We must not think too savagely of the *Comite*; only the exceptional man revolts against the abuses to which he has been brought up, and the *Comite*, had he been steam-minded, would have seen in himself nothing more than a chief engineer—half-speed ahead, one uses one's cane on the rowers' backs; full ahead, one substitutes for the cane the bull-sinew whip. *Et voilà tout*. The galley in the early spring was a mere shell, there being little on board but the ballast, and fitting out began by removing this from the hold and washing it on the quayside. The lightened galley was then careened, scraped, and recoated with pitch. Then came the overhaul of the cables, anchors, rigging, sails, and the repair of the awnings, the last an important feature in the interior economy of the galley. Lastly, the guns, masts, ammunition, and a thousand and one other things must be carried down from the arsenal and stowed on board. About April, or later if the season was a bad one, the order would come from Versailles for the galleys to put to sea.

Life on board when the galley was at sea was a sort of Hell's picnic, for there was really no accommodation for anyone. For the convicts, there was, of course, no question of sleep; the petty officers did the best they could on the forecastle head, the soldiers huddled into the hold, or under the deck awning if the weather was fine, and even the officers had no sleeping-place except on their camp chairs under the poop awning. And so crank were the ships that, to avoid risk of capsizing, the awnings could only be spread in the finest weather. Cooking facilities were primitive, and, as no one ever washed, the ship crawled with vermin from stem to stern. From below came the constant clank of chains, the crack of whips on bare flesh, screams of pain, and savage growls. At each oar all five men must rise as one at each stroke, push the eighteen-feet oar forward, dip it in the water, and pull with all their force, dropping into a sitting position at the end of each stroke. "One would not think," says a Huguenot convict, "that it was possible to keep it up for half an hour, and yet I have rowed full out for twenty-four hours without pausing for a single moment." On these occasions the rowers were fed on biscuits soaked in wine, thrust into their mouths by the *Comites* as they rowed. Those who died, or even who fainted at their posts, were cut adrift from the bench and flung overboard without further ceremony. But such a peak of suffering was never attained except in the heat of an action; had it been normal so to abuse the rowers, the whole criminal and Huguenot populations of France combined would soon have proved insufficient to keep the galleys in commission. In normal cruising, sail was set whenever possible, or, if there was no wind, only each alternate oar was pulled, so that each bench rested for one and one-half hours in every three. Not all *galériens* were rowers; in each ship a few privileged men, who were usually Huguenots, would be employed as storekeepers, stewards, cooks, and the like. The only pleasant feature of this sorry story is the almost overt sympathy shown in most cases by Roman Catholic officers and *Comites* to the Huguenots; it was the comfortably lodged mission priests ashore in Marseilles and Dunkirk who were always on the look-out to make the Huguenots' lives harder, not the men who had to work with them. There were even cases in which something that might be called friendship sprang up between the captains and their convict secretaries and servants. Even the convicts proper, the criminal convicts, pitied and respected the Huguenots: and never failed, we are told, to address a Huguenot as *Monsieur* and pull off their bonnets when speaking to one.

In 1709 the hero of Willington's narrative reached the haven of secretary to de Langeron, captain of his galley, and for the first time in eight years found himself freed from his chains, newly clothed, and allowed to grow his hair, with a corner of the store-room to sleep in; nay, more, "the captain ordered his steward to serve me a dish from his table at each meal, with a bottle of wine a day. . . . I was honoured and respected by the officers, loved and cherished by my captain." This same de Langeron was prepared to take considerable risks for his Huguenots, though himself, of course, a Roman Catholic; when the search gun was fired from the flagship it was his duty to have each Huguenot instantly seized and searched for Protestant devotional books; but de Langeron would remark on hearing the gun to his steward— "My friend, the cock has crowed." The steward ran forward with the news, and the *Comites* would look the other way before beginning their search, whilst each Huguenot handed over his Bible to the Turkish headman of his oar. How real was the risk that de Langeron ran may be gauged by the case of Marolles' neighbour at the oar in 1686, "a dragoon officer whose name was Bonvalet, a very mild and discreet man," who was there for life for having connived at the escape of a Huguenot woman of quality from France. Marolles, too, after the horrors of his journey from Paris to Marseilles, ultimately fell on his feet when posted to the galley *Magnifique.*

I live at present all alone [he writes], they bring me food from abroad (i.e. from the town) and I am furnished with wine in the galley for nothing, and with some of the King's bread. . . . I am treated with civility by all on board the galley, seeing that the officers visit me . . . we have the honestest *patron* of all the galleys. He treats me with all manner of civility and respect, and he hath promised me that when it is cold he will let me lie in his cabbin.

The privilege of getting food from ashore was a considerable one, for the diet of the *galériens* was, as might be imagined, spare. At eight in the morning an allowance of biscuit was issued for the day, "of which indeed they have enough, and pretty good." The only other meal was a soup made of beans or peas, with salad oil, at ten in the morning, to which when at sea there was added two-thirds of a pint of wine, morning and evening. Even during the campaigning season a galley spent much more time in port than at sea, and when in Marseilles or Dunkirk life was less hard for all concerned. Food was obtainable from the town, even by convicts, all of whom had some trade, and at night it was possible to sleep. Easily dismantled tables were erected over the convicts' benches for the officers and petty officers, on which they placed their beds, and each table became a sort of light tent by the aid of stuff curtains hung from a line fore and aft. It was then that a convict began to appreciate the privilege of rowing on the *Comite's* own bench, if such was his good fortune; for the *Comite's* table was built over that bench in port, and his men fed well on the leavings of his table: to say nothing of the prestige accruing from the enjoyment of the great man's conversation in his unbuttoned hours. "He was," says our anonymous authority of his *Comite*, "the cruellest man on duty I ever saw, but off duty very reasonable and filled with judicious thoughts."

After the galleys came into port in the autumn and had been laid up for the winter, the life of the convict became almost endurable. To begin with, the officers, sailors, and marines were billeted ashore, and there was much more elbow room, a general spreading out; beds were improvised in the bottom of the ship, and a huge cover on battens was pulled over the open deck, converting the ship into a sort of giant camping punt. Marolles on *La Fierce* found himself the possessor of one of the "two little cabbins at the head of the galley. This favour was procured me by a young officer whom I teach algebra. . . . I have bought coals, which are very dear, and I make a little fire in our apartment." *La Fierce* must, however, have been a slack galley, for another convict, while commenting on the comparative comfort of winter quarters, adds that the chief drawback is that no fire is ever allowed in a galley in any circumstances.

Not only was the winter a time of comparative freedom, it was also the *galérien's* commercial harvest during which he earned the money for his *menus plaisirs*. Every *galérien* had a trade; if he had no manual dexterity he knitted stockings; if he refused to learn to knit stockings he was flogged every day until he did. But it was only the lowest class of *galérien*, the submerged tenth, that knitted stockings; tailors, wigmakers, clock-menders, almost every trade was represented in the average galley. A week ashore was allowed by an ordinance of 1630 to the convicts of each galley in rotation, during which time they might freely peddle their wares and services through the town. Some were itinerant musicians and did well at the taverns, others hawked quack remedies, others set up stalls on the quay, others had good wigmaking connections, and all stole whatever they could lay their hands upon. For there was at least one advantage in being a *galérien*: there was no extradition from the galleys for any crime whatsoever: the criminal law had washed its hands of the man sent to the galleys. To be sure he might be flogged on board for a theft or a murder if the necessary social pressure could be brought to bear on his captain, but he could not be claimed by a magistrate for even the most flagrant crime. Hence the hideous scenes in Marseilles during the great plague under the Regency, when a more than usually fatuous minister inaugurated the brilliant scheme of releasing the *galériens* to help nurse the sick and dispose of the dead.

In addition to what may be somewhat loosely described as their honest tradesmen, the galleys supplied Marseilles and Dunkirk during the winter months with a plentiful infusion of swindlers of every type: apparently without the naval authorities concerning themselves about the matter. The light-fingered gentlemen in fetters who wanted change for a crown and kept both crown and change: forgers of wills, marriage certificates, and leave passes for soldiers: dealers in the seals of towns, bishoprics, corporations, and private gentlemen: renovators and adapters of legal instruments—there was no need to look far in the port for skilled professional assistance in any fraud you might be planning. Indeed, Huguenots apart, the only tolerably honest men in the galleys were the Turks, who confined themselves to a safe conservative business as receivers of stolen goods.

Such in brief outline was the life of the galleys. There is a tendency, purely English, I suspect, to assume that because a man is ill-treated, he must be a good fellow; in our indignation against the whole system, we unconsciously draw a false picture of the *galérien*, on whom we need in fact waste no sympathy. The seventeenth-century criminal is not a sympathetic object, and his Huguenot fellows have left ample record of the horrors and atrocities which he boasted of having perpetrated. Whether the system made the criminal or the criminal made the system it is here irrelevant to enquire. It is all over now. The tumult and the shouting dies; the galley in all its gilded splendour and hidden misery has followed the age it symbolizes into oblivion. No more will French criminals "write on the water with a pen eighteen feet long." New horrors have displaced the old, but at least the bloody chapter of the oared navies is closed for ever.

XI

Sea Travel

By the middle of the century an increasing interest in the sea is discernible in France: contemporary accounts of voyages become the popular reading, adventurous souls begin to seek easy wealth in the fabulous East, nobles are allowed to officer merchant vessels without losing caste, and the state-controlled mercantile marine rapidly expands. In a word, whilst no one yet goes to sea for pleasure, it becomes possible to go to sea with pleasure. The day of scheduled services is still far off, but by the 'sixties there are fairly frequent cargo and passenger services to Canada, the West Indies, West and South Africa, and the Far East. In addition there is a large expansion in the older-established Baltic and Levant trades, and, after the Restoration, in cross channel services.

Many of us still regard the trip from Dover to Calais with distaste, but to the seventeenth-century passenger it was a fearsome ordeal. Take, for instance, the attempted crossing of the Queen of England in 1644, when, after a nine-day gale, the ship was driven into a Dutch port. The unfortunate woman "suffered the terrors of almost certain death, tied down in a little bed, with her ladies tied down around her in theirs." (We may note in passing that the cabins of all ships at this period were mere empty boxes which had to be furnished by the passenger.) When the unfortunate Queen got ashore, it was "in a state so strange that it was disagreeable to approach her," says Mme. de Motteville, who adds a number of details better omitted. Let us leave her with a shudder and turn to the pleasanter experiences of some deep sea travellers.

In 1653 the eighteen-year-old Chevalier d'Arvieux was appointed to the French Consular service, and embarked for Smyrna at Marseilles in *Postillion*, 44 guns, with a total complement of one hundred and seventy, passengers included. *Postillion* was a King's ship, making her first commercial voyage, which presumably means that she was on charter to a business house, a not unusual arrangement at the time, if a fighting ship would otherwise have been lying idle. D'Arvieux was a man of an admirable curiosity, a confirmed memoir writer, determined to miss no detail of his first voyage. And as we turn over his account we reflect how alike and yet how different it is to a similar diary to-day: the officers' assurance after a spell of heavy weather that it was "the worst storm in all their sea-going experience": the ship's wag who assures him that the ship's bulldog can run up and down the rigging as handily as the smartest man on board: the increasingly nautical phrasing of the entries. Many of us have written such diaries ourselves. D'Arvieux deserves translating and editing, for his voyages form but a small part of his fascinating account of life in the Near East in the second half of the century. This is not the place to treat of his land travels, but we may note his first impression of the interior of a mosque for the significant light it throws òn the state of a French church in his day. "Not a scrap of excrement anywhere," he cries, "and no one spits: or if he has to, he does it into a handkerchief without making any noise."

In 1658 he takes passage to Egypt in an English ship, where the strictness of the discipline astonishes him; he cannot sufficiently admire the *honnête* conduct of the captain in ordering a flogging for a sailor who has stolen a pot of honey from a Turkish passenger, in spite of the prayers of the Turk that he should be pardoned. But if English discipline arouses his admiration, English cookery certainly does not. *"Mauvaise cuisine des Anglois,"* he notes moodily in the margin of his text, and then proceeds to describe its horrors.

One must be accustomed to their way of living to put up with it. Their meats, boiled or roast, were not half cooked, their pudding was detestable. It is a composition of pounded biscuit or flour, lard, raisins, salt and pepper, of which they make a pudding which is tied up in a cloth and cooked in the same pot as the soup; it is then served on a plate, and old cheese grated over it, which produces a most intolerable stench. Without the cheese, the thing itself is not absolutely bad, and is very nourishing.

However, he finds the biscuit good, the beer excellent, and very good wine, dried fruit, and mutton; also good poultry. He concludes grimly, "all that we lacked was a French chef."

On this occasion meals seem to have been included in the passage money, but when d'Arvieux went on home leave in 1665, he victualled himself; perhaps with memories of the *table d'hôte* of 1658. In 1665, "amongst all sorts of refreshments," he took for his private use "two bullocks, some sheep, kids, and chickens, biscuits, and a stock of wine."

By 1672 d'Arvieux has become a person of importance, Consul-General of the Levant, and his rise in the world is indicated by the fact that when he embarks he finds that the purser of the *Diamond* has had his cabin carpeted and tapestried for his reception; *fort proprement* as he tells us with a touch of complacency. It would have greatly surprised the worthy Consular official to know that the accident of his having gone on leave in 1669 has conferred on him the precarious immortality of a footnote. In that year he was summoned to Versailles to give the King some account of the Turkish way of life: and in doing so, amused the King so much that he suggested to Molière that he should take advantage of d'Arvieux's stories to write a burlesque Turkish comedy. The outcome of Louis' hint was *Le Bourgeois Gentilhomme*, for which d'Arvieux arranged the Turkish scene and designed the costumes.

The Abbé de Choisy (1644–1724), Peter Pan of the Grand Century, member of the Academy and Church historian, was as odd a fish as even that age, so rich in eccentrics, could show. From his earliest years until he was well into his thirties, this dean and holder of three priories, found his chief pleasure in dressing as a woman, hanging himself with jewellery, and sitting in front of his mirror admiring his own beauty, in the midst of a circle of female friends. Had the matter stopped there, it would have been absurd enough; but, incredible though it may seem, he lived openly in Paris for a considerable time as "the Comtesse de Sancey," and even appeared at the opera in full female dress. This last exploit, however, was beyond the limit of toleration of even that tolerant age, and he found it prudent to exile himself to the provinces, where he continued to lead the same sort of life as "the Comtesse des Barres." Oddest fact of all, Choisy was not addicted to the vice which distinguished his "girl friend" Monsieur, the King's brother; he kept a succession of mistresses, with whom he had normal relations, except that he insisted on their always wearing male dress.

In 1683 he became converted after a serious illness, and flung himself into the Christian life with that childish impetuosity which characterized all his actions; and in 1685 got himself attached to the embassy which was about to sail for Siam. On 3rd March of that year he left Brest in *L'Oiseau*, a navy ship of 46 guns.

If Choisy had no marked vocation for the priesthood, he certainly had one for long sea voyages. In his complete ability to live contentedly from day to day, his sunny good nature, his conciliatory manner, his unselfish cheerfulness, we find the secret of the indulgent amusement with which he was regarded by his contemporaries. Before the ship passes Finisterre he is loud in his praises of his companions, and of the various excellences of *L'Oiseau*; and the discovery that Lent has to be faced on "bad butter, and very salt cod," only moves him to laughter, gourmet though he is. Every incident of the voyage delights him: a ball given by the officers, which he and the other priests watch "from the amphitheatre of the rigging"; the "delightful liberty"; the good company; "the trumpets, which lend animation to our meals." Life at sea, he concludes, is "delicious"; and he adds, "many a French town has a poorer array of talent than our ship." A month later "his days are passing like minutes." Epic games of chess are played, the Jesuits teach him the rudiments of astron-

omy, an hour a day is devoted to learning Portuguese, two to
Siamese, and a further hour to Euclid; he has the *Essais de Morale* to get through, his Gospel to read, his music to keep up—
"we are pretty good at Plain song." Then there is the evening
stroll on the poop, the chart to be inspected, public and private
prayers. Three times a week there is a religious discussion on a
previously announced theme, at which Choisy assisted "in the
silence of profound ignorance." Father Fontenay lectures on
navigation, and shows that not only is longitude undiscovered,
but why it is undiscoverable. In parentheses, the inability to fix
the longitude is of course a main reason for what strikes us as
the extraordinarily haphazard nature of seventeenth-century navigation; a navigation so inaccurate that Forbin, Choisy's fellow-
passenger, and himself a naval officer, congratulates the ship's
navigator on making his landfall at the Cape, "only 45 miles out
in his reckoning." It comes as a surprise to us to discover that the
ship's officers neither knew, nor were expected to know, even the
rudiments of navigation; this was the work of the two petty officers called "pilots." Timekeeping was another perpetual problem
in the ships of this period. The usual method was by sand glass,
running for thirty minutes, and the sand glass was entrusted to
the quartermaster at the helm; eight turns of the glass, and the
watch was relieved. Under this too confiding arrangement, all
quartermasters were naturally given to the crime known in the
slang of the sea as "eating the sand": that is to say, turning the
glass before all the sand had run through it. One can imagine
the confusion that resulted from this practice when for perhaps
several consecutive days the weather had been too thick to take
a sight; Duguay-Trouin, cruising off Spitzbergen in 1703, did not
get a sight for eight days, and when he did, ship's time was found
to be eleven hours fast. No wonder, he adds, that we wanted to go
to bed at mealtimes, and to eat when we were going to bed.

But to return to Choisy. Even when becalmed in the tropics,
under conditions in which ill-temper might be excused, he remains his cheerful self, though he admits he cannot now study
for two hours on end. "The cod is bad, the oil stinks, and the biscuit is bitter": he is woefully disappointed in turtle meat, of
which he had heard such enticing accounts: the motionless ship
is battened down at sunset to keep out the night air, which as

everyone knows, brings on paralysis: his tropical diet is salt herring, brandy, and anchovies: yet he comes smiling through it all. There is sound stuff somewhere in our eccentric abbé.

At length the Line is crossed, the event being celebrated with a burlesque of the baptismal service, which scandalizes even Choisy, and at which the passengers buy themselves off from baptism by dropping a handful of money into the "font." As they catch the favouring wind south of the Line, a new note of cheerfulness is apparent in the diary. "Our meals are better than on shore . . . the mutton fatter, fresh eggs, and fresh bread daily, the hens are quails, we have fresh cream." Only wine is short, and "shortness" appears to be a relative term, for their consumption is "five or six big bottles daily"; "which," says Choisy with a sigh, "are gone in a flash." By 16th May the ship has half a gale of wind behind her: "We eat flying. You take three spoonfuls of soup and throw them into your stomach. You pull off the leg of a fowl. To drink, you must know all the laws of counterpoise. And we remain in good humour through it all."

With such an array of talent on board, sermons were not neglected, and each Sunday and Holy day had its discourse, giving rise in the cabin to those interminable theological arguments of which the age was so fond. Even Choisy ventured to preach, with what success he does not tell us; perhaps with little, for with unwonted seriousness he goes on to remark that a heavy sea, with "little white sheep," or as we should say "white horses," is a better preacher than any of them. The death of Robin, a famous sheep that had been to America and back, provides the text for a long disputation on the theory that animals are merely machines; and each has an animal story to tell which disproves the theory. A week later they have thirty cases of scurvy, and within a few days the figure rises to fifty-five. They are now becalmed in the Sunda Strait, and their sufferings are aggravated by the fact that they can almost touch the lush green coast of Sumatra. Even in Choisy's narrative the longings for a salad are prominent, though he keeps his cheerfulness, and he is active in the distribution of cabin stores among the sick. At long last, on the 18th August *L'Oiseau* anchors at Batavia, 168 days out from Brest.

There is a curiously pre-1939 flavour about Choisy's account of the capital of the Dutch East Indies, much of the same Far

Eastern atmosphere which survived up to the outbreak of World
War II. He finds everything very dear, and everybody very rich.
"Detestable" French wine sells at a crown a pint, but in spite of
this, "life is a perpetual passage from French wine to Rhine,
from Spanish to Persian, and now and then to beer." He enjoys
the exotic food, is moderately interested in the strange fruits,
and takes kindly to "patates," which I assume to be potatoes. Having watered and victualled, they sail on the last leg of their long
passage, and on 27th August they are attacked by pirates, an
incident worth mentioning, as it gives rise to the only flash of
malice which the good-natured abbé permits himself throughout
the diary, and the objects of it are, of course, the hated Jesuits.
"While they were praying at the bottom of the hold," he says,
"the mission priests were manning the poop, sword in hand." On
22nd September *L'Oiseau* anchored in Siamese waters, 203 days
out from France.

Choisy came home with the ship in due course, but his friend
Forbin stayed behind, a cog in the machinery of Louis XIV's
vast plans. The real object of this ostensible embassy of compliment was that the *corps d'élite* of missionaries should convert
the Siamese King and his leading subjects with all convenient
speed, the ambassador should negotiate a Franco-Siamese pact,
and Forbin should reorganize—which he found meant create—
the Siamese navy, which was, henceforth, to be at the disposal of
Louis for harrying the English and the Dutch in Far Eastern waters.
Owing to a revolution, the plan ultimately failed, but Forbin
was made Admiral of Siam with the title of Opra Sac Disom Cram
—which has a vague suggestion of a half-baked limerick—and
spent a troublesome twelve months in that inhospitable country, where *inter alia* he took to eating crocodile, which he describes as "not bad," and adds the appetizing comment that in
appearance its flesh resembles that of a sick dog. But even Forbin's
catholic taste in food rejected the invitation of a Siamese to join
him in a snack of live white worms; though he afterwards reproached himself for his fastidiousness in not sampling the deli-
cacy. After all, he says, don't we eat live oysters?

But Forbin, though evidently no delicate feeder, could do things
in style when the occasion called for it. In 1708 he commanded
the French squadron that carried the unlucky James III on his

abortive expedition to Scotland, and had the honour of carrying the King and his staff on board his flagship—an honour which he tells us cost him over 40,000 livres.

I had (he says), to feed a king, a marshal of France, milords, a large suite of *seigneurs* of the first rank, general officers, and also eighty servants. The king's table of twelve covers was magnificently served, and I also had three tables of fifteen covers, and my own of ten. Beef, mutton, and poultry were put in a large boiler from which sufficient liquor was drawn off for the soups. I had taken on board a number of little stoves, on which *ragoûts* were cooked. The ship's company dined at ten o'clock, when one of the cabin tables was served. Two more were served at eleven, and the king dined at midday. My own table, which was not the worst, a few moments later. I had taken with me four chefs and a number of assistants, who worked practically without a break, and were helped by the crew who worked in the kitchens a good deal of their time. The king's table was always served with partridge and pheasant, of which I had taken care to bring a good quantity on board. When the enemy chased us, I was much badgered to throw my oxen, sheep, calves, and so forth, overboard . . . and was wise to ignore this sage advice . . . for without them we should have been reduced to eating lard.

In 1690 we make the acquaintance of Robert Challes (1659–1719), "King's writer" to H.M. ship *L'Ecueil*, one of a convoy of six vessels about to sail under Duquesne-Guiton for the Far East, "half as King's ships, half as merchantmen." Challes is one of the best of our travellers, a diarist of considerable merit, and a man whose character strongly reminds us of Pepys. In him we find the same indefatigable pursuit of women, the same all-embracing curiosity, the same gusto, the same love of good eating and drinking, and, we may add, the same standard of official honesty. Had they met, I feel they would have become friends, in spite of the Frenchman's anti-English prejudices, for we have scarcely been introduced to Challes before we find him remarking of the war then raging: "Damn all Englishmen, what does it matter to me whether their king is called James or William?"

The King's writer was a very busy man. Not only was he responsible for the victualling of the ship and the payment of the crew, but also for the ship's gear and ammunition, as well as for the loading, stowage, and discharge of cargo; so that a writer of Challes' tastes, when in port, needed to have the Pepysian capac-

ity for going without sleep if he was to have any private amusement. The convoy sailed from Port Louis at dawn on 2nd
March, and, having already met Challes on shore, we are not surprised to notice that he arrives on board as the anchor is coming up, having spent the night ashore in the unsuccessful pursuit
of an apothecary's wife. He, and we, can now take breath and
look around the ship. *L'Ecueil* was a 38-gun ship, of about 500
tons, with a complement of 350 men, commanded by one Captain
Hurtain, an "old tarpaulin" and a nominally converted Huguenot; he and the officer of marines, a tough old ranker called La
Chassée, were Challes' particular cronies, and it is naturally of
them that we hear most. They were, in the writer's phrase, "three
heads in one hat." The other officers and passengers are somewhat shadowy figures, though there are occasional and characteristic references to the aloof Siamese "mandarins"; how on earth,
wonders Challes, will they manage in Siam, they who take so
kindly to the good wines of France? In addition to the mandarins
and the ship's company, *L'Ecueil* was carrying a number of priests
and a military draft, to say nothing of a ship's surgeon, described
by our author as "that excrement of Esculapius."

The first thing that Challes notices is that it is difficult to get
about the decks for cages and pens; "the ship is a farmyard," he
says, and this was no exaggerated description, for they were carrying 8 bullocks, 2 cows, 6 calves, 12 pigs, 24 sheep, 500 hens, 24
turkeys, 48 ducks, 12 geese and 36 pigeons. His second and much
more serious observation is that while they are amply victualled,
wine is none too plentiful, at least by the standards of the captain, *qui aime à boire le petit coup,* as do those equally thirsty
souls, the writer and the marine. But Challes' ingenuity easily
solves the problem. Under cover of darkness the chief steward descends into the hold, where he taps the ship's wine barrels and
draws off and bottles sufficient *graves* to last the precious three—
and doubtless himself also—for the passage. The plunder is stored
in the writer's cabin, together with a few snacks such as ham, salt
tongues, and so forth (also stolen), and the writer breathes again.
This strikes us as bad enough, but there is worse to follow.

Next day at dinner the scoundrel makes a solemn speech to
the company in which he enlarges on the disagreeableness of
running out of wine on the homeward passage, and asks them to
join him in petitioning the captain to put them on a daily wine

ration. The captain, newly come from a refreshing *petit coup* in Challes' cabin, gravely thanks the writer for his valuable suggestion; the passengers, not being interested in the problem of supplies homeward bound, look blank; but Challes stills the incipient murmur by saying that he is only suggesting what has already been put into effect in the flagship. "That shut their beaks," he says. The proposal is carried, and from thenceforth when one of the conspirators felt thirsty, the secret sign was to place the forefinger and thumb of the right hand on the throat—a signal which becomes increasingly frequent as the ship gets down to the tropics.

It is typical of the century that the same Challes who so prides himself on this shabby trick, was a strictly honest accountant, keeping his innumerable ledgers with meticulous accuracy, vigilant in checking his stores, and a terror in arguments with the lax shore staff about short-landed or short-loaded cargo.

Choisy's account of his voyage to Siam had been published before Challes sailed, and by a curious chance Choisy's ship *L'Oiseau* was in the present convoy. Challes, with all the seaman's amused contempt for the nautical enthusiasms of the landsman, thinks very little of Choisy or of his book; *L'Oiseau*, whatever the abbé may say to the contrary, is notoriously the worst sailer in the fleet, and as for Choisy's remarks about the sweetness of her hold, he knows for a fact that Choisy never was in *L'Oiseau's* hold. It is not surprising anyway that he did not like Choisy's book, for a peep into his cabin shows that in literature he preferred the solid to the ephemeral: travelling with Petronius, Ovid, Horace, Juvenal, Corneille, Racine, and Molière for recreation, and St. Bernard and Thomas à Kempis for his rare serious moments. For the rest, when Challes is not working or attending a secret drinking party, he cuts a considerable figure in the endless debates which take place under the poop awning as the ship crawls through the tropic seas. He scoffs at the doctrine of Papal infallibility, and a Jesuit is to him as a red rag to a bull; their only reason for going overseas, he tells us, is to swindle the natives, debauch their women, and amass a fortune. It, however, ill becomes our author to prefer the second charge, for when the ship touches at the Cape Verde Islands, seventeen days out, he finds nothing good there except the wine and the women.

A long calm near the Line gave *L'Ecueil* the opportunity of dining the admiral and the officers of the flagship on 3rd April.

The menu, which was of Challes' devising, was a formidable one; a *compôte* of twelve pigeons, four ox tongues, and a ham formed the *entrée* whilst waiting for the soup. Soup was followed by tripe, after which came sucking pig, supported by two turkeys, a goose, and a dozen chickens. Dessert consisted of a ham—whether a fresh one or the remains of the previous one is not stated—a duck pie, *gruyère* and Dutch cheese, with two salads. At the high table wine of Cahors is drunk, and at the others, *graves* and Bordeaux—Cahors, as Challes observes reverently, not being a wine to offer to the first comer. All drinks were un-rationed for the day, both for crew and afterguard, the former drinking Nantes and Anjou. By 9th April the heat is such that "to breathe is to burn one's entrails"; but after the hazardous ex-periment of a bath, the marine and the writer feel sufficiently re-freshed to adjourn to the former's cabin for two helpings of tongue and three bottles of wine. Captain Hurtain, we notice, no longer makes a third. Poor man, his drinking days are done, and he lies in a coma which is to end in death a fortnight later. On the 17th all the surgeons of the fleet hold a consultation on him—for we are still becalmed—rather to the irritation of Challes, who asks, "Does it need so many ignoramuses to kill one sick old man in this climate?" Having seen their old friend die, he and La Chassée make a solemn compact that when one is ill, the other will mount guard over him to prevent any "professor of the homi-cidal science" from approaching him. We must do Challes the justice to say that, unlike so many sceptics, his scepticism did not desert him in the moment of danger; later in the voyage, when very ill himself, he flatly refused the surgeon's ministrations: "I excused myself from putting myself in his hands on the plea that I had promised my family that I would return to France."

To fill the vacancy caused by Captain Hurtain's death the flag-ship's first lieutenant is promoted acting captain, and, the ever-lasting calm continuing, the admiral brings the new captain over to introduce him to his ship's company. "A very handsome man, much of my own appearance," is Challes' first comment on his new commander. Needless to say the occasion does not pass with-out a banquet, at which the *pièce de resistance* is a sucking pig, born on board, stuffed with boned chicken and anchovies. Speeches were made, healths drunk, salutes fired, and the new captain presented the crew with a dozen of brandy. Challes and

La Chassée are much relieved to find on the first day of the new régime that poor Hurtain's successor has no pedantic views on the wine swindle, and the parties *à trois* in the writer's cabin continue as heretofore. A day or two later they cross the Line with the usual ceremonies, which, rather to our surprise, Challes finds blasphemous, though apparently none of the priests objected to being "baptized." We glean a new detail of the proceedings from this account; if the ship had never crossed the Line before, the petty officers made a pretence of cutting down the mizzen mast, and the vessel had to be ransomed by the officers with half a pig and an *abordage d'artimon:* in English, splicing the main brace.

Two or three days later there is a court martial on an officer who has struck a soldier, and the sentence shows an interesting difference between the modern and *ancien régime* concepts of the nature of the offence. In our day the whole significance of the matter would be that the officer was guilty of disgraceful conduct, but the seventeenth-century court saw the crime rather in terms of civil law; the important aspect of the case is the compensation of the assaulted soldier. The finding was that the officer be reprimanded, and his jewellery given to the man he had struck.

Seventy days out *L'Ecueil* passes the Cape without calling, as France is at war with Holland, and by 10th June is into Indian waters, where writs do not run, and might is right; and where the French squadron prudently hoist Dutch colours whenever they sight a ship. Off the East African coast they sink the troopship *Philip Herbert*, London for Bombay, getting some hard knocks in the process, and losing all their cattle. Survivors from the English ship have a tale to tell which explains the smallness of the foreign garrisons maintained by the European powers in those days; the *Herbert* had sailed in February with 500 soldiers to reinforce the Bombay garrison, and when she fell in with *L'Ecueil* on 3rd July, all but 130 of them were already dead of disease.

Off Ceylon on 28th July *L'Ecueil* captured the Dutch ship *Montfort*, and there was a wild scramble to loot her. Challes, in two pages of invective, anathemizes his boatmen, who did not succeed in getting him on board in time to share in the choicest pieces; and then, changing front with breath-taking impudence, enlarges on the dignity of a King's writer, who should be above such low practices as looting. The admiral, however, subsequently allots him a share of the spoil, and he records the fact in a sentence worthy of Pepys: "So I keep my reputation as a man who does not loot, while I in fact get a reasonable share of the booty." La Chassée had come off rather better, having pursued the Dutch longboat ashore, and stripped a pretty girl of her jewels; and on returning to his own ship, plumes himself greatly on his chivalry in not having extended his conquest to her person. This puts the finishing touch to the exasperation of Challes, who sets the cabin in a roar by remarking that La Chassée's abstinence was due not to chivalry but to his having had a tureen of boiling soup upset into his lap in heavy weather the day before. The writer is still in a very moderate humour when they reach Pondicherry on 12th August. He finds Lascars (Lascar women, I presume) "frightful," and Pondicherry mutton "not worth a damn, while the famous fowls are very ordinary." Indeed, Challes has no good to say of the Bay of Bengal in the monsoon; off the Hoogly he is eaten alive with "heath flies"; the weather is abominable; some of his own (by which of course he means his stolen) wine gets broken; Bengal cow is "harder than a man's teeth." In fact "he will let himself be hanged before he will serve in these waters again." From 19th September to 14th October the ship lies at Negrales Island, off the western coast of Siam, where Challes is a little consoled to find good oysters and partridges; but on the other hand, the crew are on cabin rations, sixty-four men are down with fever, and "the ship is a hospital." It is by the way amusing to note that on a low island in the tropics in the rainy season, the ship's surgeon attributes the epidemic of fever entirely to the consumption of turtle meat.

On 4th December they begin to load for home at Balassor, in Bengal, where Challes buys a stock of thirty-five pints of Persian wine, wine of Shiraz, as he tells us, smacking his lips; a prudent purchase as it turned out, for by the end of January he had drunk the last of his stolen liquor, and was forced to start on the Shiraz. He found it excellent, but remarks sadly that "wine does not taste so good when you are drinking your own money." La Chassée, who had not laid in a stock at Balassor, enlarges daily on the bad keeping qualities of Shiraz, and urges the immediate consumption of the whole barrel. But the ship's stock must have been replenished, for on 23rd February the writer cures himself of a bad fever by tossing off five pints of *graves*.

By 16th April *L'Ecueil* is well out into the Atlantic, bound not

for France but for the West Indies. Fish, butter, and vegetables
have disappeared from the menu, there are worms in the biscuit,
there is much sickness, but the afterguard has still enough spirits
to stage a mock court martial on the chaplain. On 22nd May
plague breaks out, which Challes escapes, attributing his immunity to the use of frequent glasses of brandy and garlic.

At last on 4th June *L'Ecueil* anchors at Martinique, where they
remain in port for a month, and a distinctly more cheerful tone
is apparent in the diary; not unconnected with the fact that at
Port Royal Challes meets an old Parisian friend, a lady of dubious
reputation whom he calls Fanchon. Our author thinks well of
the West Indies, though after the first day he discovers that lemonade is an unhealthy drink, and reverts to his favourite *graves*.
On 3rd July they sail for home in a convoy of twenty-three ships.
One is intrigued by the *très belle dame*, a near relation of Mme.
de Maintenon's, who was a passenger in the fleet. Who was she,
and why is she never mentioned by Mme. de Maintenon? This, so
far as I know, is the only contemporary reference to such a person.

On 19th August 1691 the voyage ended at Belleisle, and the
last we see of Challes he is going ashore to eat, at La Chassée's
expense, a dinner whose menu they have been planning at intervals
for the last fortnight.

Father Labat, sent to the West Indies in 1693, was, I think, ill-
advised to make his own portrait the frontispiece to his book.
The bulbous nose, the thick blubber lips, and the double chin
rather prejudice us against one who on better acquaintance proves
to be excellent company, and of a charity not usual amongst his
clerical brethren; he likes Spaniards, Englishmen, and even Jesuits, though he is a shade apologetic over his refusal to cold-
shoulder the latter.

To go overseas as a missionary was in the France of Louis XIV
to travel *de luxe*. A passage for a missionary priest was either provided in a King's ship, or else at the King's expense in a mer-
chantman; the King paid for an outfit which included a mattress,
bedding, a white suit, a cassock, six shirts, six pairs of drawers,
twelve handkerchiefs, twelve nightshirts, twelve pairs of thread
stockings, a hat, three pairs of shoes, a sea-chest, and one spirit
case to every two priests. Finally, he gave each of them fifty francs
for incidental travelling expenses. Labat was given a passage in
a small naval vessel, a *flûte* called *La Gloire*, loaded with stores

for the garrison of Martinique, and carrying a complement of eighty, with thirty soldier recruits, and twenty-five passengers. The ship was so full that no cabin was available for him, but he lived quite happily in a sort of canvas cubicle between two guns on the lower deck. He sailed from Rochelle on 28th November 1693.

For the first week Labat is "more dead than alive," but by 8th December he has sufficiently recovered to dispute before an interested audience Father Holly's assertion that everyone believes in the doctrine of the Immaculate Conception; no one of the school of St. Thomas, says Labat, believes anything of the sort. The voyage follows the usual routine with which we are now tolerably familiar, and which need not be gone into in any detail: the meals are much the same as in *L'Oiseau* and *L'Ecueil,* as are the methods of killing the time. There is, however, one interesting amenity which neither of the other travellers had. Two large boxes of earth were carried on deck, forming a portable garden in which they raised enough green stuff to keep them in salads for the whole passage. Another unexpected refinement is that on the first day out, the captain requested that each passenger should always occupy the same seat in order that the stewards could be sure of giving each his own napkin; and the napkins, he tells us, were changed twice a week.

Herronière, the captain, seems to have been an *honnête homme,* observing on the same day that the steward had locked his wine locker, the captain called for the key, opened the locker, and then threw the key out of the window, saying that he wished his wine to be at the disposal of any passenger who cared to use it. This example was followed by everyone except the King's writer, who made "feeble excuses"; excuses which did him little service, for the young officers managed to open his locker, drink his wine, and recork the bottles filled with sea water. Labat's voyage, though I touch on it rather more lightly than the others, was on the whole the happiest of the lot. It is, of course, much the shortest, only sixty-three days, but credit for the comfort of all on board must be given to the tact and *savoir faire* of the captain, as instanced by his discouraging the formation of cliques, and his prohibition of card playing and gambling. There appears, too, to have been a good deal less junketing on board *La Gloire* than in the Eastern trading ships; indeed, the only festivities were the baptismal ceremonies when entering the tropics—when Labat was christened *Le Prêcheur*, at a cost of three crowns and six pots of brandy—and the traditional French merrymaking on *Jour des Rois*, the Eve of the Epiphany. On the latter occasion "fifteen to twenty quarts of brandy" were distributed amongst the crew, and Father Holly had to leave the dinner table at ten o'clock "in order to be in a fitting state to say Mass on the following morning": and we are not surprised to learn that next morning "Mass was rather late."

On 28th January 1694 they make their landfall at Martinique, this "frightful mountain," as Labat calls it, and on the following day he goes ashore to begin his missionary duties, shaved, and "in my new black clothes and my new black hat." Good luck to him.

XII

Female Education

In 1686 the Abbé de Fénelon, then in his thirty-fifth year, published a short pamphlet entitled *Traité de l'Education des Filles*, and in April of the same year Louis XIV, at the request of Mme. de Maintenon, opened St. Cyr as the first French boarding school for girls. Fénelon had revolutionized the theory of female education, and Mme. de Maintenon was to revolutionize its practice.

With the opening of St. Cyr begins the cult of the child, that attempt to take seriously the problems of child welfare and training, which must have so astonished the conservative elements in seventeenth-century society; for before 1686 the only theory entertained about children was that they were a nuisance, so much locked-up capital on which no dividend in the shape of family aggrandizement could be expected for the first twelve or fourteen years of the child's life. Consequently, education, such as it was, aimed only at turning the child into an adult with the least possible delay; precociousness was considered the most desirable quality in a child, and especially in a girl, whose business it was to marry the man of her father's choice or take the veil as soon as she was out of the schoolroom. Sometimes, indeed, she was married, not from the schoolroom, but from the nursery; Claire de Mailly-Brézé was still playing with her dolls when she was married to the Great Condé in the earlier part of the century. Girls so educated naturally married with no better equipment for the battle of life than a knowledge of the rules of precedence (the only indispensable knowledge), an ability to dance, to scrawl a badly written and worse spelt letter of compliment, to enter and leave a room gracefully, and to repeat a little of the parrot talk of society. Of the duties of a wife and a mother she was generally quite ignorant; a little fancy needlework, and perhaps a smattering of Italian made up the sum of her accomplishments. Her religious ideas were both vague and formal, and in the case of at least one family, seem to have solidified into a hazy belief that God was in some way related to most of the great houses of France; often there was a total indifference to religion.

Monsieur's second wife, Madame Palatine, in a gossiping letter remarks casually that she has taken to snoring so loudly that she has had to give up going to Mass.

Girls' ignorance of domestic economy and finance was unbelievable; "I wish," laments Mlle. de Scudéry in middle life, "that someone had taught me *something* when I was a girl." Another lady congratulates herself on her acumen in exchanging "a lot of wretched fields that did nothing but grow corn" for a handsome Venetian mirror. When the Duchess of Burgundy was promoted to the control of her own household, her wardrobe expenditure increased until in 1712 it was more than double that of the late Queen: and in spite of this her appearance was a scandal, and she could never appear in public without borrowing clothes from her ladies-in-waiting. A whole chapter could easily be written on the depth of the average woman's ignorance of the essentials of household management.

During the greater part of the century it was the exception to find a mother who took any interest in her daughter's education; the girl was either provided with a *gouvernante* at home, or sent as a boarder to a convent. The conventual method had at least the advantage of keeping the precocious girl out of serious mischief until the father could transfer the responsibility for her conduct to a husband; but the education given in most convents was deplorable. The reason for this is not far to seek; the average convent was poor, and lived under constant temptation to improve its finances by setting up as a boarding school, regardless of whether there were any nuns qualified to act as instructresses or not. In consequence, many convents turned out a girl determined not to take the veil, too *gauche* to cut a figure in society, and infected with the characteristic silliness and littlenesses of the small convent, which Mme. de Maintenon, herself bred in one, never tires of denouncing, and of which she used to give two characteristic examples: a convent-bred girl who nearly fainted with horror at the gross indecency of her father in using the word *breeches* in her presence: and another, a candidate for St. Cyr, who, when asked by Mme. de Maintenon to give a list of the Sacraments, stopped short at marriage. On being prompted, she giggled and said that all references to that Sacrament had been forbidden in her convent.

The governess was hardly a more satisfactory solution of the problem, for the professional governess did not yet exist. A seventeenth-century governess might be anyone from a duchess in the case of royal children, to a sharp-witted peasant girl in the case of the country squire's daughter, and the odds were that both were ignorant of and profoundly uninterested in education; both regarded their posts as a jumping-off place for higher things. Of the two, the village girl was probably the less disastrous, as she would at least bring the child at an impressionable age into touch with the lives of the common people, and help to strengthen and prolong the ties which bound it to its foster-brothers and sisters; as often as not, indeed, she might be the foster-sister of her own pupil. Educationally, the child would lose nothing, for kings' daughters, except in the externals of good breeding, were not a bit better educated than those of country squires. Louis XIV's mother could read and write, but that was about the extent of her learning. Her niece, Mademoiselle, tells us that her own good qualities are innate, and not the fruits of her education; and as she was in the habit of locking her governess up in her own room when annoyed with her, we may well believe it. The result was that when she made her début, no one could read her handwriting, and indeed she often could not read it herself. Nor in the sphere of moral training does the high-bred governess seem to have shone. The Duchess of Orléans, daughter of Louis XIV and Mme. de Montespan, at the age of nineteen, was getting "as drunk as a bell-ringer" three or four times a week; and the cynical immorality of her daughter, the Duchess of Berri, was the most notorious scandal of the end of the century.

Nothing shows more clearly the state of female education in the earlier part of the reign than the lavish praise awarded to the handful of women who had acquired a little learning: Mme. de Lafayette, who could read the Latin poets in the original, and who knew Italian, Mlle. de Scudéry, Mme. de Sévigné, Mme. des Houlières and a few others. Mlle. de Scudéry, *Sappho* as she was called, seems to have had the most elaborate education of all the learned ladies; brought up in the country by an uncle, she learnt dancing, painting, writing, spelling, designing, gardening, music, Italian, and domestic science, including the preparation of "useful and gallant" perfumes. Mme. de Sévigné, also educated by an uncle, had a less showy but perhaps better education than the professed bluestocking; Latin and Italian she knew well, and she had a taste for philosophy and theology, while throughout her life she is almost unique in good society in being an omnivorous reader. Tasso, Quintilian, St. Augustine, Josephus, Descartes, Bossuet's *Variations*, Burnet's *History*, nothing comes amiss to her, and she can comment wittily on what she reads. In these two uncles we are tempted to find support for Mme. de Maintenon's startling contention that girls should be educated by men, and boys by women; for, she says, men are implacable enemies to coquetry and silliness—while on the other hand, boys who have been brought up by a tutor are nearly always coarse and awkward. An opinion shared by her contemporary Mme. Cornuel, who once remarked that the young men of today are corpses and don't know it; they smell horrid, and can't talk.

Fénelon and Mme. de Maintenon have suffered the usual fate of pioneers. As we turn over their pages we reflect that it is all sound common sense, very well expressed, but perhaps just a little bit obvious, even occasionally platitudinous. We seem to have read very much the same sort of thing elsewhere, and forget its astonishing novelty to a society in which education, where it was attempted at all, consisted in cramming into boys and girls with the aid of a cane, a number of unexplained and disconnected facts. Only rarely in Fénelon's pamphlet are we brought to an abrupt realization that we are listening to a man of another country and another century: as for instance when he says that a girl should have *une pudeur sur la science presque aussi delicate que celle qui inspire l'horreur du vice*: or again, when he tells us that a girl may learn enough Latin to follow the Missal but she must be careful to conceal the fact that she understands it.

Awakened by such passages, our attention is called to the fact that in both writers, along with much that seems modern, there is a something curiously alien to the whole spirit of present day theory; it is as if we were reading a poem in a new metre, in which the stress appears always to fall upon the unexpected word. The explanation proves simple. Both to Fénelon and to Mme. de Maintenon, the only object of education is to lead souls to God. In the light of this discovery, their theories show themselves consistent and clear cut; their trivialities cease to be trivialities, and their apparent obscurantism proves to be deliberate. Granted their definition of the object of education, it is clear that the advantages of teaching or not teaching a certain subject cannot be considered *in vacuo*, but only in relation to its influence on the fundamental object of all education. Given the premiss, we can now understand Fénelon's advice that Spanish and Italian should never be taught to girls; to teach it is to give them access to dangerous literature, of which there is already more than enough in French. Music, too, he places on his index, regarding it as a *divertissement empoisonné*, probably with the sensuous melodies of Lulli in his mind; but he goes on to say that if a girl is incurably musical, it is wiser to permit her Church music than to forbid music altogether. Romances are, of course, forbidden, but rather surprisingly on practical not moral grounds; they are so unlike real life, he says, that a girl nourished on them will be inevitably disillusioned by the real world.

Fénelon's pamphlet was written as a practical manual for the use of mothers and governesses, and he begins encouragingly by telling them what a girl need *not* know; let her, he says, know nothing of politics, military matters, philosophy, and theology— especially theology, which for a woman is the most disastrous of all subjects. Teach her book-keeping, he urges, but don't let her dabble in subtleties about grace.

What are the radical faults of the Frenchwoman? Being a fashionable confessor, Fénelon no doubt speaks as an expert when he proceeds to answer his own question: unscrupulousness, dissimulation, affected timidity, gushing friendships, flattery, jealousy, and mistaking mere garrulity for an overflowing wit.

These defects, he says, become apparent at a very early age, and the girl's education must begin before she can speak. Even then, according to our author, a child can be taught by a smile or a frown to prefer the good to the bad, the reasonable to the unreasonable. But it is, of course, when the child reaches the stage of asking questions that its real education begins. "Open, gay, and familiar" is the conduct prescribed for the instructress, whose main task must be to win her pupil's affection, for a sombre and terrifying idea of religion is often the only legacy of a harsh upbringing. Never deceive a child under any circumstances; answer its questions truthfully if you can (being, however, careful to avoid "an indiscreet exactitude"), or else say frankly that you don't know. Remember that a child is just as much aware of your failings as you are of hers, and do not therefore adopt an austere and masterful air, which she will recognize as mere pedantry and affectation. And never forget that no one is as quick as a child to detect insincerity. A child should never be punished until all other methods of treatment have been exhausted, and, if you have to punish, never on any account do so while either you or the child have lost your tempers. On the other hand, never threaten, always punish. The governess must have as few rules as possible, the reasons for them must be explained to the child, and they must be obeyed implicitly. The good teacher, he goes on to say, is the one who has the skill to give as little formal instruction as possible, whilst making her casual conversation instructive; work and play should merge insensibly into each other, contrary to the usual practice of letting the child regard the day as divided between the boredom of the classroom and the exhilaration of the nursery. Above all, remember that what is repeated often enough to a young child it remembers all its life, and this is the time to hammer into a girl contempt for the body and reverence for the soul. Not that contempt for the body is to be interpreted as allowing personal uncleanliness or slovenliness in dress. If, says Fénelon, no one can remember what you are wearing, you are then well dressed. A startling axiom for the period, and one which must have provoked the derision of men and women alike at Versailles.

As the child grows into the young lady, further lessons have to be taught. The young lady must show no aversion to the company of dull persons; there is no one who has not one subject on which he is worth hearing, and it is for the lady to draw the man out on that subject. The governess must not now suppress her charge's reasonable curiosity: for, if she does, the girl will merely substitute unreasonable curiosities. If she is handsome, the governess will constantly impress upon her that beauty deceives its owner more than it does those whom it dazzles. A lady must not gossip with her servants, but she must talk to them frequently and kindly about their own affairs. She must remember that servitude is contrary to the natural equality of man, and therefore she will always strive to make the yoke as easy for her servants as possible. Above all, the young lady must be kept from basking in the servile admiration of her mother's waiting women.

Of education, in the sense of mere book-learning, Fénelon has much less to say, and indeed is obviously not keenly interested in the subject. Reading, writing, and arithemetic are the secular subjects for the earlier years, especially reading and writing; it is common but shameful, he remarks, to find women of quality who cannot pronounce French correctly, and whose writing is worse than their pronunciation. By way of recreational study, a girl may read Roman history, or even French, which, says Fénelon apologetically, "has also its beauties"; also a little carefully selected French eloquence and poetry is permitted. As, however, the girl nears the end of her education, a surprising series of new subjects emerges, which suggest a matriarchal background in the French household which I had not suspected. She must then acquire at least a bowing acquaintance with the form for the letting of farms, the receipt of rents, the law of inheritance, wills and donations; must be familiar with the nature of a contract, the customs of her province, and understand seigneurial rights. Truly a paragon among governesses would be needed to give Fénelon's ideal education!

Let us see how the new theories were to be translated into practice by Mme. de Maintenon.

St. Cyr was far from being her *coup d'essai* in educational matters; children and their upbringing had for long been the deepest interests of her busy life. She had educated the King's favourite bastard, the Duc du Maine, with conspicuous success, and also her own niece, Mme. de Caylus. She was in fact a schoolmistress with a frustrated vocation, and St. Cyr was merely the final result of many years' experience of practical teaching. As early as 1674 she had already begun to educate poor children, and by 1680 was the patroness of Mme. de Brinon's school at Montmorency, to which she paid frequent visits. In 1682 she established Mme. de Brinon in a better house at Rueil, gave her three assistants, and by her own exertions raised the number of her pupils to sixty. Her visits became more frequent—"I am infatuated with Rueil," she writes about this time. But her expenses were heavy and her income was still modest. Something must be done, and in 1684 she appealed to the King to come to her aid. Those were the days when Louis could refuse her nothing, and he came royally to the rescue. The school was transferred to the *château* of Noisy, near Versailles, and there Louis undertook the expense of educating and boarding a hundred girls out of his own private charities. On 3rd February 1684 the new school opened, and a few months later the King paid it a surprise visit. "Open to the King," shouted the ushers as the royal carriage drew up; the portress replied that she would enquire if mother superior could see him. He was admitted and shown over the classrooms; no girl turned her head to look at him. Gravity and decorum were dear to Louis' heart; his love for them was fully satisfied by this reception, and any lingering doubts of Mme. de Maintenon's fitness to play headmistress were finally dispelled. The King returned to Versailles determined to do something more worthy of his own grandeur than Noisy. Mme. de Maintenon's great opportunity had arrived.

Perhaps the hardest lot under the *ancien régime* was that of the poor *noblesse*, and especially that of the poor *demoiselle*. Mme. de Maintenon had herself been one, and the sufferings of her early life had left an indelible mark upon her character; true, she was a d'Aubigné, but she had been born in a common country jail; she had known want and hunger, and the bitterness of the bread offered by a grudging charity. Out of her hard, controlled resentment had grown the determination that if ever God gave her the power, she would do what she could to ease the lot of the unhappy class from which she herself had sprung. At Rueil and Noisy little attention had been paid to the class from which the pupils were drawn, but when in 1684 the question of extending the work of Noisy was mooted, Mme. de Maintenon, supported by Father de La Chaise, the royal confessor, made an urgent and ultimately successful appeal for a new and larger school, exclusively for the daughters of the poor nobility. It needed all her eloquence to win over Louis, who countered with the characteristic objection that no Queen of France had ever undertaken such a work. But Louis was a lover all his life; barely three months had elapsed since his marriage to Mme. de Maintenon; he capitulated, and having done so, was soon as enthusiastic about the proposed new school as was his wife. In April 1685 the estate of St. Cyr was bought, and the work of building began at once. Louis, as usual, wanted magnificence, Mme. de Maintenon wanted a plain and commodious school; as she remarks sourly to a friend, "I know *MM. les architectes du Roi*; they will give me a palace of exquisite external symmetry, lacking in every single convenience of a school." As she had foreseen, St. Cyr was built entirely with an eye to its external magnificence, and she had to make the best of it.

St. Cyr was something quite novel in French life, and both the Church and the law regarded it rather dubiously. What exactly was it? A new convent, and if so, of what order? Or a charity? Louis, who disliked convents, made it plain that St. Cyr was not to become one, and was supported by Father de La Chaise, who remarked that France had enough good religious, and too few good mothers. Mme. de Maintenon leant rather to the foundation of a new teaching order under absolute vows, but ultimately agreed to the King's suggestion that the mistresses should take simple vows, with a fourth vow to devote themselves to the education of the girls. The entrance age for St. Cyr was to be not younger than seven or older than twelve, the leaving age twenty; proofs of both poverty and nobility were to be demanded from any candidate for admission; and the establishment was to be under the conduct of Mme. de Brinon as superior or headmistress, assisted by four choir ladies and eight novices, all under simple vows. It is pleasant to notice that amidst the general excitement, Noisy was not forgotten. All the girls of the old school were provided for, either by admittance to St. Cyr, by marriage, or by paying their dowries in the convents of their choice.

On 2nd August 1686 St. Cyr opened with two hundred and fifty girls, all personally selected by the King from a batch of applications far in excess of the number of places at his disposal.

Under the deed of foundation Mme. de Maintenon was made spiritual foundress, but was in fact really the headmistress; an arrangement unavoidable under the circumstances, but one which did not make the superior's position an easy one, and, as we shall see, there was friction.

Nowhere do we find a better illustration of the amazing energy of the seventeenth century than in the long story of Mme. de Maintenon's dealings with St. Cyr. Had her St. Cyr correspondence perished and her general correspondence survived, we should think of her as the lady patroness, the chairman of the board of governors of a large public school, visiting the place perhaps once a year. If only the St. Cyr letters had survived, we should picture her a recluse, wholly devoted to her school, and paying occasional visits to Versailles. The fact is that this very busy woman, the wife of an exigent husband, the arbitress of every Bourbon family quarrel, pestered by visits of ceremony and by suppliants, the confidante of ministers, racked with chronic malaria, managed to spend at least two whole days a week at the school, and to visit it nearly every morning. And with Mme. de Maintenon a whole day means a whole day. She would arrive in time to assist in getting the younger girls dressed at six o'clock, and from then until her departure twelve hours later, it was a constant round of activity—taking classes, interviewing the household officers, visiting the sick-room, praising, exhorting, consoling and reprimanding. And in the earlier years, while her mistresses were young and inexperienced, she had to instruct them at least as often and as thoroughly as she did their pupils. The burden would have been too heavy for even her inexhaustible vitality but for the lucky chance that the King developed almost as strong a passion for St. Cyr as she did.

At St. Cyr, we are told, the King *a toujours l'air d'être chez lui*, and his visits become more and more frequent; with the smallest girls he was a distinct favourite, and at recreation time in the summer, might often be found with one of them sitting on his knees in the garden, chatting without constraint. To find himself liked for his own sake must have been a welcome novelty after the honeyed flattery of Versailles.

When Mme. de Maintenon was not at St. Cyr, she was writing to it: to the superior, to the mistresses, to classes, and to individual girls. Somehow in the course of her busy day, time is found for this

immense outpouring of letters, and we notice with astonishment
that any girl in the school was free to write to her whenever she
pleased, and that the letters were always fully answered; they came
to her with their difficulties and disappointments and received wise,
sympathetic answers which—fortunately for us—they treasured
for the rest of their lives. There is a freedom, almost a negligence,
about the St. Cyr letters, which is lacking from Mme. de Maintenon's general correspondence: at times almost a warmth, which
deludes us into the hope that in a page or two we shall get under
her guard and see what kind of woman she really was: but we
never do. We see only that they are the work of a very busy woman,
and full of swift transitions as the many aspects of the school's
daily life pass through her mind. There is something almost
Pauline in the impetuosity of the St. Cyr epistles, and in their
abrupt change of subject. Destroy the spirit of the world in the
girls, she writes, show them the vexations which afflict the worldly;
and then she goes on, "What's this I hear about girls in the sick-
room making a fuss about taking their quinine?" *Lâcheté* is a fault
which she cannot tolerate; meaning thereby a sensitiveness under
rebuke, anger at finding self-correction difficult, or, in the physical
sense, annoyance over stormy weather, smoking chimneys, cold
and bad smells, all of which she classes as disobedience to the will
of God. Then without any transition she continues, "You can't
make all the soup you want on a pound of meat per head per day;
you need one and a half pounds. And see that the sick have their
main meal in the morning, not the evening." A few pages further
on, the flow of another letter is broken with the interjection "Mlle.
de Grimonville is getting positively hump-backed, and I find that
her corsets haven't been seen to for eighteen months. Why?"

In the earliest years Mme. de Maintenon's chief task was to instill into her young and inexperienced mistresses her own ideas
of the theory and practice of education; daily letters flow out from
Versailles to St. Cyr in which we get a vivid picture of the anxieties
of the spiritual foundress. The *raison d'être* for St. Cyr, she tells
them, is to give an education in which instruction is regarded as
unimportant compared with the building of a Christian character.
Her ideal *Dames de St. Louis*, as the mistresses were officially styled,
is firm, mild, grave, taciturn, and of course *solide*; a favourite quality with Mme. de Maintenon, whose husband, that unrivalled
judge of character, did not christen her V*ôtre Solidité* without good

reason. The ideal mistress will begin by instilling into the new girls a love of the catechism and a conviction that nothing is so important as the reception of the Sacraments ("once every eight days is too often for girls to communicate"). These are the only foundations on which a St. Cyr education can be built; then, in somewhat startling parentheses the teacher is reminded that most new girls will arrive disingenuous, thieves, and liars, and with no real understanding of the doctrines of the Church. They will repeat parrot fashion "One God only shalt thou worship," and will be found to be worshipping the Virgin; they know "Thou shalt not steal," but will maintain that it is no sin to steal from the King. No mercy is to be shown to falsehood, which should be regarded with horror, not only by the mistresses, but by the other girls. A love of silence and work is to be inculcated, and above all, modesty and decorum. But let the *dames* remember that St. Cyr is not a convent, and that the pupils are not novices; the aim must be to fit girls for the world not for the cloister; the training must be not only Christian, but in the best sense of the word, worldly. There must be books, *honnêtes et agréables*, to give them the tone of the best society; there must be poetry recitations to develop their taste and teach them correct pronunciation; there must be letter writing and group conversations supervised by the class mistress, though in fact the conversation class was generally taken by Mme. de Maintenon herself. The mistress must school herself to adopt an air of what may be called kindness towards her charges, always equable, always a little aloof, devoid of any suspicion of favouritism, losing all interest in a girl as soon as she has left her class, and avoiding the slightest familiarity with the elder girls. They will always take advantage of it, says Mme. de Maintenon. The prohibition is more reasonable than at first sight appears when we realize that the eldest girls were in their late teens and the mistresses in their middle twenties. Of course, she adds, girls will take a violent affection to a particular mistress, but there is nothing to worry about in this; it is a passing phase. A mistress, on the other hand, must never attempt to make herself pleasant to a girl; the way to gain the only esteem worth having is to be both faultless in your own conduct, and to let it be uniform. A girl must never get the idea that a mistress is approachable at one time, and not at another, or that she can play one mistress off against another; for which reason the good mistress will never comment on the ignorance of a girl newly promoted to her class, or make any remark reflecting on her predecessor's management when taking over a new class. The good mistress will know how to join in the children's games and recreation hours without attempting to come down to their level, whilst so conducting herself that the girls do not feel constraint in her presence; and though she will not talk to them about God in playtime, she will, if she has *savoir faire,* give the conversation such a turn that the girls will press her to talk to them about Him. And let the mistress always remember that it is the children's recreation time, not hers; she takes her recreation with her sisters when she is off duty. For no mistress can ever afford to relax under the critical eyes of youth.

The young *Dames de St. Louis* seem in their first enthusiasm to have been indiscreetly zealous in the interpretation of their duties, and before long Mme. de Maintenon finds herself forced to preach tolerance; a mistress, she says, must not hear everything, or rather she must not let it be seen that she hears everything. Let the girls have every liberty consistent with obedience to the rules, and let the mistress conceal the iron hand in the velvet glove whenever possible. "You will never," she writes to one of them "instill a love of God by punishing and scolding: remember what St. François de Sales says, you catch flies with honey, not with vinegar." Never scold, she goes on to say, always punish; only let punishment be rare and severe. In a general letter, the mistresses are warned never to refuse a girl's request without giving a full explanation for the reason, and never in any circumstances to give way to importunity. She shows an affectionate contempt for those mistresses who are horrified at petty misdemeanours such as making a disturbance in the refectory or playing the fool in the corridors; girls have always behaved like that, and girls always will. Nor has she any patience with the mistress who reprimands a girl for being interested in dress; what girl isn't, she asks?

From the very outset, St. Cyr was embarrassingly successful; the King liked it, and therefore the new school became the rage at Court. Ladies of quality flocked to the parlour with offers of assistance, which in fact meant that they hoped to play at schoolmarming under the eye of the King himself. Their offers were politely but very firmly declined. Nor were the great nobles more fortunate in their entreaties to be allowed to place their daugh-

ters in St. Cyr, though many of them offered the holders of nomi-
nations large sums to exchange places with them. Louis stood
firm; praise, money and flattery were all unavailing, and poverty
remained one of the two essential conditions for admission to the
school. Once only was the rule broken, and that was in favour of
the adored Duchess of Burgundy, the child wife of the King's
grandson, who in 1697 was admitted to the bottom class, the reds,
under the incognito of Mlle. de Lastic, in order, in the words of
Mme. de Maintenon, "that she might acquire dignity without
pride." The experiment was a complete success, and at St. Cyr,
as at Court, the princess won all hearts. In later years she always
recalled her school days with delight, and any red of her year,
however humble her subsequent state, remained her friend for
life.

But all was not well with the school which was outwardly so
flourishing, and by the beginning of 1688 Mme. de Maintenon
was beginning to feel seriously uneasy. The root of the trouble
was the character of the superior, Mme. de Brinon. An Ursuline
nun, who had entered religion without a vocation, eloquent, arrogant, with what was known as the grand manner, she had begun
as the protégée of Mme. de Maintenon; but within two years she
seems to have lost her head completely under the combined influence of the King's friendship and the flatteries of the Court,
and was now challenging Mme. de Maintenon's position as spiritual foundress. The foundress argued with her in vain; but in
October the superior committed the crowning folly of offending
the King by the almost regal pomp with which she behaved
whilst taking the waters at Bourbon. Few people better understood the art of waiting for the psychological moment than did
Mme. de Maintenon—and then striking hard. On 10th December Mme. de Brinon received her dismissal in a *lettre de cachet*,
and withdrew, "stupefied and in tears" to a convent.

But it was one thing to get rid of Mme. de Brinon, quite another
to eradicate the spirit of pride and haughtiness which her influence had spread throughout the school. Matters came to a head
after the public performances of the school play, *Esther*, in January 1689, whose effect on the young actresses increased Mme. de
Maintenon's alarm. The King witnessed every performance, and
so did every courtier who could manage to scrape admission,
especially the young courtiers. *Esther* was the rage of the season;

at Versailles young guardsmen on winter leave could be heard criticizing and contrasting the charms of the performers in a tone which, to say the least of it, was not *convenable*; worse still, Mme. de Maintenon saw, or thought she saw, glances of intelligence being exchanged between the actresses on the stage and the young officers in the pit. Nor did the evil end there: the poisonous breath of the Court crossed the footlights and infected the convent; the girls talked of nothing but the delights of the Court and its charming young men, and all indulged in daydreams in which they saw themselves countesses, princesses, or even wives of dukes. Discipline relaxed daily, and it became increasingly common for girls to refuse to sing in chapel, for fear of hurting their voices for the stage. St. Cyr was in fact dropping to the level of a fashionable convent school. The soberer elements in society took fright, and a revulsion against the St. Cyr tone set in; Hébert, *curé* of Versailles, who had an influence out of all proportion to his modest preferment, openly denounced all play-acting by schoolgirls as immodest, if not indecent, and was supported in his protest by Godet Desmarets, special confessor to St. Cyr. Scandalous old women, who disliked Mme. de Maintenon, began to tell each other that no one but an idiot would have built a girls' school within a stone's throw of Versailles, and separated from it only by a practicable wall. And, the final straw, news reached Holland, where the gutter press sensationalized the story and distributed it throughout Europe. The Dutch version of the doings at St. Cyr was that Mme. de Maintenon, now that her own charms were *passé*, was seeking to retain her hold on Louis by turning procuress, and had established St. Cyr as a training school for royal mistresses.

Once convinced that a grave blunder had been made, Mme. de Maintenon wasted no time in putting her school on an entirely new footing. Generously ignoring the dismissed superior's responsibility for the existing state of affairs, she writes to the *dames* early in 1691—"It is I who have spread the sin of pride through our house, and I shall be very fortunate if God does not punish me for it; He knows that I sought nothing but virtue, but I have built upon sand"; and she next proceeds to examine the results of her own imprudence: "You mistresses," she says, "have yourselves developed a demeanour which would ill become a community of German canonesses, and as for the girls, I find a pride and haughtiness in them which would not be tolerated at Versailles in women of the very first quality. They talk about simplicity instead of practising it." Order and simplicity are to be the keynotes of the new St. Cyr, and then follows the first of the new rules: "Don't let any man—rich, poor, old, young, parent, or priest—see the amateur theatricals." As day follows day, the stream of prohibitions increases; the conversation classes disappear, so do the *honnêtes et agréables* books; poetry and letter-writing are dropped from the curriculum; periods of silence are lengthened; the use of jewellery is forbidden. It must have been a grim time for those girls whom the reform caught half-way through their school days, and yet there is ample evidence that Mme. de Maintenon did not lose her place in their affections. The tone of old girls' letters shows it, and more than once we find her having to reprove an old pupil for expressing home-sickness for St. Cyr.

The new instructions underline that distrust for all girls, which is as marked a feature of Mme. de Maintenon's character as is her liking for them. Four mistresses, or at any rate, two mistresses and two lay sisters, are appointed to each class, and two are always to be on duty, day and night; at no time is a girl to be out of sight of a mistress or a lay sister, and the lay sister is to act as an additional pair of eyes and ears for the mistress. Friendships between girls are to be discouraged, for girl's conversation among themselves is always dangerous. But, she says, it is useless to forbid a girl to have a particular friend, and this result must be achieved by so filling up the day with collective activities that a girl has no opportunity to make a confidante. There are to be no dark corners in St. Cyr, no pettifogging economy with candles. For where there is a dark corner you will find two girls whispering, and where you find a girl whispering, she is saying something which she would be ashamed to say out loud. Plenty of indoor and outdoor games are the means to stop girls from whispering in corners. And at this point, as earlier with Fénelon, we are brought up with a jerk to a realization of how remote the period is to us—"I can't imagine why dice are forbidden in convents, seeing that we are allowed to use ladders, lanterns, spears and all other things which were used in the Passion." Of all the new regulations there is one which is particularly repugnant to English sentiment, namely, that girls are to be encouraged in tale-bearing, and that any girl who resents the activities of the informer must be severely punished. There is a fresh insistence on the importance of girls practising the utmost modesty of act and speech toward each other, balanced by a warning against the false prudery of the ordinary convent. It comes to Mme. de Maintenon's ears that a girl has *whispered* the news that her married sister is pregnant—"Does she wish to be more modest than Our Lord?" asks Mme. de Maintenon indignantly. "Teach them to distinguish between words which are immodest, that is to say sinful, and those which are merely gross, or impolite. Don't be always lecturing on convents, but explain frankly to the bigger girls what are the duties of the married state." More and more obsessed with the importance of unending watchfulness grows Mme. de Maintenon as the time goes on; even at night the all-seeing eye is not to be taken off the girls; a mistress is always to sleep in a cubicle in the dormitory, and it is the unfortunate woman's duty to get up at intervals and make the round of her charges.

Was there perchance more than mere scandal in the old ladies' references to that practicable wall which separated St. Cyr gardens from Versailles park? Or could Mme. de Maintenon, if she had chosen, have told us some curious stories of the Ursuline convent in the *faubourg St. Jacques* where she herself had been educated? We don't know.

The Church had never entirely approved of the unorthodox establishment of St. Cyr, and now, headed by Godet Desmarets, took advantage of the general *bouleversement* to obtain a far-reaching reform in the founder's constitutions. On 1st December 1692 St. Cyr became a regular Ursuline convent, and though the *Dames de St. Louis* retained their distinctive dress and titles, they were obliged to take full vows; those who declined to do so were discharged with pensions. Louis yielded most reluctantly to the change, and agreed to it only in deference to Desmarets' contention that if the position was not regularized, there was no guarantee that the school would not be closed after the King's death. This change brought with it new anxieties for Mme. de Maintenon; she foresaw the danger of the *dames* becoming mere nuns who would regard the education and care of the girls as a task to be compressed into what time they could spare from prayer and contemplation; again and again she impresses on them that the order has no *raison d'être* except the school. She is constantly on the watch to see that the bursar is not economizing by employing girls on domestic work at the expense of their education; household tasks, she lays down, are to be given as a reward to the bigger girls, whose education is nearly completed, though all girls may be set to dusting and sweeping when they would otherwise be idle. Classes are, we notice, not to be mixed when doing housework; each class is to have its own task, and, for the juniors, collecting flowers to make syrup is suggested as a suitable occupation.

Before the turn of the century St. Cyr was firmly established, and the school entered upon its golden age. In its final form it had a somewhat elaborate organization. At the head of the hierarchy stood the superior, a remote and awful figure, rarely seen by any but the naughtiest girls; she concerned herself mainly with the conventual side of the establishment and its contacts with the outer world. Next in seniority and importance came the *Maîtresse Générale des Classes*, who may be said to have been the real headmistress. She supervised and revised the syllabus, watched over the teaching, distributed rewards and punishments, compiled the diet sheets, controlled the wardrobe, and was responsible for the conduct of the mistresses. She was an *ex officio* member of the governing body, where, in Mme. de Maintenon's words, she was the girls' protectress, advocate, and person of business. Next came the four class mistresses, each with three assistants, two of the four being always on duty. In chapel, classroom, playground or dormitory, no girl was ever to be out of sight of two of the four. Next came a large number of officials, some purely conventual, others with mixed responsibilities—the portress, the librarian, the *infirmière*, the mistress of the wardrobe, and so forth.

Class mistresses seem to have had a pretty free hand. The subjects for each class were laid down for her, but there was nothing corresponding to the progressive course in a subject which we find in a modern school syllabus. Christianity came first, and whatever subject was being taught seems to have been regarded primarily as a quarry from which texts could be dug for lectures on the girls' religious duties. If the routine seems to us a little bleak, it does not seem to have been so regarded by the girls themselves; perhaps because Mme. de Maintenon insisted on the dismissal of any girl who was found to have come to St. Cyr against her own wish, and the transfer of her nomination to a younger sister. The girls rose at six, and went to Mass at eight, accompanied by the *dames*, each armed with a notebook and pencil to take the names of any girl whose eyes wandered, or who slouched when kneeling —"It is the heart and not the body which should be prostrated before God," says Mme. de Maintenon. After the chapel came morning school until midday—no mention of *petit dejeuner* one notices—and then dinner and recreation filled in the time until two, when the girls went back to the classrooms until six. Bed was at 9:00 P.M. During their fifteen-hour day, the girls were permitted a total of three and a half hours' talking. The practical interpretation of the foundress' theories that girls should be kept amused and that their periods of instruction should be short, does not at first sight seem to have erred on the side of lenience; but we must remember that much of the so-called schooltime was actually employed in conversation—religious conversation no doubt, but still conversation; and also that many of the bigger girls were often absent from class altogether, assisting the portress on the door, or in the linen room and suchlike. Feast days, royal visits, and parents and relations in the parlour helped to break the somewhat monotonous life; though even when seeing her parents, the girl was accompanied to the parlour by a mistress to watch for breaches of deportment—"Nothing," says Mme. de Maintenon, "looks so bad in a girl as any familiarity, even with the closest relations." Every now and then the good girl could count on what must have been an exciting whole day's holiday —"Send one of your girls to dine with me at Versailles as a little treat," is a frequent command to class mistresses.

Having secured her nomination, a girl entered St. Cyr between her seventh and twelfth birthdays, and was placed in the bottom class, the *Red*, so-called because her school uniform was decorated with ribbons of that colour, as were also her classroom and her class dormitory. The other three classes also had their distinctive colours—house colours, as we would call them. In the red class, the subjects were catechism, elementary sacred history, reading, writing, arithmetic, and the elements of music—the last subject a concession to the taste of Louis XIV, who was passionately devoted to it, and insisted on its inclusion. Mme. de Maintenon was distrustful of it, but had to yield, and even to allow Louis to give periodical school concerts at which either his own orchestra or one of the cavalry bands performed for the amusement of the girls.

The red and each of the other three classes numbered about sixty girls each, and were subdivided into five or six "families" under a *Fille de Mme. de Maintenon,* or in our language, a school prefect, and as we study the organization it becomes apparent that school hours must have been much less monotonous than at first sight they appeared to be. There was a large amount of devolution, and the six "families" seem really to have been almost separate classes, perhaps collected under the class mistress only for a lecture. The next class, the *Green,* contained girls from eleven to fourteen, and in it, geography and mythology were added to the red class syllabus; mythology may at first sight appear a surprising choice, but it must be remembered that a smattering of classical knowledge was an indispensable part of every educated lady's equipment. Next came what Mme. de Maintenon always considered the most difficult class in the school, the *Yellow,* which took the girls between fourteen and seventeen. It was in this class, whose members were no longer children, but were not yet broken in to being young ladies, that boredom with St. Cyr was apt to manifest itself, and the yellows contained most of the girls who found themselves in periodic collision with the *maîtresse générale.* The yellow's curriculum added to that of the two lower forms the study of the French language, advanced religious instruction, deportment, and dancing. Then came the *Blue* class, girls of seventeen to twenty, whose time was largely devoted to moral instruction and advanced needlework. Whilst mainly concerned with the yellows, as being the class in which character is formed, Mme. de Maintenon realized that a blue was already more than a little tired of St. Cyr, and is merciless in hounding on their unlucky class mistress to find virtuous amusements for them, a task of no little difficulty in a school where talking was usually forbidden, and reading discouraged. Amateur theatricals, poetry readings, and helping the officers of the household seem to have been the stock palliatives of boredom.

Lastly came the *Blacks,* or school prefects, selected from the blue class, and nominally working with them in school hours, though, in fact, a separate class for all practical purposes, under the direct supervision of the *maîtresse générale.* The blacks were rarely seen in school at all, except in their capacity as assistant mistresses. Their day began with dressing and combing the hair of the younger children, then making their beds. From chapel onwards they were usually to be found at work in one of the offices, kitchen, infirmary, or stores; such at least was the theory, but we find Mme. de Maintenon complaining to the *maîtresse générale* that whenever she catches sight of two or three blacks, they seem to be doing nothing but chattering. And she adds—she is now in her sixties—that young people seem to be much lazier today than they were when she was a girl.

To the best of the blacks went the greatest prize St. Cyr had to offer, the post of secretary to Mme. de Maintenon; and it speaks well for the St. Cyr training that no holder of the position seems to have lost her head on finding herself at Versailles, and on terms of familiarity with the King. But no doubt Mme. de Maintenon kept a very watchful eye on the secretary's conduct.

When at last the time came for a girl to leave St. Cyr, she did so with many valuable privileges; if she had a vocation, she would be admitted at the King's charge to one of the royal abbeys; had she developed a taste for the life of a schoolmistress, she could fill the first vacancy in the ranks of the *Dames de St. Louis*, and continue to live at St. Cyr as a novice until a vacancy occurred; if she married, Mme. de Maintenon paid the wedding expenses, and, most coveted privilege of all, Louis XIV signed her marriage contract, thereby putting her on the same footing as the daughters of the most illustrious houses in France. And whatever she became, she was given a complete outfit of clothes and a dowry of three thousand francs.

Mme. de Maintenon lived long enough to see her dreams realized; before she died, St. Cyr had become what she had hoped it would become, not only the best girls' school in France, but a teachers' training college sending out an annual batch of St. Cyr girls to breathe the St. Cyr spirit on the dry bones of the old-fashioned convent schools. By the turn of the century St. Cyr girls were everywhere in demand, orders were competing with each other for novices from St. Cyr, and even St. Cyr schoolgirls were begged on loan to re-model convent schools on the new educational lines. This last experiment proved a complete success, all the more remarkable when we note the age of some of the reformers; Gomerfontaine, which was to become the *bourgeois* St. Cyr, was re-modelled by a girl of fifteen, and the convent of Bisy was set on the right path by a fourteen-year-old yellow.

So soundly had Mme. de Maintenon built that when in 1719 she was laid beside those of her beloved children who had died at the school, it made little difference. Her spirit lingered on, her words were handed down from *dame* to *dame*; the momentum which she had imparted to her creation kept the machine running until that fatal day in 1792 when the new rulers of France ordered the closure of St. Cyr. In 1794 some workmen, engaged in the demolition of the chapel, discovered Mme. de Maintenon's grave, pulled out her body, still in a state of perfect preservation, dragged and kicked it about the grounds, and finally threw it into a pit. At last, as her great-nephew observes, the uncrowned wife of Louis XIV found herself treated as a Queen of France.

XIII

The World of

Letters

"Sir," said Johnson, "the French have a couple of tragic poets who go round the world, and one comic poet." But would the contemporaries of Corneille, Racine, and Molière have accorded them the same unquestioned pre-eminence? What did their contemporaries read? And what was being read in the earlier part of the century? For, after all, the French Classic Age, which we are apt to confound with the reign of Louis XIV, in fact covers only the latter half of it. It is significant that in 1695, in the heyday of the *Grand Siècle*, Boileau can write, "Malherbe's reputation is growing all the time"; it is to Malherbe that the modern poet's thoughts turn, rather than to the three whose names go round the world. It is evident that we must hark back to Malherbe.

The earlier part of the century seems to us a tentative, rather fumbling period when, even among those who paid allegiance to the classics, it is not easy to discover any canon of criticism. Malherbe himself (*c.* 1555–1628), for instance, thought little of Virgil,

much preferring Statius: considered Petrarch the most important of the Italians: disliked all the Greeks, especially Pindar,
whom he dismissed as *galimatias*, balderdash: and had a poor
opinion of Ronsard. His favourite authors were Horace, Juvenal,
Martial, Ovid and Seneca. Virgil indeed seems, though much
read, to have ranked low in the first half of the century; Corneille
(1606–84), for example, tells us he preferred Lucan. Cicero,
as one would expect, was generally popular, and the favourite
book of Ménage (1613–92) was the *De Senectute*. La Fontaine
(1621–95), always travelled with the letters to Atticus in his
pocket: and is labelled a bore by Racine's sister because he either
would not talk at all at table, or else would talk of no one but
Plato. La Fontaine recommends the study of Cicero, Horace, and
Virgil to his son as authors who will teach him to write *avec jus-
tesse et netteté*. The inclusion of the two poets is odd, in view of
the fact that he has just been urging the young man to resist the
temptation of writing verse. Molière (1622–73) prided himself,
with what justice I do not know, on being an imitator of
Terence, but found his chief intellectual relaxation in the works
of Descartes. Pellisson (1624–93) surprises us with the information that much Latin, and even Greek, was to be met with in
the days of his youth in the provinces; translating from the classics
was a favourite pastime, and the composition of *galant* epigrams
in both languages a common amusement. He himself, by the time
he was twenty-five, had already written his *Remarks on Homer*,
though I do not recollect he showed any subsequent interest in
the Greeks; Terence and Cicero were his favourite authors, from
whom he drew support for his theory that *le bel air* is fundamentally the same in all ages: meaning by *le bel air*, we may suppose, that talent "for writing trifles in language which shall not
be low, constrained, or hard" for which he strove in his own
works. Terence, Horace, Cicero, Ariosto, and Ronsard are the
old authors whom he mentions most frequently; and he envies
Horace his freedom from the "thousand scrupulous maxims" of
his own time. For Ronsard he has a genuine, if slightly apologetic,
admiration. The reading of his friend Lamoignon may perhaps be
taken as typical of a lawyer of the old school; he knew Plutarch,
Cicero and Tacitus "almost by heart." Though Plutarch, by the
way, seems to have been known inside out by anyone who read
at all. Even those who could not read the original had read the

French translation, and it is one of the very few books which was appreciated by Louis XIV himself.

With Mme. de Sévigné (1627–96) two new names appear on the select list of classics. That of Tasso, whom in 1671 she is finding "most amusing"; and a couple of years later she applies the same words to Quintilian. In 1677 she is reading Lucan; in 1680 she is enquiring for a copy of Terence, "wishing to see the original, whose copies have given me so much pleasure."

Of her contemporary, Charles Perrault (1628–1703), the defender of the moderns, we shall have more to say in due course; but it may here be noted that, if he undervalued the ancients, his opinion cannot be attributed to ignorance of their works. For by the time he left school, he had read Virgil, Horace, and Tacitus, to say nothing of Tertullian, "and most of the other classics." His great opponent, Boileau (1636–1711), undoubtedly the ablest defender of the ancients, and after the publication of the *Art Poétique* in 1674 "the great authority on Parnassus," was reared on Virgil and Horace, though his own style was confessedly formed on that of Juvenal. But Virgil and Horace he knew practically by heart, as did so many of his contemporaries. Their peculiar excellence, he maintained, and also that of Homer, consisted in saying what is "dry and difficult to say in verse"; whereas the moderns confined themselves to abstractions which had been used before, and for which there was a ready-made vocabulary. His friend Racine (1639–99), like their common friend La Fontaine, always had Cicero's letters in his pocket on a journey, and, unlike the other two, had by the time he was eighteen, read much in Spanish and Italian literature, in addition to the classics. He was, too, a Greek scholar of no little merit, and left college with a thorough understanding of Sophocles and Euripides. Racine's own work may owe a larger debt to Boileau than is usually admitted: for in their forty years of unclouded friendship, the two men read each other their manuscripts and exchanged the frankest criticism upon them. Racine lived and died faithful to his beloved classics; when in 1677 he was appointed Historian to the King, his first care is to read Lucan to fit himself for his duties: and in the last year of his life, we find him reading Cicero's letters "for the hundredth time."

But if the pure scholar and man of letters tended to be preoccupied with the classics, to the exclusion of less solid fare, this was not the case with men and women of the world. Romances, burlesques, plays, minor poetry, letters, polemical divinity and sermons were eagerly devoured throughout the whole period, even after the coming of the new classical age; though sermons should perhaps rank as a branch of the theatre rather than as an arm-chair pleasure. For the sermon was a thing acted, an appeal to the emotions rather than to the intellect, and a vehicle for the display of a tedious wealth of classical imagery. How tedious, not to say indecent, the classical ornaments of a sermon could be, it is now difficult for us to realize. Conrart (1603–75) mentions a Passion sermon in which the preacher described the descent of Venus from Olympus to the foot of the Cross to distract the grief of the Virgin by telling her the story of the death of Adonis. This Conrart, by the way, was a true bibliophile, and we may here stop for a moment to glance at his library; for we are unlikely to find any that will give us a better idea of what the semi-educated man of wide tastes was reading between 1620 and 1675. Semi-educated I suppose we must call him, for he knew no Latin, and often and bitterly complains of the handicap of being unable to read the latest books until they have been translated into French. And translations came slowly, for as late as 1645 the book-sellers were still making a larger profit on works published in Latin than on those in the vernacular.

But to his books. Balzac (Jean Louis Guez de Balzac), of course, and Mlle. de Scudéry, whom he considers "one of the most precious ornaments of her sex." *Fulvio Testi* and *Vasari* he is hunting for in the second-hand market, and in 1647 the book of the moment— "Book of the Month" we should call it—is Corneille's *Heraclius*.

Sixteen forty-seven was in fact a good year for book collectors; for there was also Vaugelas' *Remarks on the French Language*, Andilly's *Confessions of St. Augustine*, Allancourt's *Retreat of the Ten Thousand*, and Sorlin's *Histoire des Dieux de l'Antiquité*. In 1648 Conrart is hunting for Camoëns' *Lusiad*, of which he has very favourable reports, and he is still bothering his bookseller for *Vasari*: but it must be a tall copy, with wide margins. And this year he buys Giustiniani's *History of Genoa*—he has had tracers out for it for a long time—and Scarron's *Virgile travesti*. In 1650 he is making enquiries about the works of an Englishman called Hobbes.

Mme. de Sévigné had an equally catholic taste. In addition to the classics, sermons, and romances, we find her reading Nicole's *Essais de Morale*, Columbus' *Discovery of the Indies*, Balzac's *Socrate Chrétien*, St. Augustine, *Don Quixote*, Pascal, Racine, Corneille, Molière, and Bossuet's *Variations*. Of the dramatists she placed Corneille easily first, and could not understand the current enthusiasm for Racine. The taste for his works was, she thought, a craze which would pass, like that for coffee. Incidentally, be it noted, Racine always maintained that Corneille's works were superior to his own. Boileau, on the other hand, preferred Molière to either of them. A still more remarkable judgment is that of Richelieu, who preferred both Georges de Scudéry and Hardi to Corneille, and exerted his influence to damn *Le Cid*.

Much of the popular reading matter of the earlier part of the century was ephemeral, and died before the end of Louis XIV's reign. Balzac (1597–1655) made his reputation in 1628 with his *Apologie pour M. de Balzac*, and enhanced it with his *Lettres Choisies* published in the middle of the century, with a characteristically eulogistic preface written by himself under a false name, and containing many letters composed for the occasion. But in 1700, a bare fifty years later, the French Academy abandons its review of Balzac's work as not being worth examination, though Boileau demurred, it is true, on the ground that Balzac's "beauties are vicious, but still beauties." Chapelain (1595–1674) kept society on the tiptoe of expectation and lived for twenty years on the wonders of his impending epic, *La Pucelle*, from which he would read excerpts to favoured audiences. It was usually received with approbation, though Mme. de Longueville unkindly described it as *parfaitement beau, et très ennuyeux*. When at last the great work was published, it proved to be "a fire of straw." Still, we need waste no pity on Chapelain; *La Pucelle* had a big sale at thirty-six francs a copy, and its preliminary puffing by the poet and his friends secured him a pension from the Duc de Longueville, another from the Crown, and yet a third on Church benefices.

Who now remembers Vincent Voiture (1598–1648)? And yet this wine merchant's son from the provinces moved in the highest social circles as the most admired poet letter-writer of his day: behaved, too, with an arrogance which astonishes us, taking off his shoes in the presence of a Princess of the Blood to warm his toes at her fire, and living at free quarters in the Hôtel de Rambouillet, though he was earning 800 louis d'or a year by his pen.

Sarrazin, poet, buffoon, and sponger, made a great deal of noise before his death in 1654, but where is his fame now? Pierre Costar (1603–60), sham man of quality, son of a Paris hatter, and a poor imitation of Voiture, secured a pension of 300 louis d'or a year and had his admirers; but this "most *galant* of pedants and most pedantic of *galants*" was forgotten in his own lifetime. Still, there is evidence that all through this period, literature of a better quality than that produced by the Voitures and Costars was in steady demand; Conrart, for instance, in 1645 recommends a young publisher to play safe by re-issuing those books for which there is always a sale, such as Montaigne's *Essays*, Commines' *Memoirs*, and the collected works of Marot.

Paul Scarron (1610–60) stands out rather more clearly than most of these minor writers, largely in virtue of the fact that he was the husband of the future Mme. de Maintenon. But not entirely for that reason. His *Roman Comique*, published in 1649, marks the beginning of the reaction against the dominance of the romance, of which we must now speak. For the romance was for many decades a steady best seller and publisher's standby. Everyone read romances, and a surprising number of people of all ranks tried their hand at writing them.

The fashion may, roughly speaking, be said to start with d'Urfé's *Astrée*, which appeared between 1600 and 1610, and which took the reading public by storm: for it was a novelty. It is the first of a long series of works which preach a love of refinement and a refinement of love: which inculcated a kind of sentimental playing at love, a subtlety of sighing for the unattainable loved one, with apparently no very genuine desire for her possession; a love which advertised itself in *salons* rather than pleaded its cause *tête-à-tête*. The writing world was quick to exploit the new craze, and generally speaking, did uncommonly well out of it; Gomberville (1600–74), who made a hit with his *Polexandre*, died worth some 750 louis d'or a year, whilst the better known La Calprenède did at least as well with his *Cassandre* and *Cléopatre*: to say nothing of winning a bride who married him on the express condition that he finished *Cléopatre*. Calprenède might well have boggled at the task, having already given the world ten volumes of *Cassandre*; but he faithfully performed his contract, and between 1647 and 1656 completed *Cléopatre* in twelve volumes. Both books sold well, and continued to sell for many years; as late as 1671 Mme. de Sévigné is re-reading Calprenède, apologetically, it is true, for she confesses that it is dreadful to have to admit that his works still amuse her. But in another letter she says that, while the style is detestable, she is ensnared by these novels: "The beauty of the sentiments, the violence of the passions, the grandeur of the incidents, and the miraculous success of their redoubtable swords, all this carries me away as if I were a child."

When such language is used of Calprenède, it becomes easier to understand the immense vogue of Mlle. de Scudéry (1607–1701), whose famous romances were the fine flower and culminating point of the school. *Femmes Illustres, L'Illustre Basso, Clélie, Le Grand Cyrus* not only raised her from poverty to comfort, but gave her a position in the social and literary worlds in which she exercised a very real influence upon manners and taste. The mid-century craze for writing portraits of oneself and of one's friends is of her making, and by the time the final instalment of *Le Grand Cyrus* appeared in 1653, it is hardly an exaggeration to say that she had forced an esoteric language upon fashionable France. Allusions to her characters were everywhere understood, and the world was endeavouring to live *à la Scudéry*. Everyone has a name borrowed from romance, Aminte and Orondate exchange sighs, and to be ignorant of the geography of the *Carte du Tendre* is much more discreditable than to be ignorant of that of France. It was a mental climate favourable to the growth of that life of the *salon* where tortured madrigals were exchanged and disputations were staged about the position of a comma; where love's casuists met to examine a text from *Clélie*, or to defend a word from the charge of vulgarity with illustrations drawn from *Le Grand Cyrus*.

Of these early *salons* only one is now remembered, or indeed deserves to be, that of the Marquise de Rambouillet (1588–1665). Mme. de Rambouillet, born Catherine de Vivonne, was a very remarkable woman, whose activities were by no means confined to literature. Her mother was a Savelli, and in the cosmopolitan atmosphere of Italy, Catherine became bi-lingual, knowing French and Italian perfectly, and had acquired a competent knowledge of Spanish before she made a happy marriage at the age of twelve with the twenty-three-year-old Charles d'Angennes, who was to remain her lover until his death in 1652. On coming to France as a young bride, one glance at the dirty, barrack-room Court of

Henri IV was enough for her; she determined to make her own circle of friends in mentally and physically cleaner surroundings, and, not content with such houses as offered, herself designed the Hôtel de Rambouillet. The house departed from accepted patterns as radically as did the society. New colour schemes were introduced, the hitherto inevitable central hall and staircase were moved to the side of the building, and lofty rooms, each with two vast doors and windows opposite each other, were erected in place of the huddle of irregular little apartments in the older houses. Not an unmixed blessing these improvements, for though a noble vista of reception rooms was thus obtained, a merciless draught must have played upon the company. The design set the standard for those town houses in which at least one great lady of the next generation accepts it as normal that the winter months should be spent in her sedan chair, brought into her living-room and placed as near the fire as possible. Another of the Marquise's innovations was the *ruelle* or alcove which plays such a large part in the memoirs and letters of pre-Revolutionary France. Mme. de Rambouillet invented it in consequence of a peculiar disease from which she suffered; exposure to heat, whether of the sun in summer or a fire in winter, invariably made her faint. And in order that her guests should not find the cold of her rooms intolerable in winter, she installed alcoves with day-beds, where she lay in her bearskin sleeping bag, within range of the conversation of those sitting around the fire.

It was in this house that in 1618 she opened her famous *salon* where for more than thirty years the fine flower of French life congregated, and where literary reputations were made and lost. Here came the aspirant to read his first work, and the established man to judge it; and he who had been stamped with the approval of the Hôtel de Rambouillet carried a *cachet* which virtually ensured his success in the larger world. Here came Chapelain in 1627, and the egregious Voiture, "the father of badinage." Here an adverse verdict was given on Corneille's *Polyeucte*, and here the sixteen-year-old Bossuet is said to have preached his first sermon.

It was, under the serious and all-pervading topic of refined love, an unexpectedly light-hearted society, fond even of practical jokes. Gramont is observed to make an exceptionally hearty supper, so during the night his clothes are stolen and taken in two inches round the waist, to the great diversion of the house-party. But

enough was enough, thought Mme. de Rambouillet, and the limit
appeared to her to have been reached when Voiture introduced
a couple of bears into her room, with himself as interpreter of
their high-flown compliment to the tutelary goddess of the house.
He was not encouraged to give further rein to his ingenuity in the
devising of gallant surprises. To us, indeed, this round of gallant
surprises seems as tiresome as would have been those in fashion at
the Court of King Réné of Provence; if you visited the Rambouillet
country estate, and were taken through the largest park in France,
where once Rabelais had sauntered, it was long odds that you
could not enter a solemn grove without finding a troop of wood
nymphs posed on rocks, who would burst into a cantata of welcome. What must have been worse, when Rambouillet went on
a visit, some gallant surprise was devised for the unsuspecting host.

In 1634 the whole company decides to visit the Abbé Arnauld
at Pomponne, and this is how they set about it. At five in the evening, two or three men reach Pomponne, announce that they
are billeting officers, and demand accommodation for a troop of
horse; whilst the infuriated abbé is arguing with them, the sound
of a trumpet is heard, and there enters the dwarf Godeau, *armé
à l'antique* and mounted on a cart horse, who charges the abbé
at full gallop, breaks his straw lance upon him, and throws down a
challenge couched in *vers fort galants*. We are on the whole pleased
to learn that while Arnauld received the company with a warmer
welcome than he would have shown to a cavalry regiment, he
treated Godeau to a severe cuffing.

The outbreak of the Civil War in 1649 swept the Hôtel de Rambouillet out of existence; when the country settled down again in
1653, a new world had grown up. The Marquise was now an ailing
woman of sixty-five, and her famous daughter, "the incompa-
rable Julie," who had yielded to her lover's flame after a twelve-
year courtship, was no longer living in Paris. The Hôtel de Rambouillet had served its purpose in refining speech and manners;
but it had always carried within itself the seeds of its own decay.
Its ostentatious refinement had always hovered on the verge of
the ridiculous, and in the hands of its successors and imitators,
refinement speedily degenerated into a *préciosité* which was a
legitimate target for the satire of a generation which had substituted *le bon sens* for *le bel air* as the chief literary merit.

Of these derivative *salons* the best known was that of Mlle. de

Scudéry; at her Saturdays the Duc de St. Aignan generally presided, while the chief lion was Paul Pellisson (1624–93), who paraded a sentimental and gallant attachment for his hostess until her death in 1667. Pellisson was an unrepentant champion of *le bel air*, a man of fastidious, too fastidious, taste, and of some judgment, but who unfortunately had nothing to say. To him it was the turn of a phrase and not its content which was the important thing. He had made his reputation with an eloquent *History of the French Academy* in 1653, and was now resting on his oars in Mlle. de Scudéry's drawing-room, enunciating such apothegms as "a thought is worthless if it can be understood by the vulgar," and turning out an endless succession of empty sonnets, rondeaux, madrigals, and enigmas. For the Scudéry clique was nothing if not poetical. The shortest journey of one of its members must be described in verse: their letters to each other were in verse; they exchanged presents containing verses: and of course they were under the direct protection of Olympus. Pellisson—*Acante* to the faithful—records of one meeting in the secretary's minute book that "the spirit of Apollo descended upon the room, and the whole company was aware of his presence." Unfortunately Apollo does not seem to have been aware of theirs; for the outpourings of the Saturday muses become ever drearier and more lifeless. It was time, more than time, for the extinction of such coteries, and the agents for their destruction were at hand. Scarron had attacked them in 1649, but it was left to Boileau and Molière to complete the work. In 1659 Molière struck a mortal blow with the *Précieuses Ridicules*, and in 1664 Boileau administered the *coup de grâce*. The old-time *salon* collapsed under the victory of *le bon sens*.

It is 1661, a turning point in the history of the century. The young, handsome, extravagantly popular Louis XIV is in the saddle at last. "The course," as the late Kaiser was fond of saying, "is full speed ahead." In future there will be no place in France for coteries, literary or otherwise, for the arch-planner Colbert (1619–83) has supplanted Fouquet, and is now in control of all matters other than war and foreign policy. (Incidentally, he has sent our poor Pellisson, the disgraced Fouquet's chief clerk, to cool his heels in the Bastille for five years.) Colbert has other plans for literature than the formation of *salons à la Rambouillet*. Literature, like all other departments of the national life, must be keyed up to maximum output under planned controls; the men of letters must swing into their appointed place in the marching column which thrusts onward for the glory of France.

We get many hints of the impact of the new France upon the world of letters from Perrault's memoirs.

Charles Perrault (1628–1703), now chiefly known as author of the fairy tales *Contes de la Mère d'Oie*, not published until 1697, was a remarkably clever and versatile man: brimful of ideas, bubbling over with vitality, with a touch of genius in the practical; an unabashed modern, who did not hesitate to say openly that he thought Versailles infinitely superior to the Parthenon, and who considered Quinault a better poet than Racine. And above all, a man of insatiable curiosity in every field of knowledge. It is, for instance, entirely characteristic of him that, having persuaded the French Academy that vacancies should in future be filled by formal election, he should have presented it with a patent ballot box of his own invention and construction. Perrault's chance came in 1663, when Colbert, who was, amongst many other things, Comptroller of Buildings, appointed him his clerk of works, a post which Perrault rapidly expanded into that of general factotum and second-in-command. He was, for instance, a founder-member of Colbert's Academy, whose main business it was to compose classical inscriptions for medals, portraits, and statues of the King; he reviewed and corrected the already considerable output of prose and poetry in praise of the King; next we find him at work designing tapestries to be woven at the Gobelins' factory; and when he had nothing better to do, he tinkered at his history of the King. Nor was his post as clerk of the works neglected; a year or so later he is designing a fountain and grotto for Versailles, where *Apollo va se coucher chez Thétis*, symbolical of Louis XIV "reposing himself at Versailles after working for the good of the whole world." And he had a hand in the construction of Mme. de Montespan's artistic masterpiece, the bronze tree which perpetually dripped water from its white-metal leaves.

But Perrault's overriding task was to second Colbert's effort to integrate French artists and men of letters into the new economy. Perrault is probably the author of the instructions for Poussin who, quietly painting in Rome, was to be transformed overnight into Louis XIV's art ambassador to Italy and director of a royal academy of French students. The plan and elevation of the Louvre is sent to Poussin, with a curt intimation that the building is to be reconstructed in a nobler style; he, Poussin, will therefore consult every leading architect in Rome on the matter. When each has had time to digest the project, they are to be assembled to discuss it. Each is to submit his opinions in writing, giving his reasons in detail for approving or condemning the plans of his *confrères*. And nowhere in the latter is there the slightest suspicion that these distinguished foreigners, much less Poussin, will hesitate to take orders from Versailles; *Le Roi le veut*: there is nothing more to be said. And as for the art students, Poussin will be held personally responsible for their progress and conduct: "I do not doubt that His Majesty will obtain from you every kind of satisfaction in the execution of the two important projects with which you are charged."

But it is in his dealings with the French Academy that Colbert's passion for regimentation is seen most clearly. It was not until 1671 that he discovered that Perrault was not an academician, but having done so, he took prompt steps to secure his election. Colbert was horrified at the state of affairs disclosed by his protégé's first report; the academy, it appeared, had no regular days or hours of assembly, kept no minutes, nor any register of attendance and absence. Colbert's first step was to order it to meet in future in the Louvre where he could keep an eye upon its slackness. In future, he said, the academy sessions would be from three till five, and would not disperse until five o'clock had struck; and that there might be no excuses, he presents them with a clock, issuing at the same time another order, to the King's Clockmaker this time, that he will be responsible for the clock's maintenance. Next, each academician is issued with a desk, and the secretary with a morocco-bound minute book; also a suitable ration of candles and firewood. Here is surely regulation enough in all conscience, but there is more to follow. Medals are to be struck, forty of them available for each session, and no one arriving after the clock had struck three is to be issued with a medal; on the other hand, the good boys who are there on time may keep their medals, which now become their own property. Colbert could now turn to other tasks with the comfortable knowledge that he had a docile, well-ordered academy, in which Perrault's suggestions were invariably adopted, on the often erroneous assumption that he was acting as Colbert's mouthpiece.

But though the drawbacks are obvious, this regimentation, the enforcement of the principle that only one hand should feed the dog, was for the artist and writer not without compensating advantages. Praise is no doubt warming, but then so is pudding; and under the new régime pudding was much more plentiful than it had been heretofore. And, more important perhaps, the enforced association with the Court, which was an immediate result of Colbert's conscription of the literary world, permanently enhanced the social status of the man of letters. The "ragged regiment of Parnassus" still existed, but its leaders had moved from the precarious neighbourhood of Grub Street into the royal circle. Until the beginning of Louis XIV's personal reign, it is broadly true to say that the literary man, though welcomed in the highest class of society, was there received on a footing which wavered between that of a jester and a domestic pet. Voiture, for instance, sprung from the lower *bourgeoisie*, made love to every woman of quality who came his way. It was expected of him. Condé, First Prince of the Blood, once found him on his knees before Condé's beautiful sister, the Duchesse de Longueville; had Voiture been noble he would probably have paid a visit to the Bastille; had he been a social climber he would most likely have been caned. But it was only little Voiture, the poet, and Condé says to his sister with a burst of laughter, "If the fellow were of our quality, there would be no enduring him." And we find the same Voiture on another occasion supping with the Duc d'Orléans, at whose table a gentleman, *en badinant*, throws a plate at his head. This kind of treatment of the literary man died hard; as late as 1697 Santeuil, whose hymns are still sung in the Church of England, was killed by the Duc de Bourbon's joke of emptying his snuff box into Santeuil's wine. But then the duke was a man who ought to have been by rights in a lunatic asylum.

Some of the earlier men of letters, however, protected themselves from the insolence of the great by sheer force of personality; Malherbe for one, that misanthropic *esprit fort*, who said little, but whose every word counted. When the old Duc de Bellegarde, who was living in fear of excommunication, unburdened himself to Malherbe, the only consolation he got was, "Good! You'll turn black like all excommunicates, and no longer have to dye your beard." And it was Malherbe who, invited to hear the Archbishop of Paris read a sermon, fell asleep shortly after the reading began. His indignant host woke him up: "It's all right," said Malherbe, "I can sleep quite well without it": and went to sleep again. But Malherbe was an original, whose position was so strong that he could even afford to risk the censures of the Church. He was once detected eating meat at seven in the morning on a Fast of the Virgin, and when rebuked for doing so, replied airily that he was running no risk, for ladies were never up so early as that. It was risky to talk to him about his poetry; for if he smelt any condescension in your praise, he would growl that the only two things he understood were music and gloves.

A more typical specimen of the struggling man of letters of earlier times was Boisrobert (1592–1662), an imperturbably impudent provincial, who by sheer persistence forced himself upon an unwilling Richelieu in the capacity of household jester. Boisrobert was a man who could extract money from a Norman, or a treasury pay warrant from Mazarin. Having billeted himself on Richelieu, his first exploit was to beg books from the courtiers to enable him to pursue his studies; and being protected by the cardinal, his mendacity was very successful. Having thus acquired a library, he at once sold it for five thousand francs, no inconsiderable sum of money at this time. Another of his ingenious ideas was to sell parts to the stage struck in an amateur performance of his own tragedy, *The Blood of Abel*. At the last moment a wealthy woman offered him a large fee if he would find a rôle for her son; a lesser man would have ejected an actor who had paid a smaller fee, or at least put a part up to auction; but not Boisrobert. He replied at once that the most important rôle, that of Abel's blood, was still unfilled; pocketed his fee; and had the boy, wrapped in a crimson cloak, rolled across the stage, shouting, "Vengeance, vengeance!" When Richelieu founded the French Academy, Boisrobert managed to sell several seats in return for pensions, but the day of retribution was drawing near; he was, amongst other things, director of Richelieu's private theatre, and was turned adrift by his patron after the evening when, at a royal command performance, he admitted a bevy of Paris street-walkers in return for large bribes. Incidentally, this worthy man was a priest and a canon of St. Ouen; but, as de Retz remarked, "his priesthood sat on him like flour on a buffoon: it made him more diverting." But still, even Boisrobert had his troubles; "how I envy Melchisedech," he used to say, "he had no brothers or nephews."

If society was cavalier in its treatment of the earlier writers, that was not entirely society's fault, for many of them were intolerable. For example, Mlle. de Scudéry's brother, Georges (1601–67), second-rate playwright and swaggering down-at-heels Gascon, of obscure birth, who, as the Court complained, talked of the overthrow of *his House* as if it had been the Byzantine Empire; and who, after he had pestered the Queen into giving him the sinecure command of a ruined tower near Marseilles, behaved as if he was the shield and buckler of France. Sarrazin, sham noble and adventurer, who made a lucky hit with his *Pompe Funèbre de Voiture*, was accorded a contemptuous tolerance in virtue of his status as buffoon to the Prince de Conti. Pierre Costar, in spite of his unceasing flattery, and the useful accomplishment of being able to cry at will, was steadily refused admission to the Hôtel de Rambouillet. Calprenède, a man of some real eminence, was another sham gentleman, who made himself ridiculous by his gasconades; he was constantly showing courtiers an architect's drawings of the palace which he was building on his estate at La Calprenède, or inviting their opinion on some piece of tawdry jewellery. The crippled Paul Scarron held a very different position from such men as these; he cannot properly be said to have been of the Court, though on familiar terms with Anne of Austria, who paid him a pension, nor did he in the strict sense maintain a *salon*. But his house was the rendezvous of the smartest courtiers, drawn there perhaps as much by the charm of Mme. Scarron as by the wit of her husband. And we may note in passing that in her teens the future Mme. de Maintenon was already a person to be reckoned with. "If," said a courtier, "I had to be disrespectful to either the Queen or Mme. Scarron, I should choose the Queen."

In Corneille (1606–84) we see the world of letters in its transitional state. Corneille has a foot in both camps, is of the Court though not a courtier, yet has a smack of the old hand-to-mouth school, but without either its rascality or its buffoonery. The fact that he himself disliked the Court and was never comfortable there, yet felt his frequent attendance obligatory, is significant of the change that was coming over the literary world. And indeed a man less suited to a court it would have been hard to find; a dull, brusque, melancholy man, who spoke French badly and read it worse, with a common appearance, and no conversation. "He should be listened to through the mouth of an actor," was the verdict of a society lady after making his acquaintance. But he knew his own worth; when his friends reproached him with his slovenliness, he would retort, *Je n'en suis pas moins pour cela Pierre Corneille*. His slovenliness was not only bodily, but mental. The actor Baron, unable to make any sense of four lines of *Tite et Bérénice*, at last had to appeal to Corneille. The author pored over the lines for some time, and then admitted that he could not make any sense of them either.

As a critic of his own works, Corneille has all the objectivity of Trollope, but his judgments on his contemporaries are not always happy; when Racine showed him his *Alexandre*, he advised him to discontinue his attempts, as it was obvious that he had no talent for the stage. Though Corneille showed himself regularly at Court, his happiest times were spent at Rouen, where he and his brother Thomas, who had married sisters, kept house together, and where Pierre from his study would shout to Thomas in his, to give him a rhyme; for Thomas, a playwright of infinitely less genius, had the livelier wit of the two.

Molière was unique in having inherited a humble niche of his own at Court as Royal Upholsterer, and as such could rely upon that benevolent protection which Louis extended to all his servants with whom he was brought into personal contact. Everyone at Court knew who Molière was, and his position was further strengthened by the friendship of Condé, who would often spend three or four hours with him. But with all his advantages, Molière endured rather than enjoyed the society of Versailles; the good fellow and witty talker whom the courtiers saw was a very different man from the real Molière. The real Molière was a rootless man, disliking crowds and constraint, yet finding no comfort in domesticity with his unhappy wife who was a source of constant unhappiness to her husband. It is customary to place the whole blame for the failure of the marriage on the wife, but certainly Molière cannot have been an easy man to live with. "I am not supple enough for domesticity," he had said years earlier when refusing an appointment as secretary to the Prince de Conti. And he needed a great deal of attention. One of the first uses he made of affluence was to engage a valet, and thereafter his valet always dressed him; "he would not himself," we are told, "even arrange the fold of his cravat." He was, too, "of a fatiguing regularity" and fidgety to a degree. A window opened or shut before the hour appointed in his household regulations threw him into convulsions, and a book out of its ordained place upset him for a fortnight. Nor does he seem to have been able to find any consolation in his great fame. Often he would say that if he had his life to live over again, he would choose some other profession; and at the height of his reputation he confessed that he had never done anything that satisfied him.

On the whole one would have much sooner known Molière's lifelong friend Boileau, about whom there is an atmosphere of virility, a masculine humour and common sense which often reminds us of Samuel Johnson; and the resemblance is underlined by the fact that Boileau, too, had his Boswell. The parallel is a really striking one. On 3rd October 1698, Boileau, then sixty-two years old and in the fullness of his fame, was waited upon by an unknown provincial barrister, one Claude Brossette, aged twenty-seven, who explained to the great man that he had come to solicit the honour of his friendship. He would have perhaps spoken more honestly if he had said to demand Boileau's friendship, for Brossette had that first requisite of a Boswell, the ingenuous, friendly, unsnubbable persistence of a high-pressure salesman. Boileau capitulated, and found himself a regular correspondent of Brossette's for the rest of his life. Interrogatories pour in upon him from Brossette at Lyons: can Boileau send him a copy of his genealogical tree? Can Boileau provide him with a suitable motto for a portrait? What is Boileau's opinion of such and such a writer? How does Boileau translate such and such a Latin phrase? May he trouble Boileau with details of a very interesting lawsuit now before the Lyons courts? The whole spiced with a flattering deference not unappreciated by Boileau, who "did not hate that people should talk to him of his own works." Before long Brossette has established his position as the future editor and commentator of the definitive edition of Boileau's works, and the questions multiply, whilst Boileau's answers take on a new freedom—"Can it be possible that you are unable to see that . . ." "Your letter, or rather your dissertation. . . ." And the sheets are sprinkled with "How, sir!" and "What then, sir?" in the true

Johnsonian manner. Brossette hazards the opinion that Horace's style is "negligent" and receives a castigation; Boileau, asked for his opinion of *Télémaque*, replies: "I wish Mentor preached a little less, and that the moral had been inculcated less perceptibly, and with more art . . . Fénelon is a better poet than theologian."

"And what of Godeau, sir?" asks Brossette. BOILEAU: "Godeau writes with great ease: that is to say, with too much ease." It is in the anecdotal department that Brossette is weakest, no doubt because he had less frequent opportunity of meeting his hero than had Boswell; but there are stories scattered through the book which we are glad to have preserved. Boileau is reproving the Abbé de Dangeau for holding several benefices: "But it is so pleasant for living," pleads the abbé. BOILEAU: "I don't doubt it: but for dying, sir, for dying?"

Boileau was much given to dining out, and set much store by the virtue of punctuality—"A man's faults, sir, are always brought up when he keeps the company waiting." He had a great contempt for low wit, and especially for the still fashionable burlesque. "Your father," he said to the young Racine, "read Scarron's *Virgile Travesti:* but he took care not to let me catch him at it." When his old friend Molière was obviously nearing his end, Boileau urged him to give up the stage and take some rest; Molière replied that honour demanded that he should continue to play. BOILEAU: "Honour, sir! To daub your face with a great black Sganarelle moustache and offer your back to a caning for the diversion of the pit!" Unlike Molière, Boileau was a tranquil man; if not a contented man, at least a cheerfully resigned one, seeing much that was bad in life, but seeing no use in whining about it. As the eleventh child of a lawyer, he had had his own way to make in the world, and after trying both the Bar and the Sorbonne, which he disliked about equally, had raised himself to a competence as a professional writer. He had a disinterestedness rare in any period, but specially at the Court of Louis XIV. The King, who liked and appreciated him, gave him a priory in his earlier days; several years later Boileau, finding his conscience pricking him over the matter, not only resigned the priory, but insisted upon refunding the stipend from the date on which he had first drawn it.

For without being a *dévot*, Boileau had a solid and unostentatious piety that never wavered. But there was nothing austere about the man; he loved wine and good company, and did not object to hearing the story of his own attempt to reform Chapelle. Chapelle was a witty debauchee, still remembered for the burlesque *voyage* which he wrote in conjunction with Bachaumont. Boileau, meeting him one day in the street, started to reprove him for his dissipation in general, and for his drunkenness in particular. Chapelle was most penitent, felt the force of Boileau's words, but suggested that the street was hardly the place for such a serious conversation; here was a handy tavern in which they could talk undisturbed. The upshot of the matter was that moralist and penitent got so drunk together that they both had to be sent home in chairs. Boileau was generous to his fellow-authors—always excepting defenders of the moderns—and charitable to the Grub Street hacks, even when he knew that his kindness was being abused; he continued, for instance, to support one Linières, though well aware that whenever he gave Linières money, the first use he made of it was to enter the nearest tavern and there entertain the company with satirical slanders on his benefactor. Boileau was a man, said his contemporaries, who knew not how to dissimulate or to flatter, and too blunt to be a successful courtier. But it is difficult to find any evidence in support of the latter contention. It rests presumably on the incident of his continuing to abuse Scarron's works in the presence of Scarron's former wife, Mme. de Maintenon, in spite of the kicks and nudges of Racine. Incidentally, St. Simon (1675–1755) makes Racine the blunderer, and attributes his disgrace to the affair, a typical example of that hasty recording of ill-digested or badly authenticated stories which mars so much of St. Simon's best work. So far from being an unsuccessful courtier, Boileau was always on excellent terms with the King: "Remember," said Louis to him, "I have always an hour a week for you when you care to come." And Louis liked nothing better than to get Boileau aside and draw him on to mimic the courtiers, for he was amongst other things an excellent mimic. Nay more, Louis even encouraged him to read his verse to him, and though Boileau read admirably, it is hard to believe that the King really enjoyed the performance. The statement that Boileau was incapable of flattery seems simply untrue. After his appointment as King's Historian in 1677, it became his duty to accompany Louis on active service; once, seeing him in a somewhat exposed position, he went up to him and said: "Sire, do not put an end to my history so early." At one time it was fashionable slang to use the word *gros* for grand; the King asked Boileau what he thought of the innovation. "Sire," said Boileau, "I can see all the difference in the world between Louis-le-Gros and Louis-le-Grand." On another occasion he was asked his age by Louis. "I came into the world, sire, a year before Your Majesty to announce the marvels of your reign." If this is the language of a plain, blunt man, incapable of flattery, what must have been the language of the flatterers?

With Boileau the arbiter of the national taste, and his close allies Racine, Molière and La Fontaine as warm admirers of the ancients as he, it might have been thought that there was no room for revolt on the part of those who held by the moderns. But the seeds of revolt were germinating; as early as 1667 Le Labourer had published a work with the significant title *Advantages de la langue française sur la langue latine,* and another book on the same theme, *De l'excellence de la langue française,* had appeared in 1683. And there was the nimblewitted, busy Perrault, who, since last we heard of him, had tired of his slavery under Colbert and was now loose again in the world of letters and of the French Academy. Perrault it was who may be said to have opened the battle for the moderns in 1687, when he read to the Academy his *Siècle de Louis-le-Grand,* in which he bluntly denies the superiority of the ancients. The session was a stormy one; Boileau, rising from his chair, hotly observed that it was a disgrace to the Academy to listen to such stuff, whilst the cooler Racine countered much more effectively by pretending to believe that Perrault had written with his tongue in his cheek, and, on this assumption, congratulating him on his poem. But Perrault had by no means finished with his opponents. Towards the end of 1688 he began to publish his *Parallèle des Anciens et des Modernes,* in which, if he shows much ignorance, he also displays a good-humoured wit which contrasts pleasantly with the wrath of his enemies. They, as he complains, behave as if they were descended in the direct line from Homer and Plato. And whilst Perrault may not say much to convince the impartial reader of the superiority of the moderns, his rejection of his adversaries' dogmatic claims is reasonable. Are we to be forbidden, he asks, to form an opinion on Homer which differs from that of other men? Authority, he insists, is valid only in theology and jurisprudence. The quarrel was to drag on for another six years, until August 1694, when a personal reconciliation took place between Boileau and Perrault. It had been a drawn battle; for if Boileau has rather the better of the quarrel, Perrault secured the emancipation of the literary conscience from the dogmas of the high priests of classicism.

Boileau's most intimate friend, Racine (1639–99), had little of his happy equanimity of temperament; a melancholy, foreboding man, who himself confessed that one adverse criticism of his work destroyed all his satisfaction at the praise which he had received. There clings to Racine throughout life much of the grim atmosphere of his foster-mother, Port Royal, to whose care he had been entrusted at the age of four. Though Racine, too, had heard the chimes at midnight in many a meeting at Boileau's lodgings, or in convivial gatherings at the *Mouton Blanc* where they and Molière would unite in affectionate teasing of the simple, absent-minded La Fontaine (1621–95), *le bonhomme*, as they called him, and where the penalty for a breach of the rules was to read a verse of Chapelain's poetry, or, in aggravated circumstances, a whole page. Which, in Racine's case at any rate, was unkindly, for it was Chapelain who had brought him into notice as a young man, and had got him a gratuity of 100 louis d'or for his poem on Louis XIV's marriage in 1660. In 1664 Racine made his first appearance at Court, where he was to prove himself the most successful of the new generation of literary men who lived on easy terms at Versailles. For though he passed for an indifferent courtier, no man surpassed him in expert knowledge of human nature. Corneille had talked of his own works and bored his listeners; and perhaps even Boileau was too ready to speak of himself. But Racine avoided the topic and reaped his reward. *Mon talent avec eux* (the courtiers) *n'est pas de leur faire sentir que j'ai l'esprit, mais de leur apprendre qu'ils en ont*. Men were soon saying that "whilst one found the poet easily in Boileau, in Racine one had to hunt for him." But to do Racine justice, his reluctance to talk about his own work was not entirely a subtle piece of flattery; for ignorant and undiscriminating praise of his writings irritated rather than flattered him. With Louis XIV he was an immediate success, and to Louis he must, I think, have borne a marked physical resemblance; for early in their acquaintance the King observed that Racine was one of the handsomest men at his Court. Be that as it may, Racine certainly did better at Versailles than any others of the literary world, possibly because, unlike his *confrères*, he really enjoyed the life; for he had that admiration, or rather adoration, for the King which is the mark of the seventeenth-century *bourgeois*, and which so startles us when it breaks out from time to time in Bossuet. Racine's progress at Court was steady; in 1664 he was given a pension; in 1677 he was, conjointly with Boileau, made Historian to the King; and in 1690 he was appointed a gentleman-in-ordinary. In 1687 he was invited to Marly, a distinction usually granted only to courtiers of the highest standing, and was delighted with his visit—"Everything there is quite different to Versailles," he reports proudly. Racine was now the complete courtier. Louis liked having him read to him, particularly Plutarch's *Lives*. He and the King exchange compliments. When Racine misses a siege in the Low Countries in 1677, he explains his absence with, "Sire, before my tailor had finished my country clothes, Your Majesty had finished the siege"; and when he reads his academy oration to the King, Louis replies: "I could praise you more if you had praised me less." But Racine's head is not turned; he remains at heart the affectionate family man, playing with his children, refusing to dine with the Duc de Bourbon because he cannot disappoint his family, and cherishing the wife who did not know what a verse was, and with whom, in his son's words, he had made a marriage in which "neither love nor interest, but reason only, was his guide."

Racine was not only a great poet, but also a great man of the theatre, the first of the modern school of producers; he it was who "made" Champmeslé, the leading tragedienne of the day. She was no born actress, but owed her artistry to the patience with which Racine rehearsed her every word, action, and gesture with all the meticulousness of a Hollywood director.

We are first surprised that a man who wrote so well as Racine did should have written so little, until we realize that he gave up writing for the stage at the height of his powers, when he was only thirty-eight. His retirement, often attributed unjustly to pique, was without doubt due to qualms of conscience. He never shook off his Port Royal training, and had never been quite easy in his mind about the question of stage plays; as early as the 'sixties Nicole had stabbed him with the remark that "a writer of romances or of theatrical poetry is a public poisoner," and though Racine counter-attacked in 1667, the wound festered. His aunt, too, the

Abbess of Port Royal, was unwearied in her exhortations that he should abandon the sinful life of a dramatic writer. The pressure was successful, and after 1677 Racine wrote no more for the public stage; no longer was he to be seen walking up and down his garden, loudly versifying the play which, in accordance with his invariable custom, he had already written out in prose. Family prayers and a daily exposition of the Scriptures to his household are now his chief concern; and he seems to have had no regrets. In 1696 this man, formerly so thin-skinned, can write, "long ago by the Grace of God I became completely indifferent to any criticisms of my tragedies."

But he remained a courtier, and still kept his post as Royal Historian; though perhaps as time went on, a little of the gilt wore off the ginger-bread of office. In 1692 he writes from the front to Boileau, detained in Paris by ill-health: "No doubt you have found reviews of an army in epics, long and boring: but in real life they are even longer and more boring."

It is usual to say that Racine died in 1699 of a heart broken by his disgrace at Court. But the celebrated "disgrace" of which we hear so much amounted to no more than a certain coolness on the King's part, which was in itself evidence of the great esteem in which Louis continued to hold him. For Racine had certainly been guilty of the normally unpardonable offence of having written some indiscreet comments on political matters, and these had fallen into the King's hands. Yet not only was he not exiled, but he was not even forbidden the Court; and when he continued to appear there, he was not *foudroyé d'un regard*, given that silent level stare which had struck dead so many unfortunate courtiers. In his last illness Louis frequently sent him kindly messages, and when he died, pensioned his widow and children. But the whole episode is significant of the change which had come about in the status of the man of letters in the past fifty years. A Sarrazin, a Costar, even a Calprenède, though he might be thrown out of a royal *château*, could not be disgraced; he was as much beneath disgrace as was a footman. Whereas Racine's misfortune was a society topic, as was the disgrace of the Duc de Lauzun or the Comte de Guiche.

Of the noble authors, authors by accident as we may call them, I feel that this is not the place to speak. Without going into the vexed question, What is literature? it is I think evident that La

Rochefoucauld, Mme. de Sévigné, de Retz, Mlle. de Montpensier and the rest, cannot possibly be described as writers in the sense in which I have throughout employed that term. It is not a question of their merit, still less of their charm; indeed, I suspect that we turn more often to Sévigné's letters than we do to Corneille, and read de Retz more frequently than we do Racine. But none of them wrote for the public; one and all they would have taken it very ill if they had been described as authors. They are by many, of whom I confess myself one, more loved than are the professed writers; but their work does not fall within the limits prescribed for this chapter.

Nor have I attempted a fresh critical assessment of the great literary figures of the period. Firstly, because I have endeavoured throughout this book to keep to tracks and bridlepaths rather than to ride post on the highway; and secondly, because all that can be said of Corneille, Racine, Molière and their peers has already been said. To attempt to add anything to that corpus of criticism would be at best presumptuous, at worst to paraphrase the opinions of abler writers than myself. The position of the giants is fixed; and at this time of day one no longer offers conjectures on the height of Mount Everest. The gold lace of Louis' Life Guard is tarnished, and the famous regiments, Artois, Picardy, Navarre, whose very names once stirred French blood like a trumpet call, are grown dim to us. The last glint of the great gilded ships which fought under the White Flag at Malaga and La Hogue has vanished below the horizon of history. Versailles itself has gone the way of Babylon the Great. Louis XIV, though he still shines palely in the twilight of time, is ever receding towards the ultimate darkness. But the writers of his age stand securely established, not far from the supreme heights of the huge central massif which is the literature of the world. Corneille, Racine, Molière, Fénelon, Bossuet, La Bruyère, the list seems endless; not even the Victorians can out-top it. And it is the writers, not the soldiers, grandees and politicians, who give the century its enduring place in the history of civilization; on their shoulders rests the claim of the *Grand Siècle* to the title of "the splendid century."

Notes
for Further
Reading

CHAPTER I

The King

The Age of Louis XIV, Vol. V. of *Cambridge Modern History*, eds.
Ward, Prothero, Leathes, Cambridge: C.U.P., 1908

AVAUX, *Négociations de M. le Comte d'Avaux en Hollande*. Paris:
Durand, 1752–53.

BOULENGER, JACQUES, *The Seventeenth Century*. London: W. Heinemann, 1920.

BUSSY-RABUTIN, *Histoire Amoureuse des Gaules*, intro. A. Poitevin.
Paris: Delahays, 1857–58.

CAYLUS, *Souvenirs et Correspondance de Mme. de Caylus*. Paris:
Raunié, n.d.

DANGEAU, *Journal du Marquis de Dangeau*. Paris, 1817.

EUGÈNE, *Mémoires du Prince Eugène*. Paris, 1810.

FARE, *Mémoires du Marquis de la Fare*, (*Collection des Mémoires
relatifs à l'Histoire de France*, ed. C. B. Petitot). Paris, 1828.

FEDERN, KARL, *Mazarin, 1602–1661*. Paris: Payot, 1934.

FEILING, K., *British Foreign Policy, 1660–1672*. London: Macmillan, 1930.

HARTMANN, C. H., *Charles II and Madame*. London: W. Heinemann, 1934.

HÉRBERT, *Mémoires de François Hérbert*. Paris: Girard, 1827.

LAIR, J. A., *Louise de la Vallière et la Jeunesse de Louis XIV*. Paris: Plon, Nourrit & Cie., 1880.

LOUIS XIV, *Concordance de l'Etat Sanitaire de Louis XIV*, ed. P. Lacroix. Paris, 1839.

————, *La Mort de Louis XIV*, ed. Antoine. Paris: Drumont, 1880.

————, *Oeuvres de Louis XIV*. 6 Vols. Paris: Treutel & Wertz, 1806.

MAINTENON, *Correspondance Générale de Mme. de Maintenon*, ed. T. Lavallée. Paris: Charpentier, 1865.

————, *Lettres inédites de Mme. de Maintenon et de Mme. La Princesse des Ursins*. Paris: Bossange, 1826.

MARCOU, F. L., *Etude sur la vie et les oeuvres de Pellisson*. Paris, 1859.

MONTPENSIER, *Mémoires de Mlle. de Montpensier*, notes by A. Chéruel. Paris: Charpentier, 1858–59.

NOAILLES, DUC DE, *Histoire de Mme. de Maintenon*. Paris, 1848.

NOBILI-VITELLESCHI, MARCHESA DE, *The Romance of Savoy*. London, 1905.

OGG, D., *Europe in the Seventeenth Century*. London: Black, 1931.

ORLÉANS, *Correspondance complète de Mme. la Duchesse d'Orléans née Princesse Palatine, mère du régent*, intro., notes by G. Brunet. Paris: Charpentier, 1863.

————, *Lettres inédites de la Princesse Palatine*, trans. Rolland. Paris: Hetzel, (1863?).

PEREY, L., *Le Roman du Grand Roi*. Paris, 1894.

PERRAULT, CHARLES, *Mémoires de Perrault*, ed. P. Lacroix. Paris, 1878.

ROUSSET, CAMILLE, *Histoire de Louvois*. Paris, 1872.

ST. MAURICE, *Lettres sur La Cour de Louis XIV, 1667–1670*, intro., notes by J. Lemoine. Paris: Lévy, 1910.

ST. SIMON, *The Memoirs of the Duke of St. Simon*. Various editions.

STE. BEUVE, "Maintenon," *Causeries du Lundi*, 28 July 1851.

SPANHEIM, E., *Relations de La Cour de France en 1690*. Paris: Renouard, 1882.

TORCY, *Journal inédit de J. B. Colbert, Marquis de Torcy*, ed. F. Masson. Paris: Plon, Nourrit & Cie., 1884.

————, *Mémoires du Marquis de Torcy*. Paris, 1758.

VALFREY, J., *Hugues de Lionne*. Paris, 1827.

VILLARS, CLAUDE, *Mémoires du Maréchal de Villars*, with additional material by Le Marquis de Voqué. 6 Vols. Paris: Renouard, 1884–1904.

Visconti, Primi, *Mémoires sur La Cour de Louis XIV*, trans., intro., notes by J. Lemoine. Paris: Lévy, 1908.

CHAPTER II
The Court

Bièvre, Cte. de, *Georges Mareschal, Seigneur de Bièvre*. Paris, 1906.
Boulenger, Jacques, *The Seventeenth Century*. London: W. Heinemann, 1920.
Caylus, *Souvenirs et Correspondance de Mme. de Caylus*. Paris: Raunié, n.d.
Dangeau, *Journal du Marquis de Dangeau*. Paris: 1817.
Etat de France. Paris, 1665.
Franklin, Alfred, *La Cuisine*. Paris, 1888; *Les Repas*. Paris, 1889; *Les Soins de la Toilette et le Savoir Vivre*. Paris, 1887; *Variétés Gastronomiques*. Paris, 1891 (from series *La Vie Privée d'Autrefois*).
Hugon, C., *Social France in the Seventeenth Century*. London: Methuen & Co., 1911.
Lair, J. A., *Louise de La Vallière et la Jeunesse de Louis XIV*. Paris: Plon, Nourrit & Cie., 1880.
Maintenon, *Correspondance Générale de Mme. de Maintenon*, ed. T. Lavallée. Paris: Charpentier, 1865.
Montpensier, *Mémoires de Mlle. de Montpensier*, notes by A. Chéruel. Paris: Charpentier, 1858–59.
Motteville, *Mémoires de Mme. de Motteville*. Paris, 1869.
Orléans, *Correspondance complète de Mme. la Duchesse d'Orléans née Princesse Palatine, mère du régent*, intro., notes by G. Brunet. Paris: Charpentier, 1863.
———, *Lettres inédites de La Princesse Palatine*, trans. Rolland. Paris: Hetzel, (1863?).
St. Maurice, *Lettres sur La Cour de Louis XIV, 1660–1672*, intro., notes by J. Lemoine. Paris: Lévy, 1910.
"St. Simon," *Encyclopaedia Britannica* (ninth ed.).
St. Simon, *The Memoirs of the Duke of St. Simon*. Various editions.
Sévigné, *Lettres de Mme. de Sévigné*, ed. L. Aimé-Martin. 6 Vols. Paris, 1876.
Spanheim, E., *Relations de La Cour de France en 1690*. Paris: Renouard, 1882.
Torcy, *Journal inédit de J. B. Colbert, Marquis de Torcy*, ed. F. Masson. Paris: Plon, Nourrit & Cie., 1884.

VISCONTI, PRIMI, *Mémoires sur La Cour de Louis XIV*, trans., intro., notes by J. Lemoine. Paris: Lévy, 1908.

CHAPTER III
The Base of the Pyramid

BABEAU, A., *Le Village sous l'Ancien Régime*. Paris: Didier & Cie., 1878.

BOISGUILLEBERT, PIERRE, *Détail de La France*, ed. E. Daire. Paris: Guillaumin, 1851.

———, *Factum de La France*, ed. E. Daire. Paris: Guillaumin, 1851.

BOISLILE, A. DE, *Correspondance de contrôleurs-généraux des finances avec les intendants des provinces*. Paris: Impr. Nat., 1874–97.

BOULENGER, JACQUES, *The Seventeenth Century*. London: W. Heinemann, 1920.

CALONNE D'AVESNE, *La Vie Agricole sous l'Ancien Régime dans le nord de la France*. Paris: Picard, 1920.

CLÉMENT, P., *La Gouvernement de Louis XIV*. Paris, 1848.

EVELYN, JOHN, *Diary*. Simkin, Marshall, Hamilton, Kent & Co., n.d.

FLÉCHER, *Mémoires sur les Grands Jours d'Auvergne*. Paris: Dauphin, 1930.

FUNCK-BRENTANO, FRANTZ, *The Old Régime in France*, trans. H. Wilson. London: Arnold & Co., 1930.

SÉVIGNÉ, *Lettres de Mme. de Sévigné*, ed. L. Aimé-Martin. 6 Vols. Paris, 1876.

TOCQUEVILLE, ALEXIS DE, *L'Ancien Régime et La Revolution*. Paris: Lévy, 1856.

VAUBAN, SÉBASTIEN, *Project d'une Dîme Royale*. Paris, 1851.

CHAPTER IV
The Church

ARBOUZE, *La Vie de la Vénérable Mère*. Paris, 1685.

ARNAULD, ANGÉLIQUE, *Mémoires pour servir à l'Histoire de Port Royal et de la Revde. Mère Angélique Arnauld*. 3 Vols. Utrecht, 1742.

BOSSUET, J. B., *Lettres de Bossuet*, ed. H. Massis. Paris, n.d.

BOULENGER, JACQUES, *The Seventeenth Century*. London: W. Heinemann, 1920.

BRÉMOND, HENRI, *The Thundering Abbot*, trans. F. J. Sheed, London: Sheed & Ward, 1930.

Brodrick, James, *The Economic Morals of the Jesuits*. London: O.U.P., 1934.

———, *The Progress of the Jesuits* (1556–1579). London: Longmans, Green & Co., 1946.

Chérot, P., *La Première Jeunesse de Louis XIV*. Lille, 1892.

Fénelon, Francois de, *Oeuvres de Fénelon*. Paris, 1828.

Fouqueray, H., *Histoire de La Compagnie de Jésus en France*. Vol. V. Paris, 1925.

Higham, F. M. G., *King James the Second*. London: H. Hamilton, 1934.

Knox, R. A., *Enthusiasm*. Oxford: O.U.P., 1950.

La Chaise, *Histoire du Père*. Cologne, 1719.

Louis XIV, *Oeuvres de Louis XIV*. 6 Vols. Paris: Treutel & Wertz, 1806.

Lowndes, M. E., *The Nuns of Port Royal*. London: O.U.P., 1909.

Racine, J., *Abrégé de l'Histoire de Port Royal*. Paris, 1825.

Petitot, C. B., "Notice sur Port Royal," prefixed to *Mémoires de l'Abbé Arnauld (Collection des Mémoires relatifs à l'Histoire de France*, ed. C. B. Petitot). Paris, 1824.

Retz, *Mémoires du Cardinal de Retz adresses à Mme. de Caumartin*. 4 Vols. Paris: Charpentier, 1912–13.

Richelieu, *Mémoires du Cardinal de Richelieu, sur le règne de Louis XIII (Collection des Mémoires relatifs à l'Histoire de France*, ed. C. B. Petitot). Paris, 1823.

St. Cyres, Viscount, *François de Fénelon*. London: Methuen & Co., 1911.

———, "The Gallican Church," *Cambridge Modern History*. Vol. V., Chap. 4. Cambridge: C.U.P., 1908.

St. Simon, *The Memoirs of the Duke of St. Simon*. Various editions.

Ste. Beuve, "Fénelon," *Causeries du Lundi*, 1 April 1850.

Sanders, E. K., *Jacques Bénigne Bossuet*. London: Macmillan, 1921.

CHAPTER V

The Army

Arnauld, A., *Mémoires de l'Abbé Arnauld (Collection des Mémoires relatifs à l'Histoire de France*, ed. C. B. Petitot). Paris, 1824.

Berwick, James, *Mémoires du Maréchal de Berwick (Collection des Mémoires relatifs à l'Histoire de France*, ed. C. B. Petitot). Paris, 1828.

Boulenger, Jacques, *The Seventeenth Century*. London: W. Heinemann, 1920.

CHOUPPES, AYMAR, *Mémoires du Marquis de Chouppes*. Paris: Techener, 1861.

FEUQUIÈRES, MARQUIS DE, *Memoirs Historical and Military*. London,
1735–36.

LANGALLERIE, *Memoirs of the Marquis de Langallerie*. London: Taylor,
1710.

LOUIS XIV, *Oeuvres de Louis XIV*. 6 Vols. Paris: Treutel & Wertz,
1806.

MONTECUCULI, R., *Mémoires de Montecuculi*. Strasbourg, 1735.

MONGLAT, *Mémoires de François de Paule de Clermont, Marquis de
Montglat* (*Collection des Mémoires relatifs à l'Histoire de
France*, ed. C. B. Petitot). Paris, 1826.

NAVAILLES, *Mémoires du Marquis de Chouppes . . . suivis de mémoires du Duc de Navailles et de La Valette*. Paris: Techener,
1861.

ROUSSET, CAMILLE, *Histoire de Louvois*. Paris, 1872.

ST. SIMON, *The Memoirs of the Duke of St. Simon*. Various editions.

SÉGUR, MARQUIS DE, *Le Maréchal de Luxembourg et le Prince
d'Orange, 1668–78*. Paris: Lévy, 1902.

VILLARS, CLAUDE, *Mémoires du Maréchal de Villars*, with additional
material by Le Marquis de Voqué. 6 Vols. Paris: Renouard,
1884–1904.

CHAPTER VI
The Country Gentleman

BABEAU, A., *Le Village sous l'Ancien Régime*. Paris: Didier & Cie.,
1878.

BOISGUILLEBERT, PIERRE, *Détail de La France*, ed. E. Daire. Paris:
Guillaumin, 1851.

———, *Factum de La France*, ed. E. Daire. Paris: Guillaumin, 1851.

BOULENGER, JACQUES, *The Seventeenth Century*. London: W. Heinemann, 1920.

BUSSY-RABUTIN, *Mémoires de Roger de Rabutin*. Paris: Charpentier,
1857.

FLÉCHER, *Mémoires sur les Grands Jours d'Auvergne*. Paris: Dauphin,
1930.

FUNCK-BRENTANO, FRANTZ, *The Old Régime in France*, trans. H. Wilson. London: Arnold & Co., 1930.

GUYOT, G. A., *Observations sur les droits des patrons et les seigneurs
de paroisse*. Paris, 1751.

———, *Traité des droits, fonctions, franchises, etc.* Paris, 1786.

Hugon, C., *Social France in the Seventeenth Century*. London: Methuen & Co., 1911.

Sévigné, *Lettres de Mme. de Sévigné*, ed. L. Aimé-Martin. 6 Vols. Paris, 1876.

Tocqueville, Alexis de, *L'Ancien Régime et La Revolution*. Paris: Lévy, 1856.

Vaissière, P. de, *Gentilshommes compagnards de l'ancienne France*. Paris, 1903.

Vauban, Sébastien, *Project d'une Dîme Royale*. Paris, 1851.

CHAPTER VII
The Town

Babeau, A., *La Ville sous l'Ancien Régime*. Paris, 1884.

Berthaud, Sieur de, *La Ville de Paris en vers burlesques*. Paris, 1658.

Boileau-Despréaux, Nicolas, *Correspondance entre Boileau-Despréaux et Brossette*, ed. A. Lavardet. Paris: Techener, 1858.

Correspondance administrative sous le règne de Louis XIV, collected by G. B. Depping. Paris: Impr. Nat., 1850–55.

Estrades, *Letters and Negotiations of the Count of Estrades*. London, 1711.

Franklin, Alfred, *L'Hygiene*. Paris, 1890; *Variétés Gastronomiques*. Paris, 1891 (from series *La Vie Privée d'Autrefois*).

Furetière, A., *Le Roman Bourgeois*. Paris, 1666.

Gramont, *Mémoires du Maréchal de Gramont*. Paris, n.d.

Loret, Jean, *La Muze Historique*. Paris, 1857.

Loyseau, C., *Des Ordres et Simples Dignités*. N.d.

———, *Du Droit des Offices*. Chasteaudun, 1610.

———, *Traité des Seigneuries*. Paris, 1608.

Motteville, *Mémoires de Mme. de Motteville*. Paris, 1869.

Patin, *Correspondance de Gui Patin*. Paris, 1901.

Scarron, Paul, *The Whole Comical Works of Mons. Scarron*, trans. Brown, Savage et al. London, 1700.

CHAPTER VIII
The Medical World

Bièvre, Cte. de, *Georges Mareschal, Seigneur de Bièvre*. Paris, 1906.

Brièlle, Léon, *Archives de l'Hotel-Dieu de Paris (1157–1300)*. Paris: Impr. Nat., 1894.

Dionis, *Cours d'operations de Chirurgie*. Brussels, 1708.

FRANKLIN, ALFRED, *Recherches sur la bibliothèque de la Faculté de Médicine*. Paris, 1864.

——, *Les Chirurgiens*. Paris, 1893; *Les Médicins*. Paris, 1892; *Variétés Chirurgicales*. Paris, 1894 (from series *La Vie Privée d'Autrefois*).

GILLES DE LA TOURETTE, GEORGES, *Théophraste Renaudot d'après des documents inédits*. Paris: Plon, Nourrit & Cie., 1884.

PATIN, *Correspondance de Gui Patin*. Paris, 1901.

——, *L'Esprit de Gui Patin*. Amsterdam, 1710.

ST. SIMON, *The Memoirs of the Duke of St. Simon*. Various editions.

CHAPTER XI

The Art of Living

AUDIGER, *La Maison Réglée*. Amsterdam, 1725.

CORNEILLE, *Oeuvres de P. Corneille, avec les commentaires de Voltaire*. Paris: Renouard, 1824.

COURTIN, A. DE, *Nouveau Traité de la Civilité qui se pratique en France parmi les honnestes gens*. Paris: Josset, 1679.

COUSIN, VICTOR, *Mme. de Sablé*. Paris, 1854.

FLEURY, C., *Devoirs des Maîtres et des Domestiques*. Paris, 1688.

FRANKLIN, ALFRED, *La Cuisine*. Paris, 1888; *Les Repas*. Paris, 1889; *Variétés Gastronomiques*. Paris, 1891 (from series *La Vie Privée d'Autrefois*).

LOISEL, A., *Institutes coutumières de la France*. Paris, 1679.

MAINTENON, *Correspondance Générale de Mme. de Maintenon*, ed. T. Lavallée. Paris: Charpentier, 1865.

MOLIÈRE, *Oeuvres Complètes de Molière*. Paris: Dufour & Cie., 1826.

RIBBE, CHARLES DE, *Une grande dame dans son ménage d'après le Journal de la Ctsse. de Rochefort, 1689*. Paris, 1889.

ST. SIMON, *The Memoirs of the Duke de St. Simon*, trans. Arkwright. London, 1915.

SÉVIGNÉ, *Lettres de Mme. de Sévigné*, ed. L. Aimé-Martin. 6 Vols. Paris, 1876.

TROLLOPE, H. M., *The Life of Molière*. London: Constable & Co., 1905.

CHAPTER X

The Galleys

BOULENGER, JACQUES, *The Seventeenth Century*. London: W. Heinemann, 1920.

EVELYN, JOHN, *Diary*, entry on 7 October 1644. London: Simkin, Marshall, Hamilton, Kent & Co., n.d.

LA RONCIÈRE, CHARLES DE, *Histoire de La Marine Française*. Vol. V. Paris: Plon, Nourrit & Cie., 1934.

LAVEDAN, HENRI, *Monsieur Vincent, Aumônier des Galères*. Paris: Plon, Nourrit & Cie., 1928.

MACDOUGALL, DOROTHY, *Madeleine de Scudéry*. London: Methuen & Co., 1938.

MARTEILHE, JEAN, *The Memoirs of a Protestant condemned to the Galleys of France for his Religion*, trans. "James Willington" (O. Goldsmith). London: Griffiths & Dilly, 1758.

MAYNARD, THEODORE, *Apostle of Charity*. London: Allen & Unwin, 1920.

PRIESTLY, JOSEPH, *An History of the Sufferings of Mr. Lewis de Marolles and Mr. Isaac Le Fevre upon the Revocation, etc.* Birmingham, n.d.

SÉVIGNÉ, *Lettres de Mme. de Sévigné*, ed. L. Aimé-Martin. 6 Vols. Paris, 1876.

CHAPTER XI
Sea Travel

ARVIEUX, *Mémoires du Chevalier d'Arvieux*. Paris, 1735.

CHALLES, ROBERT, *Journal d'un voyage fait aux Indies Orientales*. Rouen, 1721.

CHOISY, ABBÉ DE, *Journal ou suite du voyage de Siam. En forme des lettres familières fait en 1685–86*. Amsterdam: Mortier, 1687.

DUGUAY-TROUIN, RÉNÉ, *Mémoires de Duguay-Trouin (Collection des Mémoires relatifs à l'Histoire de France*, eds. C. B. Petitot & L. J. N. Monmerqué). Paris, 1829.

FORBIN, CLAUDE, *Mémoires du Comte de Forbin*. Amsterdam, 1730.

LABAT, *Nouveau voyage aux Isles de l'Amérique*. Paris: Cavelier, 1742.

MOTTEVILLE, *Mémoires de Mme. de Motteville*. Paris, 1869.

STE. BEUVE, *Causeries du Lundi*, 3 March 1851.

TROLLOPE, H. M., *The Life of Molière*. London: Constable & Co., 1905.

CHAPTER XII
Female Education

CAYLUS, *Souvenirs et Correspondance de Mme. de Caylus*. Paris: Raunié, n.d.

CONRART, VALENTIN, *Mémoires de Valentin Conrart, premier secrétaire perpétuel de l'Académie Française (Collection des Mémoires relatifs à l'Histoire de France,* ed. C. B. Petitot). Paris, 1825.

FÉNELON, FRANÇOIS DE, *Oeuvres choisies de Fénelon,* ed. Mignot. London, Paris: J. M. Dent & Sons, n.d.

LAFAYETTE, *Mémoires de Mme. de Lafayette.* Paris: Flammarion, n.d.

LAVALLÉE, T., *Mme. de Maintenon et la Maison Royal de St. Cyr.* Paris: Plon, Nourrit & Cie., 1862.

MAINTENON, *Correspondance Générale de Mme. de Maintenon,* ed. T. Lavallée. Paris: Charpentier, 1865.

———, *Lettres inédites de Mme. de Maintenon et de Mme. La Princesse des Ursins.* Paris: Bossange, 1826.

———, *Lettres sur l'Education des Filles,* notes by T. Lavallée. Paris, 1854.

MONTPENSIER, *Mémoires de Mlle. de Montpensier,* notes by A. Chéruel. Paris: Charpentier, 1858–59.

ST. CYRES, VISCOUNT, *François de Fénelon.* London: Methuen & Co., 1911.

SCUDÉRY, *Lettres de Mlle. de Scudéry et de Mmes. de Salvan et de Saliez.* Paris, 1806.

SÉVIGNÉ, *Lettres de Mme. de Sévigné.* Paris, Firmin-Didot Frères, 1844.

CHAPTER XIII

The World of Letters

ARNAULD, A., *Mémoires de l'Abbé Arnauld (Collection des Mémoires relatifs à l'Histoire de France,* ed. C. B. Petitot). Paris, 1824.

BOILEAU-DESPRÉAUX, NICOLAS, *Correspondance entre Boileau-Despréaux et Brossette,* ed. A. Lavardet. Paris: Techener, 1858.

DUCLAUX, MARY, *The Life of Racine.* London, 1925.

FAGUET, EMILE, *Dix-Septième Siècle Etudes Littéraires.* Paris: Boivin & Cie., 193–.

———, "French Seventeenth Century Literature and its European Influence," *Cambridge Modern History,* Vol. V, Chap. 3. Cambridge: C.U.P., 1908.

———, *Petite Histoire de la Littérature Française.* Paris: Crès & Cie., 1913.

FONTENELLE, BERNARD, Preface to *The Works of Pierre Corneille.* Paris: Lefèvre, 1824.

GRIMAREST, JEAN L., "Vie de Molière," prefixed to *Oeuvres de Molière*, ed. L. Aimé-Martin. Paris: Lefèvre, 1845.

KERVILER, RENÉ, *Valentin Conrart*. Paris, 1881.

LA BRUYÈRE, JEAN DE, *Les Caractères de Théophraste, traduits du grec*. Amsterdam: Frères Wetsteins, 1720.

LAFAYETTE, *Lettres de M-M Pioche de la Vergne, Ctsse. de Lafayette, et de Gilles Ménage*, intro. notes H. Ashton. London: Hodder & Stoughton, 1924.

MACDOUGALL, DOROTHY, *Madeleine de Scudéry*. London: Methuen & Co., 1938.

MARCOU, F. L., *Etude sur la vie et les oeuvres de Pellisson*. Paris, 1859.

PERRAULT, CHARLES, *Les Hommes Illustres qui ont paru en France*. Paris: Dezallier, 1696–1700.

———, *Mémoires de Perrault*, ed. P. Lacroix. Paris, 1878.

ST. SIMON, *The Memoirs of the Duke of St. Simon*. Various editions.

STE. BEUVE, "Perrault," *Causeries du Lundi*, 29 December 1851.

SCARRON, PAUL, *Le Roman Comique*. Various editions.

SCUDÉRY, *Lettres de Mlle. de Scudéry et de Mmes. de Salvan et de Saliez*. Paris, 1806.

SÉVIGNÉ, *Lettres de Mme. de Sévigné*, ed. L. Aimé-Martin. 6 Vols. Paris, 1876.

TALLEMANT DES RÉAUX, GÉDÉON, *Les Historiettes de Tallemant des Réaux*. Paris, 1862.

TILLEY, A., *Decline of the Age of Louis XIV*. Cambridge: C.U.P., 1929.

TROLLOPE, H. M., *The Life of Molière*. London: Constable & Co., 1905.

VOITURE, VINCENT, *Lettres et autres oeuvres de M. Voiture*. Amsterdam, 1659.

WILSON, N. SCARLYN, *French Classic Age*. London, 1927.

Index